The Least You Should Know
About English

Writing Skills

Form C

Seventh Edition

W9-ARA-948

The LEAST

YOU SHOULD KNOW ABOUT

*E*NGLISH

WRITING SKILLS

TERESA FERSTER GLAZIER

PAIGE WILSON

PASADENA CITY COLLEGE

FORM **C**
SEVENTH EDITION

HEINLE & HEINLE
THOMSON LEARNING

Australia Canada Mexico Singapore Spain United Kingdom United States

HEINLE & HEINLE

THOMSON LEARNING

The Least You Should Know About English/Seventh Edition
Teresa Ferster Glazier, Paige Wilson

Publisher: Earl McPeek
Acquisitions Editor: Steve Dalphin
Market Strategist: John Meyers
Developmental Editor: Michell Phifer
Project Manager: Andrea Archer

Copyright © 2002, 1996, 1991, 1987,
1984, 1981 Heinle & Heinle, a division of
Thomson Learning, Inc. Thomson Learning ™ is
a trademark used herein under license.

Printed in the United States of America

2 3 4 5 6 7 8 9 10   06 05 04 03 02

For more information contact Heinle & Heinle,
25 Thomson Place, Boston, MA 02210 USA, or
you can visit our Internet site at
http://www.heinle.com

All rights reserved. No part of this work covered
by the copyright hereon may be reproduced or
used in any form or by any means—graphic,
electronic, or mechanical, including
photocopying, recording, taping, Web
distribution or information storage and retrieval
systems—without the written permission of
the publisher.

For permission to use material from this text or
product contact us:

Tel:	1-800-730-2214
Fax:	1-800-730-2215
Web:	www.thomsonrights.com

ISBN: 0-15-506986-1

Library of Congress Catalog Card Number:
00-111722

This book is for students who need to review basic English skills and who may profit from a simplified "least you should know" approach. Parts 1 to 3 cover the essentials of spelling, sentence structure, and punctuation. Part 4 on writing teaches students the basic structures of the paragraph and the essay, along with the writing skills necessary to produce them.

Throughout the book, we try to avoid the use of linguistic terminology whenever possible. A conjunction is a connecting word; gerunds and present participles are *ing* words; an infinitive is the *to* ___ form of a verb. Students work with words they know instead of learning a vocabulary they may never use again.

There are abundant exercises, including practice with writing sentences and proofreading paragraphs—enough so that students learn to use the rules automatically and thus *carry over their new skills into their writing*. Exercises consist of sets of ten thematically related, informative sentences on such subjects as Harrison Ford's real-life rescue of two hikers, Julia "Butterfly" Hill's fight to save an ancient redwood tree, the reconciliation of the Hatfields and the McCoys, the amazing life of Mike "The Headless Chicken," and so on. Such exercises reinforce the need for coherence and details in student writing. With answers provided at the back of the book, students can correct their own work and progress at their own pace.

For the seventh edition, we have completely revised Part 4 on writing, which covers the writing process and which stresses the development of the student's written "voice." Writing assignments follow each discussion, and there are samples by both student and professional writers. Part 4 ends with a section designed to help students with writing assignments based on readings. It includes articles to read, react to, and summarize. Students improve their reading by learning to spot main ideas and their writing by learning to write meaningful reactions and concise summaries.

The Least You Should Know about English functions equally well in the classroom and at home as a self-tutoring text. The simple explanations, ample exercises, and answers at the back of the book provide students with everything they need to progress on their own. Students who have previously been overwhelmed by the complexities of English should, through mastering simple rules and through writing and rewriting simple papers, gain enough competence to succeed in further composition courses.

ACKNOWLEDGMENTS

For their thoughtful commentary on the book, we would like to thank the following reviewers: Irene Badaracco, Fordham University; Cheryl Delk, Western Michigan University; Nancy Dessommes, Georgia Southern University; Donna Ross Hooley, Georgia Southern University; Sandra Jensen, Lane Community College; Anastasia Lankford, Eastfield College; Ben Larson, York College; Sue McKee, California State University at Sacramento; Karen McGuire, Pasadena City College; Kevin Nebergall, Krikwood Community College; Peggy Porter, Houston Community College; and Anne Simmons, Olean Business Institute.

For their specific contributions to Form C, we extend our gratitude to the following student writers: Eric Coffey, Amanda K. Gomez, Sherika McPeters, and Ken Slu.

In addition, we would like to thank our publishing team for their expertise and hard work: Steve Dalphin, Acquisitions Editor; Michell Phifer, Developmental Editor; Andrea Archer, Project Manager.

Finally, we are indebted to Herb and Moss Rabbin, Kenneth Glazier, and the rest of our families and friends for their support and encouragement.

Teresa Ferster Glazier

Paige Wilson

Form C differs from Forms A and B in that all of the exercises, writing samples, and assignments are new. The explanations and examples remain the same.

A **Test Packet** with additional exercises and ready-to-photocopy tests accompanies this text and is available to instructors.

CONTENTS

Writing Skills   206

What Is the Least You Should Know?

Most English textbooks try to teach you more than you need to know. This one will teach you the least you need to know—and still help you learn to write acceptably. You won't have to bother with grammatical terms like gerunds and modal auxiliary verbs and demonstrative pronouns and all those others you've been hearing about for years. You can get along without knowing these terms if you'll learn thoroughly a few basic concepts. You *do* have to know how to spell common words; you *do* have to recognize subjects and verbs to avoid writing fragments; you *do* have to know a few rules of sentence structure and punctuation—but rules will be kept to a minimum.

The English you'll learn in this book is sometimes called Standard Written English, and it may differ slightly or greatly from the spoken English you use. Standard Written English is the accepted form of writing in business and the professions. So no matter how you speak, you will communicate better in writing when you use Standard Written English. You might *say* something like "That's a whole nother problem," and everyone will understand, but you would probably want to *write,* "That's a completely different problem." Knowing the difference between spoken English and Standard Written English is essential in college, in business, and in life.

Unless you learn the least you should know, you'll have difficulty communicating in writing. Take this sentence for example:

I hope my application will be excepted by the scholarship committee.

We assume the writer will not actually be happy to be overlooked by the committee but merely failed to use the right word. If the sentence had read

I hope my application will be *accepted* by the scholarship committee.

then the writer would convey the intended meaning. Or take this sentence:

The manager fired Lee and Dave and I received a hundred dollar raise.

The sentence needs a comma.

The manager fired Lee and Dave, and I received a hundred dollar raise.

But perhaps the writer meant

The manager fired Lee, and Dave and I received a hundred dollar raise.

Punctuation makes all the difference, especially if you are Dave. What you'll learn from this text is simply to make your writing so clear that no one will misunderstand it.

As you make your way through the book, it's important to master every rule as you come to it because many rules depend on previous ones. For example, unless you learn to pick out subjects and verbs, you'll have trouble with fragments, with subject–verb agreement, and with punctuation. The rules are brief and clear, and it won't be difficult to master all of them—*if you want to*. But you do have to want to!

HERE'S THE WAY TO MASTER THE LEAST YOU SHOULD KNOW

1. Study the explanation of each rule carefully.

2. Do the first exercise. Correct your answers using the answer section at the back of the book. If you miss even one answer, study the explanation again to find out why.

3. Do the second exercise and correct it. If you miss a single answer, go back once more and study the explanation. You must have missed something. Be tough on yourself. Don't just think, "Maybe I'll get it right next time." Go back and master the rules, and *then* try the next exercise. It's important to correct each group of ten sentences before going on so that you'll discover your mistakes while you still have sentences to practice on.

4. You may be tempted to quit after you do one or two exercises perfectly. Don't! Make yourself finish another exercise. It's not enough to *understand* a rule. You have to *practice* it.

If you're positive, however, after doing several exercises that you've mastered the rule, take the next exercise as a test. If you miss even one answer, you should do all the rest of the questions. But if you again make no mistakes, move on to the proofreading and sentence-composing exercises so that your understanding of the rule carries over into your writing.

Mastering the essentials of spelling, sentence structure, and punctuation will take time. Generally, college students spend a couple of hours outside of class for each hour in class. You may need more. Undoubtedly, the more time you spend, the more your writing will improve.

Spelling

Anyone can learn to spell better. You can eliminate most of your spelling errors if you want to. It's just a matter of deciding you're going to do it. If you really intend to learn to spell, study each of the seven parts of this section until you make no more mistakes in the exercises.

Your Own List of Misspelled Words

Words Often Confused (Sets 1 and 2)

Contractions

Possessives

Words That Can Be Broken into Parts

Rule for Doubling the Final Letter

Using a Dictionary

Study these seven parts, and you'll be a better speller.

Your Own List of Misspelled Words

On the inside cover of your English notebook or in some other obvious place, write correctly all the misspelled words in the papers handed back to you. Review them until you're sure of them.

Words Often Confused (Set 1)

Learning the differences between these often-confused words will help you over-come many of your spelling problems. Study the words carefully, with their examples, before trying the exercises.

a, an　　　　Use *an* before a word that begins with a vowel *sound* (*a, e, i,* and *o,* plus *u* when it sounds like *uh*) or silent *h*.

Note that it's not the letter but the *sound* of the letter that matters.

> an apple, an essay, an inch, an onion
>
> an umpire, an ugly design (the *u*'s sound like *uh*)
>
> an hour, an honest person (silent *h*)

Use *a* before a word that begins with a consonant sound (all the sounds except the vowels, plus *u* or *eu* when they sound like *you*).

> a chart, a pie, a history book (the *h* is not silent in *history*)
>
> a union, a uniform, a unit (the *u*'s sound like *you*)
>
> a European vacation, a euphemism *(eu* sounds like *you)*

accept, except   *Accept* means "to receive willingly."

> I *accept* your apology.

Except means "excluding" or "but."

> Everyone arrived on time *except* him.

advise, advice   *Advise* is a verb (pronounce the *s* like a *z*).

> I *advise* you to take your time finding the right job.

Advice is a noun (it rhymes with *rice*).

> My counselor gave me good *advice*.

affect, effect   *Affect* is a verb and means "to alter or influence."

> All quizzes will *affect* the final grade.
>
> The happy ending *affected* the mood of the audience.

Effect is most commonly used as a noun and means "a result." If *a, an,* or *the* is in front of the word, then you'll know it isn't a verb and will use *effect*.

> The strong coffee had a powerful *effect* on me.
>
> We studied the *effects* of sleep deprivation in my psychology class.

all ready, already   If you can leave out the *all* and the sentence still makes sense, then *all ready* is the form to use. (In that form, *all* is a separate word and could be left out.)

We're *all ready* for the trip. (*We're ready for the trip* makes sense.)

The banquet is *all ready*. (*The banquet is ready* makes sense.)

But if you can't leave out the *all* and still have the sentence make sense, then use *already* (the form in which the *al* has to stay in the word).

They've *already* eaten. (*They've ready eaten* doesn't make sense.)

We have seen that movie *already*.

are, our   *Are* is a verb.

We *are* going to Colorado Springs.

Our shows we possess something.

We painted *our* fence to match the house.

brake, break   *Brake* used as a verb means "to slow or stop motion." It's also the name of the device that slows or stops motion.

I had to *brake* quickly to avoid an accident.

Luckily I just had my *brakes* fixed.

Break used as a verb means "to shatter" or "to split." It's also the name of an interruption, as in "a coffee break."

She never thought she would *break* a world record.

Enjoy your spring *break*.

choose, chose   The difference here is one of time. Use *choose* for present and future; use *chose* for past.

I will *choose* a new major this semester.

We *chose* the wrong time of year to get married.

clothes, cloths   *Clothes* are something you wear; *cloths* are pieces of material you might clean or polish something with.

I love the *clothes* that characters wear in movies.

The car-wash workers use special *cloths* to dry the cars.

coarse, course   *Coarse* describes a rough texture.

I used *coarse* sandpaper to smooth the surface of the board.

Course is used for all other meanings.

> Of *course* we saw the golf *course* when we went to Pebble Beach.

complement, compliment

The one spelled with an *e* means to complete something or bring it to perfection.

> Use a color wheel to find a *complement* for purple.

> Juliet's personality *complements* Romeo's; she is practical, and he is a dreamer.

The one spelled with an *i* has to do with praise. Remember "*I* like compliments," and you'll remember to use the *i* spelling when you mean praise.

> My evaluation included a really nice *compliment* from my coworkers.

> We *complimented* them on their new home.

conscious, conscience

Conscious means "aware."

> They weren't *conscious* of any problems before the accident.

Conscience means that inner voice of right and wrong. The extra *n* in *conscience* should remind you of *No*, which is what your conscience often says to you.

> My *conscience* told me to turn in the expensive watch I found.

dessert, desert

Dessert is the sweet one, the one you like two helpings of. So give it two helpings of *s*.

> We had a whole chocolate cheesecake for *dessert*.

The other one, *desert,* is used for all other meanings and has two pronunciations.

> I promise that I won't *desert* you.

> The snake slithered slowly across the *desert*.

do, due

Do is a verb, an action. You *do* something.

> I always *do* my best work at night.

But a payment or an assignment is *due;* it is scheduled for a certain time.

> Our first essay is *due* tomorrow.

Due can also be used before *to* in a phrase that means *because of.*

The outdoor concert was canceled *due to* rain.

feel, fill   *Feel* describes *feelings.*

Whenever I stay up late, I *feel* sleepy in class.

Fill describes what you do to a cup or a gas tank.

Did they *fill* the pitcher to the top?

fourth, forth   The word *fourth* has *four* in it. (But note that *forty* does not. Remember the word *forty-fourth.*)

This is our *fourth* quiz in two weeks.

My grandparents celebrated their *forty-fourth* anniversary.

If you don't mean a number, use *forth.*

We wrote back and *forth* many times during my trip.

have, of   *Have* is a verb. Sometimes, in a contraction, it sounds like *of.* When you say *could've,* the *have* may sound like *of,* but it is not written that way. Always write *could have, would have, should have, might have.*

We should *have* planned our vacation sooner.

Then we could *have* used our coupon for a free one-way ticket.

Use *of* only in a prepositional phrase (see p. 54).

She sent me a box *of* chocolates for my birthday.

hear, here   The last three letters of *hear* spell "ear." You *hear* with your ear.

When I listen to a sea shell, I *hear* ocean sounds.

The other spelling *here* tells "where." Note that the three words indicating a place or pointing out something all have *here* in them: *here, there, where.*

I'll be *here* for three more weeks.

it's, its   *It's* is a contraction and means "it is" or "it has."

It's hot. (*It is* hot.)

It's been hot all week. (*It has* been hot all week.)

Its is a possessive. (Pronouns such as *its, yours, hers, ours, theirs,* and *whose* are already possessive and never need an apostrophe. See p. 30.)

The jury had made *its* decision.

The dog pulled at *its* leash.

knew, new   *Knew* has to do with knowledge (both start with *k*).

New means "not old."

They *knew* that she wanted a *new* bike.

know, no   *Know* has to do with knowledge (both start with *k*).

By Friday, I must *know* all the state capitals.

No means "not any" or the opposite of "yes."

My boss has *no* patience. *No,* I need to work late.

E X E R C I S E S

Underline the correct word. Don't guess! If you aren't sure, turn back to the explanatory pages. When you've finished ten sentences, compare your answers with those at the back of the book. Correct each group of ten sentences before continuing so you'll catch your mistakes while you still have sentences to practice on.

Exercise 1

1. What (affect, effect) does a name have on (a, an) consumer product?

2. Of (coarse, course), nearly everyone has heard of Oreos.

3. But does everyone (know, no) about Hydrox?

4. Actually, (a, an) Oreo and (a, an) Hydrox were very similar (deserts, desserts).

5. For nearly ninety years, these chocolate sandwich cookies with creamy white filling competed on (are, our) grocery store shelves.

6. Surprisingly, Sunshine's Hydrox cookie got (it's, its) name from a combination of the words "hydrogen" and "oxygen."

7. However, many people did not (feel, fill) attracted by the name Hydrox.

8. Oreo was (a, an) easier name to (accept, except), and Nabisco was a larger company.

9. Therefore, even though Hydrox came onto the market in 1908 and Oreos in 1912, the Oreo was far more successful partly (do, due) to (it's, its) name.

10. (Conscious, Conscience) of the problem, Keebler, the new owner of Sunshine Biscuits, recently (choose, chose) to change the name of Hydrox cookies to Droxies.

Source: Fortune, 15 Mar. 1999

Exercise 2

1. (It's, Its) never too late to learn something (knew, new).

2. After living for nearly one hundred years without knowing how to read or write, George Dawson could (have, of) just (accepted, excepted) his life as it was.

3. But he never did (feel, fill) good about hiding his illiteracy from his children or signing his name with (a, an) X.

4. In 1996, George Dawson (choose, chose) to start school for the first time at the age of ninety-eight.

5. Dawson, who was (all ready, already) in his teens when the *Titanic* sank, worked all of his life to support his family and even outlived his (fourth, forth) wife.

6. He had enough memories to (feel, fill) a book, (accept, except) he wouldn't (have, of) been able to read it.

7. When a man in Seattle came to (hear, here) of Dawson's long life and strong desire for (a, an) education, he gave Dawson some (advise, advice).

8. Richard Glaubman, a teacher himself, suggested that Dawson share his experiences in a book; they (are, our) now coauthors of Dawson's autobiography.

9. In the (coarse, course) of his life as an African-American man and the grandson of slaves, Dawson witnessed and felt the (affects, effects) of racism and oppression.

10. But Dawson always believed that the joyful moments in life more than (complemented, complimented) the painful ones, and he titled his book *Life Is So Good.*

Source: Jet, 17 Apr. 2000

Exercise 3

1. The prospect of graduating from a university brings (fourth, forth) the emotions of pride and excitement.

2. Many graduating seniors (feel, fill) a (conscious, conscience) need to express themselves at moments like these.

3. Ryan Ruano, one of the first graduates of the year 2000, (choose, chose) to arrive at his University of Central Florida commencement ceremony in (a, an) very unusual way.

4. His secret plan involved (a, an) airplane, (a, an) parachute, and (a, an) accomplice.

5. Ruano's family didn't (know, no) that he would be parachuting into the crowd, but his girlfriend (knew, new).

6. She watched the sky, (conscious, conscience) that Ryan was (do, due) to drop out of it at any moment (all ready, already) wearing his graduation robe over his (clothes, cloths).

7. When UCF officials, graduates, and their families were (all ready, already) to begin, Ryan started his freefall.

8. Ryan's girlfriend kept looking up to see if he was on (coarse, course).

9. Happily, Ryan landed right next to his grandmother, and everyone was just glad that he didn't (brake, break) anything.

10. He imagines that someday his children will (hear, here) the story of their dad's exciting entrance to his graduation and try to top it with a stunt of their own.

Source: Wall Street Journal and Public Radio International, 10 May 2000

Exercise 4

1. I've been out of high school for two years, and I (all ready, already) miss it.

2. While I was still in high school, my parents bought my (clothes, cloths) and took care of all my necessities.

3. When my car needed to have (it's, its) (brakes, breaks) fixed, they paid the repair bills.

4. Every time I had to (choose, chose) a new elective or a summer activity, my family gave me the best (advise, advice).

5. One summer, I spent a spectacular week in the (dessert, desert) with my school's geology club.

6. That firsthand experience with nature strongly (affected, effected) me, especially the sight of the brilliant blue sky and the feeling of the (coarse, course), rocky sand.

7. Now that I am (hear, here) at college, I am (conscious, conscience) of a change in my parents' attitude.

8. (It's, Its) as if they (feel, fill) that (are, our) lives should grow apart.

9. I didn't (know, no) that this change was coming, or I would (have, of) tried to prepare myself for it.

10. Now I go back and (fourth, forth) between wishing for the past and trying to (accept, except) the future.

Exercise 5

1. (It's, Its) common to (hear, here) the expression "heart of stone" applied to someone without feeling.

2. But a real stone heart, actually the fossil of (a, an) heart, has been making news lately.

3. Such a fossil wouldn't be especially interesting, (accept, except) that (it's, its) a dinosaur heart, and (it's, its) owner lived nearly seventy million years ago.

4. Until recently, most theories imagined dinosaurs to be cold-blooded, lizard-like beasts brought to life in movies through special (affects, effects).

5. But many (knew, new) discoveries, including this intact dinosaur heart, show dinosaurs to have been warm-blooded and birdlike, possibly even covered with feathers.

6. The scientists who found the skeleton of a Thescelosaurus in 1993 (knew, new) that they had made (a, an) amazing discovery.

7. But it became even more amazing after a paleontologist/doctor from Oregon gave them some (advise, advice); he suggested that they (do, due) a CAT scan of the chest area to see what they might find.

8. The CAT scan showed scientists the first pictures of a dinosaur's heart, and (it's, its) structure surprised them: instead of three chambers like those of cold-blooded reptiles, it seemed to have four chambers like those of warm-blooded mammals or birds.

9. The discovery of a (fourth, forth) chamber in the heart of a dinosaur has had a huge (effect, affect) on dinosaur experts.

10. Some scientists believed all along that dinosaurs were warm-blooded, (accept, except) that there was (know, no) proof—until now.

Source: Los Angeles Times, 21 Apr. 2000

PROOFREADING EXERCISE

Find and correct the ten errors contained in the following student paragraph. All of the errors involve Words Often Confused (Set 1).

During my singing recital last semester, I suddenly became very self-conscience. My heart started beating faster, and I didn't no what to due. I looked around to see if my show of nerves was having an affect on the audience. Of coarse, they could here my voice shaking. I was the forth singer in the program, and everyone else had done so well. I felt my face turn red and would of run out the door if it had been closer. After my performance, people tried to give me com-plements, but I new that they weren't sincere.

SENTENCE WRITING

The surest way to learn these Words Often Confused is to use them immediately in your own writing. Choose the five pairs or groups of words that you most often confuse from Set 1. Then use each of them correctly in a new sentence. No answers are provided at the back of the book, but you can see if you are using the words correctly by comparing your sentences to the examples in the explanations.

Words Often Confused (Set 2)

Study this second set of words carefully, with their examples, before attempting the exercises. Knowing all of the word groups in these two sets will take care of many of your spelling problems.

lead, led   *Lead* is the metal that rhymes with *head*.

Old paint is dangerous because it often contains *lead*.

The past form of the verb "to lead" is *led*.

What factors *led* to your decision?

I *led* our school's debating team to victory last year.

If you don't mean past time, use *lead*, which rhymes with *bead*.

I will *lead* the debating team again this year.

loose, lose   *Loose* means "not tight." Note how *l o o s e* that word is. It has plenty of room for two *o*'s.

My dog's tooth is *loose*.

Lose is the opposite of win.

If we *lose* this game, we will be out for the season.

passed, past   The past form of the verb "to pass" is *passed*.

She easily *passed* her math class.

The runner *passed* the baton to her teammate.

We *passed* your house twice before we saw the address.

Use *past* when it's not a verb.

We drove *past* your house. (the same as "We drove *by* your house")

I always use my *past* experiences to help me solve problems.

In the *past,* he had to borrow his brother's car.

personal, personnel   Pronounce these two correctly, and you won't confuse them—*pérsonal, personnél*.

She shared her *personal* views as a parent.

Personnel means "a group of employees."

I had an appointment in the *personnel* office.

piece, peace   Remember "piece of pie." The one meaning "a *piece* of something" always begins with *pie*.

One child asked for an extra *piece* of candy.

The other one, *peace,* is the opposite of war.

The two gangs discussed the possibility of a *peace* treaty.

principal, principle

Principal means "main." Both words have *a* in them: princip*a*l, m*a*in.

The *principal* concern is safety. (main concern)

He lost both *principal* and interest. (main amount of money)

Also, think of a school's "princi*pal*" as your "*pal*."

An elementary school *principal* must be kind. (main administrator)

A *principle* is a "rule." Both words end in *le:* princip*le*, ru*le*.

I am proud of my high *principles*. (rules of conduct)

We value the *principle* of truth in advertising. (rule)

quiet, quite

Pronounce these two correctly, and you won't confuse them. *Quiet* means "free from noise" and rhymes with *diet*.

Tennis players need *quiet* in order to concentrate.

Quite means "very" and rhymes with *bite*.

It was *quite* hot in the auditorium.

right, write

Right means "correct" or "proper."

You will find your keys if you look in the *right* place.

It also means in the exact location, position, or moment.

Your keys are *right* where you left them.

Let's go *right* now.

Write means to compose sentences, poems, essays, and so forth.

I asked my teacher to *write* a letter of recommendation for me.

than, then

Than compares two things.

I am taller *than* my sister.

Then tells when (*then* and *when* rhyme, and both have *e* in them).

I always write a rough draft of a paper first; *then* I revise it.

their, there, they're

Their is a possessive, meaning belonging to them.

> *Their* cars have always been red.

There points out something. (Remember that the three words indicating a place or pointing out something all have *here* in them: *here, there, where.*)

> I know that I haven't been *there* before.

> *There* was a rainbow in the sky.

They're is a contraction and means "they are."

> *They're* living in Canada. (*They are* living in Canada.)

threw, through

Threw is the past form of "to throw."

> We *threw* snowballs at each other.

> I *threw* away my chance at a scholarship.

If you don't mean "to throw something," use *through*.

> We could see our beautiful view *through* the new curtains.

> They worked *through* their differences.

two, too, to

Two is a number.

> We have written *two* papers so far in my English class.

Too means "extra" or "also," and so it has an extra *o*.

> The movie was *too* long and *too* violent. (extra)

> They are enrolled in that biology class *too*. (also)

Use *to* for all other meanings.

> They like *to* ski. They're going *to* the mountains.

weather, whether

Weather refers to conditions of the atmosphere.

> Snowy *weather* is too cold for me.

Whether means "if."

> I don't know *whether* it is snowing there or not.

> *Whether* I travel with you or not depends on the weather.

were, wear, where

These words are pronounced differently but are often confused in writing.

Were is the past form of the verb "to be."

> We *were* interns at the time.

Wear means to have on, as in wearing clothes.

I always *wear* a scarf in winter.

Where refers to a place. (Remember that the three words indicating a place or pointing out something all have *here* in them: *here, there, where.*)

Where is the mailbox? There it is.

Where are the closing papers? Here they are.

who's, whose *Who's* is a contraction and means "who is" or "who has."

Who's responsible for signing the checks? (*Who is* responsible?)

Who's been reading my journal? (*Who has* been . . . ?)

Whose is a possessive. (Pronouns such as *whose, its, yours, hers, ours,* and *theirs* are already possessive and never take an apostrophe. See p. 30.)

Whose keys are these?

woman, women The difference here is one of number: wo*man* refers to one female; wo*men* refers to two or more females.

I know a *woman* who won eight thousand dollars on a single horse race.

I bowl with a group of *women* from my work.

you're, your *You're* is a contraction and means "you are."

You're as smart as I am. (*You are* as smart as I am.)

Your is a possessive meaning belonging to you.

I borrowed *your* lab book.

E X E R C I S E S

Underline the correct word. When you've finished ten sentences, compare your answers with those at the back of the book. Do only ten sentences at a time so you can teach yourself while you still have sentences to practice on.

Exercise 1

1. Some people think of Tupperware as thing of the (passed, past).

2. But most American homes still have an old (piece, peace) of Tupperware in (their, there, they're) cupboards.

3. For many, nothing brings back memories of childhood better (than, then) that square, flat, sandwich-shaped container tossed into a lunchbox.

4. Now museum curators around the world are hunting (threw, through) objects at flea markets and thrift stores (two, too, to) find vintage Tupperware for their collections.

5. The new demand for old Tupperware products has (lead, led) to an increase in (their, there, they're) prices.

6. For example, Tupperware poker chips made in the 1940s are now (quiet, quite) valuable; (their, there, they're) worth nearly (two, too, to) hundred dollars.

7. If (you're, your) old enough to have lived the 1950s, you might remember the first Tupperware parties, (were, wear, where) all guests (were, wear, where) urged to buy Tupperware.

8. These parties (were, wear, where) the idea of a (woman, women) named Brownie Wise.

9. Earl Silas Tupper, inventor of Tupperware, started selling his products in stores; (than, then) he made Brownie Wise vice president in charge of distribution and decided to restrict the sale of Tupperware to Tupperware parties.

10. Wise did (loose, lose) her job later, however, after Tupper accused her of feeding her dog its food in a Tupperware bowl.

Source: Traditional Home, May 2000

Exercise 2

1. As a student on financial aid, I was advised to work on campus or (loose, lose) some of my benefits.

2. At first I didn't know (were, wear, where) to work.

3. It definitely needed to be a (quiet, quite) place so that I could study or (right, write) a paper in my free time.

4. I finally chose to take a job in the (personal, personnel) office.

5. Now that I have been working (their, there, they're) for (two, too, to) months, I know that I made the (right, write) decision.

6. My (principal, principle) duties include filing documents and stuffing envelopes.

7. However, when the receptionist takes a break, I am the one (who's, whose) at the front desk.

8. Once I was sitting up front when the (principal, principle) of my old high school came in to apply for a job at the college.

9. I didn't know (weather, whether) to show that I recognized her or to keep (quiet, quite) about the (passed, past).

10. As a student, I like working on campus for financial-aid benefits better (than, then) working off campus for a tiny paycheck.

Exercise 3

1. In the (passed, past), TV commercials for exterminating companies showed cute little cartoon bugs falling over into (their, there, they're) cute little cartoon graves.

2. However, movies like *Antz* and *A Bug's Life* (lead, led) to a change in advertising strategies.

3. Audiences loved the animated critters in these films and would've been upset if any of (their, there, they're) favorite characters (passed, past) away.

4. So pest-control companies had (two, too, to) change (their, there, they're) portrayal of the "enemy" from lovable bugs to disgusting pests.

5. (You're, Your) probably already familiar with one of the first ads to show bugs in a more realistic way.

6. (You're, Your) watching what you think is a fabric softener commercial when, (quiet, quite) suddenly, a life-size cockroach appears to creep (passed, past) the image on the screen.

7. The ad agency (who's, whose) idea it was to put the pest on screen appropriately called the commercial "Fake-Out."

8. But this illusion of a big bug on the (loose, lose) in people's living rooms worked perhaps (two, too, to) well.

9. One (woman, women) was so terrified that she (thew, through) a helmet (threw, through) her TV screen.

10. Other people decided to (right, write) to the company to share (their, there, they're) (personal, personnel) reactions to the controversial ad.

Source: Wall Street Journal, 21 Apr. 1999, and Washington Post, 6 Apr. 2000

Exercise 4

1. I'm not (quiet, quite) sure (weather, whether) I should use my credit card to shop over the Internet.

2. I still have (piece, peace) of mind because I haven't bought anything with it yet.

3. I feel that once my number is (loose, lose) in cyberspace, all of my (personal, personnel) information will be available.

4. I have heard scary reports in the (passed, past) of people (who's, whose) credit-card numbers were (passed, past) on to criminals.

5. My (principal, principle) concern is that someone will steal my identity.

6. (Their, There, They're) is really a lot to (loose, lose) if that happens.

7. Victims of identity theft have to go (threw, through) a long process to clear up (their, there, they're) records.

8. It's the same problem for men and for (woman, women).

9. Stealing people's identities is much more serious (than, then) stealing (their, there, they're) property.

10. I don't know anyone (who's, whose) not worried about Internet security.

Exercise 5

1. On a beautiful morning in June, you may receive a phone call that changes (you're, your) life.

2. The caller will tell you that (you're, your) half a million dollars richer and that you don't have to do anything other (than, then) be yourself to deserve the money.

3. You might wonder (weather, whether) it is a real or a crank call.

4. Believe it or not, this wonderful (piece, peace) of news is delivered to between twenty and thirty special men and (woman, women) in America every year.

5. (Their, There, They're) unofficially called the "Genius Awards," but (their, there, they're) real title is the MacArthur Fellowships.

6. The MacArthur Foundation awards its fellowships each year based on the (principal, principle) that forward-thinking people deserve an opportunity to pursue their ideas freely and without obligation to anyone.

7. No application is necessary (two, too, to) receive the gift of $100,000 a year plus health insurance for five years, and no particular field of work receives more consideration (than, then) another.

8. The (principal, principle) characteristic that MacArthur Fellows share is (their, there, they're) creative potential—in any area.

9. Each year, the MacArthur Foundation sends about one hundred "scouts" across the country looking for people with untapped potential (two, too, to) nominate; (than, then) another anonymous group selects the year's recipients.

10. The nominees don't even know that (their, there, they're) going (threw, through) the process until the phone rings on that fateful morning in June.

PROOFREADING EXERCISE

See if you can correct the ten errors in this student paragraph. All errors involve Words Often Confused (Set 2).

Sometimes it's hard to find the write place to study on campus. The library used too be the principle location for students to do they're difficult course work, weather it was preparing research papers or writing critical essays. But now most library resources are available online, two. This change has lead students to use campus computer labs and cafés as study halls. There, students can go online, get up-to-date sources, write their reports, and have peace and quite without the stuffy atmosphere of the library. The only problem with doing research online is that it's easier to loose a piece of information on the computer then it is to lose a hard copy in the library.

SENTENCE WRITING

Write several sentences using any words you missed in doing the exercises for Words Often Confused (Set 2).

Sentence writing is a good idea not only because it will help you remember these words often confused but also because it will be a storehouse for ideas you can later use in writing papers. Here are some topics you might consider writing your sentences about:

Friends from childhood

Favorite actors/actresses

A hobby or a collection

Something you would like to accomplish this year

Your favorite getaway spot

Contractions

When two words are condensed into one, the result is called a contraction:

is not ·······➤ isn't   you have ·······➤ you've

The letter or letters that are left out are replaced with an apostrophe. For example, if the two words *do not* are condensed into one, an apostrophe is put where the *o* is left out:

do not   don't

Note how the apostrophe goes in the exact place where the letter or letters are left out in these contractions:

I am	I'm
I have	I've
I shall, I will	I'll
I would	I'd
you are	you're
you have	you've
you will	you'll
she is, she has	she's
he is, he has	he's
it is, it has	it's
we are	we're
we have	we've
we will, we shall	we'll
they are	they're
they have	they've
are not	aren't
cannot	can't
do not	don't
does not	doesn't
have not	haven't
let us	let's

who is, who has	▸ who's
where is	where's
were not	weren't
would not	wouldn't
could not	couldn't
should not	shouldn't
would have	would've
could have	could've
should have	should've
that is	that's
there is	there's
what is	what's

One contraction does not follow this rule: *will not* becomes *won't.*

In all other contractions that you're likely to use, the apostrophe goes exactly where the letter or letters are left out. Note especially *it's, they're, who's,* and *you're.* Use them when you mean two words. (See pp. 31–32 for the possessive forms—*its, their, whose,* and *your*—which don't have an apostrophe.)

E X E R C I S E S

Put an apostrophe in each contraction. Then compare your answers with those at the back of the book. Be sure to correct each group of ten sentences before going on so you'll catch your mistakes while you still have sentences to practice on.

Exercise 1

1. I bet youve never heard of a "geep"; I hadnt either until I read about it in a library book.

2. The geep is an animal thats half goat and half sheep.

3. Its not one that occurs naturally.

4. But a number of geep were produced in the early 1980s.

5. Scientists created this strange beast by combining a goat's cells with a sheep's cells at their earliest stages of development.

6. What many people couldnt believe was that the resulting geep's cells still kept either their goat or sheep qualities intact.

7. Therefore, the geep had long straight goat hair on parts of its body and fluffy sheep's wool on other parts.

8. Theres a picture of a geep in the book that I read.

9. Its so weird to look at a goat's head surrounded by curled sheep horns.

10. Lets hope that scientists dont try to make a "cog" or a "dat" in the same way.

Source: Mysteries of Planet Earth (Carlton Books, 1999)

Exercise 2

1. John Carpenter isnt only the name of a famous movie director.

2. Its also the name of the first contestant to win a million dollars on TV's *Who Wants to Be a Millionaire?*

3. Before winning the big prize, Carpenter wasnt any different from the rest of us.

4. He worked while going to college, including jobs on an assembly line and at an amusement park; after graduating, he delivered pizzas and couldve been killed by an armed robber whod ordered a pizza over the phone.

5. When Carpenter arrived, the robber asked for the pizza and Carpenter's money.

6. Carpenter didnt hesitate to give the man the pizza and all the cash in one of his pockets; then Carpenter ran back to his car and drove away.

7. What the robber didnt know was that Carpenter's other pocket was also full of money—his tips for the evening.

8. Carpenter felt that it wouldnt be fair to be robbed of his tips, so he kept them.

9. John Carpenter eventually became a tax collector and married Debbie Fong, a banker.

10. Id say the TV show couldnt have given the million dollars to a couple more qualified to manage the money well.

Source: People, 6 Dec. 1999

Exercise 3

1. The moons an amazing satellite.

2. Many experts now believe that its a chunk of the earth sent into orbit after a huge collision.

3. The core of the moon is solid, but its covered with rocks, powdery dark-gray soil, and maybe even vast areas of ice at its perpetually dark poles.

4. The crystalline center of the moon causes it to emit a long ringing sound whenever its struck by a big meteor or piece of space junk.

5. We dont hear the moon ringing because noise cant travel in a vacuum.

6. From the earth, only one side of the moons ever visible—always the same side.

7. And since the moon spins at the slow rate of ten miles per hour at its widest part, a person could hypothetically jog across its surface without ever encountering a sunrise or a sunset.

8. The months of the year, of course, are closely related to the cycles of the moon.

9. And the moons in sync with earth time in another way.

10. Both solar and lunar eclipses last one hour from start to finish because thats the time it takes for the moon to travel the distance of its own diameter.

Source: Discover, Aug. 2000

Exercise 4

1. As I was driving home the other day, I saw a fully equipped camper shell for sale on someone's front lawn, and I shouldve stopped to look at it.

2. At first, I didnt think I wanted a camper for my pickup truck, but now I wish Id gone back for it.

3. I remember that it didnt look brand new: it had a door in the back and windows with curtains that I couldve replaced if I didnt like them.

4. And there wasnt any price posted, so I dont know how much it cost.

5. Its just that, for some reason, I feel as though Ive missed an opportunity.

6. Whenever Im driving on a long trip and pass a truck with a camper on it, I always think of how much fun itd be to park on a beach and spend the night.

7. To get all of the comforts of home, I wouldnt have to stop at a hotel; theyd be right in the back of the truck.

8. A friend of mine whos got a motor home said that it was the best purchase hed ever made because it always gives him a reason to take a trip.

9. A camper shell mightve been just what I needed to bring some adventure into my life.

10. Of course, theres nothing stopping me from buying a new one.

Exercise 5

1. This week, Im helping my sister with her research paper, and shes chosen chocolate as her topic.

2. Weve been surprised by some of the things weve discovered.

3. First, the cocoa beans arent very appetizing in their natural form.

4. They grow inside an odd-shaped, alien-looking pod, and theyre surrounded by white mushy pulp.

5. Once cocoa beans have been removed from the pods, theyre dried, blended almost like coffee beans, and processed into the many types of chocolate foods available.

6. In fact, the Aztecs enjoyed chocolate as a heavily spiced hot drink that was more like coffee than the sweet, creamy chocolate thats popular today.

7. Weve also learned that white chocolate cant be called chocolate at all since it doesnt contain any cocoa solids, only cocoa butter.

8. With an interest in organic foods, wed assumed that organic chocolate would be better than conventional chocolate.

9. But thats not true either because its got to be grown on pesticide-free trees, and theyre the strongest but not the tastiest sources of chocolate.

10. Unfortunately, the best cocoa trees are also the most vulnerable to disease, so they cant be grown organically.

Source: The Chocolate Companion (Simon & Schuster, 1995)

PROOFREADING EXERCISE

Add apostrophes to the ten contractions used in the following paragraph.

If youve ever read any reviews of books sold on Amazon.com, youre probably familiar with the writings of Harriet Klausner. Klausner didnt write the books; she wrote the reviews after buying and reading the books. In fact, shes the reviewer whos ranked as the most popular on the famous website. To date, Klausners written more than five hundred reviews, but she hasnt been paid for any of them. Her responses havent gone unnoticed, however, and Amazon.com fans cant wait to see what shell recommend next.

Source: People, 19 June 2000

SENTENCE WRITING

Doing exercises helps you learn a rule, but even more helpful is using the rule in writing. Write ten sentences using contractions. You might write about your reaction to the week's big news story, or you can choose your own subject.

Possessives

The trick in writing possessives is to ask yourself the question, "Who (or what) does it belong to?" (Modern usage has made *who* acceptable when it comes first in a sentence, but some people still say, "*Whom* does it belong to?" or even "*To whom* does it belong?") If the answer to your question doesn't end in *s,* then add an apostrophe and *s.* If the answer to your question ends in *s,* add an apostrophe. Then you must see if you need another sound to make the possessive clear. If you need another *s* sound, add the apostrophe and another *s* (as in the last of the following examples).

one girl (bicycle)	Who does it belong to?	girl	Add *'s*	girl's bicycle
two girls (bicycles)	Who do they belong to?	girls	Add *'*	girls' bicycles
a man (coat)	Who does it belong to?	man	Add *'s*	man's coat
men (coats)	Who do they belong to?	men	Add *'s*	men's coats
children (game)	Who does it belong to?	children	Add *'s*	children's game
a month (pay)	What does it belong to?	month	Add *'s*	a month's pay
Brahms (lullaby)	Who does it belong to?	Brahms	Add *'*	Brahms' lullaby
my boss (office)	Who does it belong to?	boss	Add *'s*	boss's office

This trick will always work, but you must ask the question every time. Remember that the key word is *belong.* Who (or what) does it belong to? If you ask the question another way, you may get an answer that won't help you. Also, if you just look at a word without asking the question, you may think the name of the owner ends in *s* when it really doesn't.

TO MAKE A POSSESSIVE

1. Ask, "Who (or what) does it belong to?"
2. If the answer doesn't end in *s,* add an apostrophe and *s.*
3. If the answer ends in *s,* add just an apostrophe *or* an apostrophe and *s* if you need the extra sound to show a possessive (as in *boss's office*).

E X E R C I S E S

Follow the directions carefully for each of the following exercises. Because possessives can be tricky, explanations follow some exercises to help students understand them better.

Exercise 1

Cover the right column and see if you can write the following possessives correctly. Ask the question "Who (or what) does it belong to?" each time. Don't look at the answer before you try!

1. people (opinions)	_____	people's opinions
2. a jury (verdict)	_____	a jury's verdict
3. Chris (GPA)	_____	Chris' or Chris's GPA
4. Tiffany (scholarship)	_____	Tiffany's scholarship
5. the Jacksons (new roof)	_____	the Jacksons' new roof
6. Dr. Moss (advice)	_____	Dr. Moss's advice
7. patients (rights)	_____	patients' rights
8. a fish (gills)	_____	a fish's gills
9. a car (windshield)	_____	a car's windshield
10. many cars (windshields)	_____	many cars' windshields

(Sometimes you may see a couple of choices when the word ends in *s*. *Chris' career* may be written *Chris's career*. That is also correct, depending on how you want your reader to say it. Be consistent when given such choices.)

> **CAUTION-** Don't assume that any word that ends in *s* is a possessive. The *s* may indicate more than one of something, a plural noun. Make sure the word actually possesses something before you add an apostrophe.

A few commonly used words are already possessive and don't need an apostrophe added to them. Memorize this list:

our, ours	its
your, yours	their, theirs
his, her, hers	whose

Note particularly *its, their, whose,* and *your*. They are already possessive and don't take an apostrophe. (These words sound just like *it's, they're, who's,* and *you're,* which are *contractions* that use an apostrophe in place of their missing letters.)

Exercise 2

Cover the right column below and see if you can write the correct form. The answer might be a *contraction* or a *possessive*. If you miss any, go back and review the explanations.

1. Yes, (that) the one I ordered.	that's
2. (He) saving his money for summer.	He's
3. Does (you) dog bark at night?	your
4. I don't know (who) backpack that is.	whose
5. (You) been summoned for jury duty?	You've
6. My cat is so old that (it) going bald.	it's
7. (They) taking classes together this spring.	They're
8. My car's paint is losing (it) shine.	its
9. We welcomed (they) suggestions.	their
10. (Who) visiting us this weekend?	Who's

Exercise 3

Here's another chance to check your progress with possessives. Cover the right column again as you did in Exercises 1 and 2, and add apostrophes to the possessives. Each answer is followed by an explanation.

1. My twin brothers are members of our schools orchestra.	school's (You didn't add an apostrophe to *brothers* or *members,* did you? The brothers and members don't possess anything.)
2. The cashier asked to see my friends identification, too.	friend's (if it is one friend) friends' (two or more friends)
3. Both mens and womens tennis are exciting to watch.	men's, women's (Did you use the "Who does it belong to" test?)
4. I bought a bad textbook; half of its pages were printed upside down.	No apostrophe. *Its* needs no apostrophe unless it means "it is" or "it has."
5. Julias grades were higher than yours.	Julia's (*Yours* is already possessive and doesn't take an apostrophe.)

6. I decided to quit my job and gave my boss two weeks notice.	weeks' (The notice belongs to *two weeks,* and since *weeks* ends in *s,* the apostrophe goes after the *s.*)
7. The Taylors porch light burned out while they were still on vacation.	Taylors' (The house belongs to the Taylors.)
8. It is every citizens duty to vote in national elections.	citizen's (The duty belongs to *every citizen,* and since *citizen* doesn't end in *s,* we add an apostrophe and *s.*)
9. The chemistry students evaluated each others results as they cleaned up after the experiment.	each other's (*Students* is plural, not possessive.)
10. During a long trip, flight attendants attitudes can greatly affect an airline passengers experience.	attendants', passenger's (Did you use the "Who do they belong to" test?)

Exercises 4 and 5

Now you're ready to put the apostrophe in each possessive that follows. But be careful. *First,* make sure the word really possesses something; not every word ending in *s* is a possessive. *Second,* remember that certain words are already possessive and don't take an apostrophe. *Third,* remember that even though a word ends in *s,* you can't tell where the apostrophe goes until you ask the question, "Who (or what) does it belong to?" Check your answers at the back of the book after the first set.

Exercise 4

1. *The Legacy of Luna* is a book that tells the story of a twenty-three-year-old woman, a lumber company, and a thousand-year-old redwood tree.

2. The young womans name is Julia "Butterfly" Hill, and the trees name is Luna.

3. Hill came up with Lunas name when she first saw the two-hundred-foot-tall redwood on a moonlit night, realized that it would soon be turned into lumber, and decided that she had to save its life.

4. Hill wrote the book after climbing to the top of Lunas branches and not setting foot on the earths surface again for over two years.

5. The lumber companys position was that Hill was trespassing on private property and affecting peoples livelihood by halting logging in the area around Luna.

6. While living atop Lunas branches, Hill watched the clearing of trees in the distance.

7. Hills determination allowed her to persevere through the cold, the wind, the insects, the loggers taunting, and the lack of any household facilities.

8. As a result of this young womans protest and her support teams tireless efforts, Lunas life and most of the trees around her were spared after the government bought them and guaranteed their preservation.

9. *The Legacy of Luna*s epilogue was finished after Hills return to solid ground.

10. Hills book has received mostly favorable reviews for its sincere assertion that we need to take care of the earth, but some still disagree with her method.

Sources: Earth Island Journal, spring 2000, *US Weekly,* 10 Apr. 2000, and *Christian Science Monitor,* 1 June 2000

Exercise 5

1. The Hatfields and the McCoys are famous for their ancestors feud in the late 1800s.

2. One hundred years later, the two families hostile feelings have cooled considerably.

3. The Hatfields family roots are in West Virginia, and the McCoys roots are in Kentucky.

4. In June of 2000, the Hatfields and the McCoys came together at the two states border on the banks of the Big Sandy River for a sort of reunion.

5. The reunions organizers hoped that the actions of the past could be forgiven.

6. To help with healing, members of both families threw symbols of the old enemies deeds into the fork of the river.

7. The Hatfields and McCoys also faced each other in a tug-of-war and a softball game.

8. The McCoys team beat the Hatfields team in both events; the winning softball score was 14–1.

9. The Hatfields defeat seemed appropriate because most believe their ancestors to be the "winners" of the feud.

10. Many Hatfields and McCoys have married each other, and the reunion was interesting for them, for many found themselves secretly cheering for their original familys team.

Source: People, 26 June 2000

PROOFREADING EXERCISE

Find the six errors in this student paragraph. All of the errors involve possessives.

At a ski resort in Montana, residents have more than one reason to remember New Years Eve, 1999. Everyones worries about Y2K computer failures, money mishaps, and military glitches proved to be unfounded. But that didn't stop human beings from causing problems of their own. Just after midnight, the town of Whitefish was celebrating the arrival of the first day of the year 2000. But the party quickly turned into a riot because of four womens decision to run through town without wearing any clothes. The police quickly took three of the women into custody, but the officers actions upset the gathering crowd. As the crowds number grew to include nearly four hundred people, some of them started throwing everything from glass bottles to snowballs at the authorities. By the end of the night, three of the streakers and twelve of the protesters had been arrested; all were released the next day. The police never learned the fourth streakers identity, but they did receive many eyewitness descriptions of her.

Source: Los Angeles Times, 2 Jan. 2000

SENTENCE WRITING

Write ten sentences using the possessive forms of the names of members of your family or the names of your friends. You could write about a recent event where your family or friends got together. Just tell the story of what happened that day.

REVIEW OF CONTRACTIONS AND POSSESSIVES

Here are two review exercises. First, add the necessary apostrophes to the following sentences. Try to get all the correct answers. Don't excuse an error by saying, "Oh, that was just a careless mistake." A mistake is a mistake. Be tough on yourself.

1. Ive been reading about the artist Jeff Koons.

2. In the summer of 2000, I saw one of Koons art pieces unveiled on the *Today* show, and I wanted to know more about it.

3. The sculptures name was "Puppy," and it was a forty-three-foot-tall statue of a West Highland terrier that Koons placed in the middle of Rockefeller Center in New York City.

4. Puppy wasnt a traditional statue carved in stone or sculpted out of clay.

5. Instead, Puppys metal frame was completely covered with a foot of dirt and planted with more than fifty thousand flowers.

6. As Puppy sat there from June to September as if waiting for a treat, its living flower-fur grew with the help of an internal sprinkler system.

7. Many people dont know that New York City hasnt been Puppys only showplace.

8. Earlier versions of Koons Puppy have been exhibited in Germany, Australia, and Spain.

9. Puppys most dangerous location was Spain; thats where terrorists tried to blow up the huge statue.

10. Fortunately, they werent successful.

Source: New York Times, 6 June 2000

Second, add the necessary apostrophes to the following short student essay.

A Journal of My Own

Ive been keeping a journal ever since I was in high school. I dont write it for my teachers sake. I wouldnt turn it in even if they asked me to. Its mine, and it helps me remember all of the changes Ive gone through so far in my life. The way I see it, a diarys purpose isnt just to record the facts; its to capture my true feelings.

When I record the days events in my journal, they arent written in minute-by-minute details. Instead, if Ive been staying at a friends house for the weekend, Ill write something like this: "Sharons the only friend I have who listens to my whole sentence before starting hers. Shes never in a hurry to end a good conversation. Today we talked for an hour or so about the pets wed had when we were kids. We agreed that were both 'dog people.' We cant imagine our lives without dogs. Her favorites are Pomeranians, and mine are golden retrievers." Thats the kind of an entry Id make in my journal. It doesnt mean much to anyone but me, and thats the way it should be.

I know that another persons diary would be different from mine and that most people dont even keep one. Im glad that writing comes easily to me. I dont think Ill ever stop writing in my journal because it helps me believe in myself and value others beliefs as well.

Words That Can Be Broken into Parts

Breaking words into their parts will often help you spell them correctly. Each of the following words is made up of two shorter words. Note that the word then contains all the letters of the two shorter words.

chalk board	. . .	chalkboard	room mate	. . .	roommate
over due	. . .	overdue	home work	. . .	homework
super market	. . .	supermarket	under line	. . .	underline

Becoming aware of prefixes such as *dis, inter, mis,* and *un* is also helpful. When you add a prefix to a word, note that no letters are dropped, either from the prefix or from the word.

dis appear	disappear	mis represent	misrepresent
dis appoint	disappoint	mis spell	misspell
dis approve	disapprove	mis understood	misunderstood
dis satisfy	dissatisfy	un aware	unaware

inter act	interact	un involved	uninvolved
inter active	interactive	un necessary	unnecessary
inter related	interrelated	un sure	unsure

Have someone dictate the previous list for you to write and then mark any words you miss. Memorize the correct spellings by noting how each word is made up of a prefix and a word.

Rule for Doubling a Final Letter

Most spelling rules have so many exceptions that they aren't much help. But here's one worth learning because it has almost no exceptions.

Double a final letter (consonants only) when adding an ending that begins with a vowel (such as *ing, ed, er*) if all three of the following are true:

1. The word ends in a single consonant,

2. which is preceded by a single vowel (the vowels are *a, e, i, o, u*),

3. and the accent is on the last syllable (or the word only has one syllable).

We'll try the rule on a few words to which we'll add *ing, ed,* or *er.*

begin   **1.** It ends in a single consonant—*n,*
       2. preceded by a single vowel—*i,*
       3. and the accent is on the last syllable—*be gin ́.*
       Therefore, we double the final consonant and write *beginning, beginner.*

stop   **1.** It ends in a single consonant—*p,*
       2. preceded by a single vowel—*o,*
       3. and the accent is on the last syllable (there is only one).
       Therefore, we double the final consonant and write *stopping, stopped, stopper.*

filter   **1.** It ends in a single consonant—*r,*
       2. preceded by a single vowel—*e,*
       3. But the accent isn't on the last syllable. It's on the first—*fil ́ter.*
       Therefore, we don't double the final consonant. We write *filtering, filtered.*

keep   **1.** It ends in a single consonant—*p,*
2. but it isn't preceded by a single vowel. There are two *e*'s.
Therefore, we don't double the final consonant. We write *keeping, keeper.*

NOTE- Be aware that *qu* is treated as a consonant because *q* is almost never written without *u.* Think of it as *kw.* In words like *equip* and *quit,* the *qu* acts as a consonant. Therefore *equip* and *quit* both end in a single consonant preceded by a single vowel, and the final consonant is doubled in *equipped* and *quitting.*

E X E R C I S E S

Add *ing* to these words. Correct each group of ten before continuing so you'll catch any errors while you still have words to practice on.

Exercise 1

1.	bet	**6.**	admit
2.	milk	**7.**	slap
3.	wait	**8.**	think
4.	park	**9.**	tap
5.	skim	**10.**	hit

Exercise 2

1.	wrap	**6.**	order
2.	rip	**7.**	profit
3.	peel	**8.**	scream
4.	refer	**9.**	slip
5.	invest	**10.**	predict

Exercise 3

1.	pass	**6.**	print
2.	need	**7.**	look
3.	fear	**8.**	heat
4.	crush	**9.**	pot
5.	occur	**10.**	suffer

Exercise 4

1.	preview	**6.**	frost
2.	heal	**7.**	numb
3.	chug	**8.**	rush
4.	flick	**9.**	paint
5.	book	**10.**	send

Exercise 5

1.	prefer	**6.**	fish
2.	shout	**7.**	feel
3.	rest	**8.**	hiccup
4.	fasten	**9.**	sneak
5.	hold	**10.**	plead

PROGRESS TEST

This test covers everything you've studied so far. One sentence in each pair is correct. The other is incorrect. Read both sentences carefully before you decide. Then write the letter of the incorrect sentence in the blank. Try to isolate and correct the error if you can.

1. __ **A.** The tutor complemented me on my well-organized essay.

   B. She said that my examples complemented my ideas perfectly.

2. __ **A.** I took two coffee breaks at work today.

   B. Do you know wear I put my keys?

3. __ **A.** Students could of registered two days earlier if there hadn't been an error in the computer program.

   B. That would have made the first day of classes much easier.

4. __ **A.** Pat and Jill have travelled to England many times.

   B. Their trips have never been canceled.

5. __ **A.** When people lie, they are usually bothered by their conscious.

   B. We could tell that the first pianist at the recital was feeling self-conscious.

6. __ **A.** The childrens' bicycles were lined up in front of the adults' bikes.

   B. One of a child's first major accomplishments is learning to ride a bicycle.

7. __ **A.** We've always taken her advice about movies.

   B. We have all ready seen that movie.

8. __ **A.** My mother is trying to quit smoking, and it's affecting the whole family.

   B. The harmful affects of smoking are well-known.

9. __ **A.** Many people still believe in the principal "Money can't buy everything."

   B. We shouldn't invite Jenny and Joe; they're always late.

10. __ **A.** Your the happiest person I know.

   B. When I see your face, it's always got a smile on it.

Using a Dictionary

Some dictionaries are more helpful than others. A tiny pocket-sized dictionary or one that fits on a single sheet in your notebook might help you find the spelling of very common words, but for all other uses, you will need a complete, recently published dictionary. Spend some time at a bookstore looking through the dictionaries to find one that you feel comfortable reading. Look up a word that you have had trouble with in the past, and see if you understand the definition. Try looking the same word up in another dictionary and compare. If all else fails, stick with the big names, and you probably can't go wrong.

Work through the following thirteen exercises using a good dictionary. Then you will understand what a valuable resource it is.

1. Pronunciation

Look up the word *tradition* and copy the pronunciation here.

_____

_____

_____

Now under each letter with a pronunciation mark over it, write the key word having the same mark. You'll find the key words at the bottom of one of the two dictionary pages open before you. Note especially that the upside-down *e* (ə) always has the sound of *uh* like the *a* in *ago* or *about.* Remember that sound because it's found in many words.

Next, pronounce the key words you have written, and then slowly pronounce *tradition,* giving each syllable the same sound as its key word.

Finally, note which syllable has the heavy accent mark. (In most dictionaries the accent mark points to the stressed syllable, but in one dictionary it is in front of the stressed syllable.) The stressed syllable is *di.* Now say the word, letting the full force of your voice fall on that syllable.

When more than one pronunciation is given, the first is more common. If the complete pronunciation of a word isn't given, look at the word above it to find the pronunciation.

Look up the pronunciation of these words, using the key words at the bottom of the dictionary page to help you pronounce each syllable. Then note which syllable has the heavy accent mark, and say the word aloud.

rufescent   hibachi   triage   scrumptious

2. Definitions

The dictionary may give more than one meaning for a word.

Read all the meanings for each italicized word and then write a definition appropriate to the sentence.

1. Our neighbors taught their dog to *heel*. _____

_____

2. He made himself a cup of *instant* coffee. _____

_____

3. When we *land*, I will call my parents. _____

_____

4. The battery was leaking at one of its *poles*. _____

_____

3. Spelling

By making yourself look up each word you aren't sure how to spell, you'll soon become a better speller. When two spellings are given in the dictionary, the first one (or the one with the definition) is preferred.

Use a dictionary to find the preferred spelling for each of these words.

moustache, mustache   wagon, waggon

judgement, judgment   cancelled, canceled

4. Compound Words

If you want to find out whether two words are written separately, written with a hyphen between them, or written as one word, consult your dictionary. For example:

half sister   is written as two words

father-in-law   is hyphenated

stepson   is written as one word

Write each of the following correctly.

stereo type _____   half dollar _____

off shore _____   good natured _____

5. Capitalization

If a word is capitalized in the dictionary, that means it should always be capitalized. If it is not capitalized in the dictionary, then it may or may not be capitalized, depending on how it is used (see p. 190). For example, *Friday* is always capitalized, but *college* is capitalized or not, according to how it is used.

> On Friday, Beth will graduate from college.

> On Friday, Beth will graduate from Pasadena City College.

Write the following words as they're given in the dictionary (with or without a capital) to show whether they must always be capitalized or not. Take a guess before looking them up.

corvette _____   pulitzer prize _____

mars _____   scotch _____

6. Usage

Just because a word is in the dictionary doesn't mean that it's in standard use. The following labels indicate whether a word is used today and, if so, where and by whom.

obsolete	no longer used
archaic	not now used in ordinary language but still found in some biblical, literary, and legal expressions
colloquial, informal	used in informal conversation but not in formal writing
dialectal, regional	used in some localities but not everywhere
slang	popular but nonstandard expression
nonstandard, substandard	not used in Standard Written English

Look up each italicized word and write the label indicating its usage. Dictionaries differ. One may list a word as slang whereas another will call it colloquial. Still another may give no designation, thus indicating that that particular dictionary considers the word in standard use.

1. Please *gimme* some of that popcorn. _____

2. His *deadpan* delivery of the joke is what made it so funny. _____

3. The doctor called my baby sister a *butterball.* _____

4. Our teacher *freaked out* when we said that we needed more time. _____

_____

5. They went *thataway!* _____

7. Derivations

The derivations or stories behind words will often help you remember the current meanings. For example, if you read that someone is *narcissistic* and you consult your dictionary, you'll find that *narcissism* is a condition named after Narcissus, who was a handsome young man in Greek mythology. One day Narcissus fell in love with his own reflection in a pool, but when he tried to get closer to it, he fell in the water and drowned. A flower that grew nearby is now named for Narcissus. And *narcissistic* has come to mean "in love with oneself."

Look up the derivation of each of these words. You'll find it in square brackets either just before or just after the definition.

Murphy bed _____

Chihuahua _____

Goody Two-shoes _____

silhouette _____

8. Synonyms

At the end of a definition, a group of synonyms is sometimes given. For example, at the end of the definition of *injure,* you'll find several synonyms, such as *damage* or *harm.* And if you look up *damage* or *harm,* you'll be referred to the same synonyms listed under *injure.*

List the synonyms given for the following words.

fly _____

revamp _____

scoff _____

9. Abbreviations

Find the meaning of the following abbreviations.

DVD   _____   HMO   _____

SAM   _____   CDC   _____

10. Names of People

The names of famous people will be found either in the main part of your dictionary or in a separate biographical names section at the back.

Identify the following famous people.

Anna Ivanovna   _____

Gabriel García Márquez   _____

Grace Hopper   _____

Frederick Douglass   _____

11. Names of Places

The names of places will be found either in the main part of your dictionary or in a separate geographical names section at the back.

Identify the following places.

Killiecrankie   _____

Chernobyl   _____

Biolystok   _____

Zanzibar   _____

12. Foreign Words and Phrases

Find the language and the meaning of the italicized expressions.

1. The *hors d'oeuvres* at the party were delicious. _____

2. I hope to graduate *magna cum laude.* _____

3. My new sheet music said that it should be played *all' otava* _____

4. Beverly's projects were always considered the *crème de la crème.* _____

13. Miscellaneous Information

See if you can find these miscellaneous bits of information in a dictionary.

1. What duty is a *devil's advocate* supposed to perform? _____

2. In what country would you measure liquid by *mutchkin?* _____

3. Under what circumstances should someone be given *ipecac?* _____

4. Is a *macaroon* something to eat or something to wear? _____

5. What part of speech is the expression *yoo-hoo?*_____

Sentence Structure

Sentence structure refers to the way sentences are built using words, phrases, and clauses. Words are single units, and words link up in sentences to form clauses and phrases. Clauses are word groups *with* subjects and verbs, and phrases are word groups *without* subjects and verbs. Clauses are the most important because they make statements—they tell who did what (or what something is) in a sentence. Look at the following sentence, for example:

We bought oranges at the farmer's market on Main Street.

It contains ten words, each playing its own part in the meaning of the sentence. But which of the words together tell who did what? *We bought oranges* is correct. That word group is a clause. Notice that *at the farmer's market* and *on Main Street* also link up as word groups but don't have somebody (subject) doing something (verb). Instead, they are phrases to clarify *where* we bought the oranges.

Importantly, you could leave out one or both of the phrases and still have a sentence—*We bought oranges*. However, you cannot leave the clause out. Then you would just have *At the farmer's market on Main Street*. Remember, every sentence needs at least one clause that can stand by itself.

Learning about the structure of sentences helps you control your own. Once you know more about sentence structure, then you can understand writing errors and learn how to correct them.

Among the most common errors in writing are fragments, run-ons, and awkward phrasing.

Here are some fragments:

Wandering around the mall all afternoon.

Because I tried to do too many things at once.

By interviewing the applicants in groups.

They don't make complete statements—not one has a clause that can stand by itself. Who was *wandering*? What happened *because you tried to do too many things at once?* What was the result of *interviewing the applicants in groups?* These incomplete sentence structures fail to communicate a complete thought.

In contrast, here are some run-ons:

Computer prices are dropping they're still beyond my budget.

The forecast calls for rain I'll wait to wash my car.

A truck parked in front of my driveway I couldn't get to school.

Unlike fragments, run-ons make complete statements, but the trouble is they make *two* complete statements; the first *runs on* to the second without correct punctuation. The reader has to go back to see where there should have been a break.

So fragments don't include enough information, and run-ons include too much. Another problem occurs when the information in a sentence just doesn't make sense.

Here are a few sentences with awkward phrasing:

The problem from my grades started to end.

It was a time at the picnic.

She won me at chess.

Try to find the word groups that show who did what, that is, the clauses. Once you find them, then try to put the clauses and phrases together to form a precise meaning. It's difficult, isn't it? You'll see that many of the words themselves are misused or unclear, such as *from, it,* and *won.* These sentences don't communicate clearly because the clauses, phrases, and even words don't work together. They suffer from awkward phrasing.

Fragments, run-ons, awkward phrasing, and other sentence structure errors confuse the reader. Not until you get rid of them will your writing be clearer and easier to read. Unfortunately, there is no quick, effortless way to learn to avoid errors in sentence structure. First, you need to understand how clear sentences are built. Then you will be able to avoid common errors in your own writing.

This section will describe areas of sentence structure one at a time and then explain how to correct errors associated with the different areas. For instance, we start by helping you find subjects and verbs and understand dependent clauses; then we show you how to avoid fragments. You can go through the whole section yourself to master all of the areas. Or your teacher may assign only parts based on errors the class is making.

Finding Subjects and Verbs

The most important words in sentences are those that make up its independent clause, the subject and the verb. When you write a sentence, you write about *something* or *someone*. That's the subject. Then you write what the subject *does* or *is*. That's the verb.

> <u>Lightning</u> <u><u>strikes</u></u>.

The word *Lightning* is the something you are writing about. It's the subject, and we'll underline it once. *Strikes* tells what the subject does. It shows the action in the sentence. It's the verb, and we'll underline it twice. Most sentences do not include only two words—the subject and the verb. However, these two words still make up the core of the sentence even if other words and phrases are included with them.

> <u>Lightning</u> <u><u>strikes</u></u> back and forth from the clouds to the ground very quickly.

> Often <u>lightning</u> <u><u>strikes</u></u> people on golf courses or in boats.

When many words appear in sentences, the subject and verb can be hard to find. Because the verb often shows action, it's easier to spot than the subject. Therefore, always look for it first. For example, in the sentence

> The neighborhood cat folded its paws under its chest.

which word shows the action? <u><u>Folded</u></u>. It's the verb. Underline it twice. Now ask yourself who or what folded? <u>Cat</u>. It's the subject. Underline it once.

Study the following sentences until you understand how to pick out subjects and verbs.

> Tomorrow our school celebrates its fiftieth anniversary. (Which word shows the action? <u><u>Celebrates</u></u>. It's the verb. Underline it twice. Who or what celebrates? <u>School</u>. It's the subject. Underline it once.)

> The team members ate several boxes of chocolates. (Which word shows the action? <u><u>Ate</u></u>. Who or what ate? <u>Members</u> <u><u>ate</u></u>.)

> Internet users crowd the popular services. (Which word shows the action? <u><u>Crowd</u></u>. Who or what crowd? <u>Users</u> <u><u>crowd</u></u>.)

Often the verb doesn't show action but merely tells what the subject *is* or *was*. Learn to spot such verbs—*is, am, are, was, were, seems, feels, appears, becomes, looks,* and so forth. (For more information on these verbs, see the discussion of sentence patterns on p. 126).

> Marshall is a neon artist. (First spot the verb is. Then ask who or what is? <u>Marshall</u> <u><u>is</u></u>.)

The bread appears moldy. (First spot the verb appears. Then ask who or what appears? Bread appears.)

Sometimes the subject comes after the verb.

In the audience were two reviewers from the *Times*. (Who or what were in the audience? Reviewers were.)

There was a fortune-teller at the carnival. (Who or what was there? Fortune-teller was there.)

There were name tags for all the participants. (Who or what were there? Name tags were there.)

Here are the worksheets. (Who or what are here? Worksheets are here.)

NOTE- Remember that *there* and *here* (as in the last three sentences) are not subjects. They simply point to something.

In commands, often the subject is not expressed. It is *you* (understood).

Sit down. (You sit down.)

Place flap A into slot B. (You place flap A into slot B.)

Meet me at 7:00. (You meet me at 7:00.)

There may be more than one subject in a sentence.

Toys and memorabilia from the 1950s are high-priced collectibles.

Celebrity dolls, board games, and even cereal boxes from that decade line the shelves of antique stores.

There may also be more than one verb.

Water boils at a consistent temperature and freezes at another.

The ice tray fell out of my hand, skidded across the floor, and landed under the table.

As you pick out subjects in the following exercises, you may wonder whether you should say the subject is, for example, *heat* or *summer heat*. It makes no difference so long as you get the main subject, *heat,* right. In the answers at the back of the book, usually—but not always—the single word is used. Don't waste your time worrying whether to include an extra word or two with the subject. Just make sure you get the main subjects right.

E X E R C I S E S

Underline the subjects once and the verbs twice. When you've finished ten sentences, compare your answers carefully with those at the back of the book.

Exercise 1

1. The summer heat causes many problems for people.

2. Food spoils more quickly in the summer.

3. Insects and other pests seek shelter inside.

4. There are power outages due to excessive use of air conditioners and fans.

5. In some areas, smog levels increase dramatically in the summer.

6. School children suffer in overheated classrooms.

7. On the worst days, everyone searches for a swimming pool or drives to the beach.

8. Sleeping comfortably becomes impossible.

9. No activity seems worth the effort.

10. But the heat of summer fades in our minds at the first real break in the weather.

Exercise 2

1. In 1992, Jacquelyn Barrett became the sheriff of Fulton County, Georgia.

2. She was the first African-American woman sheriff in U.S. history.

3. As sheriff of Fulton County, Barrett managed the biggest system of jails in the state of Georgia.

4. Her department had a yearly budget of sixty-five million dollars.

5. Over a thousand people worked for the Fulton County Sheriff's office.

6. Barrett definitely broke the stereotype of southern sheriffs in TV and movies.

7. By 1999, there were over eleven hundred sheriffs in the South.

8. African-American men and women represented just five percent of the total.

9. Only one percent of them were women.

10. However, of the twenty-four female sheriffs in the country, nine were from the South.

Sources: USA Today, 16 Dec. 1999, and *Essence,* July 2000

Exercise 3

1. Livio De Marchi lives in Venice, Italy, with its canals and romantic gondolas.

2. Unfortunately, large power boats also crowd the canals of Venice.

3. So De Marchi built a boat of his own in response to the growing traffic problems in the canals.

4. His "boat" looks exactly like a convertible Volkswagen Beetle.

5. De Marchi carved the body of his floating VW Bug completely out of wood.

6. Even the open convertible top behind the passenger seat is wooden.

7. De Marchi's car-boat has a small motor and travels at only five miles an hour.

8. With its real headlights and glass windshield, this replica gets a lot of attention.

9. De Marchi carved other wooden cars besides the VW.

10. One of them, a Fiat, is on exhibit at a Ripley's Believe It or Not! museum in Missouri.

Source: People, 1 Nov. 1999

Exercise 4

1. I just read the American Film Institute's list of "America's Funniest Movies."

2. The list goes all the way back to the 1920s and includes one hundred great comedies.

3. A 1924 movie, *The Navigator,* is the earliest of AFI's funniest picks.

4. That one is an unknown to me.

5. I recognize 1925's *The Gold Rush* and remember Chaplin's classic shoe-eating scene.

6. The 1998 hit *There's Something about Mary* ends the list.

7. In between, some decades produced more of the best comedies than others.

8. Filmmakers in the 1980s, for instance, created twenty-two of the funniest.

9. But there are only five films from the 1990s.

10. Maybe Y2K worries shifted the focus to sci-fi thrillers.

Exercise 5

1. At the Swiss Federal Institute of Technology in Lausanne, Switzerland, teams of tiny robots roam the labs.

2. They are all about the size of a lump of sugar or a single die in a pair of dice.

3. A motor and battery from a watch power each of the teeny technological wonders.

4. They move around and navigate in mazes through the use of sensing devices.

5. And they all have the same name: Alice.

6. Yet every Alice has its own number code.

7. Upon contact, each communicates its ranking to its companion and either leads or follows the other in numerical order.

8. The Alices also send information directly back to computers in the lab.

9. Needless to say, the Alices give scientists a lot of enjoyment.

10. Even visitors to the lab's Web site play with the Alices through remote control.

Source: Discover, Aug. 2000

PARAGRAPH EXERCISE

Underline the subjects once and the verbs twice in the following student paragraph.

Stories about air travel hold many people's interest these days. Of course, there are stories with happy and unhappy endings. Some of the stories just confuse everyone. For instance, the people in charge of landings and take-offs at Chicago's O'Hare Airport have a strange story of their own. Early in 2000, the radar at O'Hare often showed false images of airplanes on the screens. The controllers took all of the necessary precautions but found no planes there at all. They called these illusions "ghosts." And no one has a good explanation for them yet.

Source: Washington Post, 21 May 2000

SENTENCE WRITING

Write ten sentences about any subject—your favorite color, for instance. Keeping your subject matter simple in these sentence-writing exercises will make it easier to find your sentence structures later. After you have written your sentences, go back and underline your subjects once and your verbs twice.

Locating Prepositional Phrases

Prepositional phrases are among the easiest structures in English to learn. Remember that a phrase is just a group of related words (at least two) without a subject and a verb. And don't let a term like *prepositional* scare you. If you look in the middle of that long word, you'll find a familiar one—*position*. In English, we tell the *positions* of people and things in sentences using prepositional phrases. Look at the following sentence with its prepositional phrases in parentheses:

Our field trip (to the desert) begins (at 6:00) (in the morning) (on Friday).

One phrase tells where the field trip is going (*to the desert*), and three phrases tell when the trip begins (*at 6:00, in the morning,* and *on Friday*). As you can see, prepositional phrases show the position of someone or something in space or in time.

Here is a list of many prepositions that can show positions in space:

under	across	outside	against
around	by	inside	at
through	beyond	over	beneath
above	among	on	in
below	near	behind	past
between	with	from	to

Here are some prepositions that can show positions in time:

before	throughout	past	within
after	by	until	in
since	at	during	for

These lists include only individual words, *not phrases*. Remember, a preposition must be followed by an object—someone or something—to create a prepositional phrase. Notice that in the added prepositional phrases that follow, the position of the plane in relation to the object, *the clouds,* changes completely.

The passenger plane flew *above the clouds.*
below the clouds.
within the clouds.
between the clouds.
past the clouds.
around the clouds.

Now notice the different positions in time:

The plane landed *at 3:30.*
by 3:30.
past 3:30.
before the thunderstorm.
during the thunderstorm.
after the thunderstorm.

> **NOTE-** A few words—such as *of, as,* and *like*—are prepositions that do not fit neatly into either the space or time category, yet they are very common prepositions (box *of candy,* note *of apology,* type *of bicycle*—act *as a substitute,* use *as an example,* testified *as an expert*—vitamins *like A, C, and E,* shaped *like a watermelon,* moved *like a snake*).

By locating prepositional phrases, you will be able to find subjects and verbs more easily. For example, you might have difficulty finding the subject and verb in a long sentence like this:

> After the rainy season, one of the windows in the attic leaked at the corners of its molding.

But if you put parentheses around all the prepositional phrases like this

> (After the rainy season), <u>one</u> (of the windows) (in the attic) <u>leaked</u> (at the corners) (of its molding).

then you have only two words left—the subject and the verb. Even in short sentences like the following, you might pick the wrong word as the subject if you don't put parentheses around the prepositional phrases first.

> <u>Many</u> (of the characters) <u>survived</u> (in that movie).

> The <u>waves</u> (around the ship) <u>looked</u> real.

NOTE- Don't mistake *to* plus a verb for a prepositional phrase. For example, *to quit* is not a prepositional phrase because *quit* is not the name of something. It's a form of verb.

E X E R C I S E S

Locate and put parentheses around the prepositional phrases in the following sentences. Be sure to start with the preposition itself (*in, on, to, at, of . . .*) and include the word or words that go with it (*in the morning, on our sidewalk, to Hawaii . . .*). Then underline the subjects once and the verbs twice. Remember that subjects and verbs are almost never inside prepositional phrases. Review the answers given at the back for each group of ten sentences before continuing.

Exercise 1

1. For nearly thirty years, a phone booth stood in the middle of the Mojave Desert with absolutely nothing around it.

2. It was far from any sign of civilization but originally served miners in camps far away.

3. The number for this pay phone became well-known over time: 760-733-9969.

4. People called it from around the world and traveled to it for fun and adventure.

5. Sites on the Internet posted the isolated phone's number and offered maps to its remote location near Baker, California.

6. Individuals camped outside the booth and waited for random calls from strangers.

7. Callers never expected an answer from a phone in the middle of nowhere.

8. On many occasions, callers panicked and said nothing for a minute or two.

9. In addition, some of its visitors vandalized the booth and the phone itself.

10. So phone-company workers removed the infamous Mojave phone booth in May 2000.

Source: Washington Post, 25 May 2000

Exercise 2

1. One of the most popular movies of the year 2000 was *Chicken Run.*

2. This stop-motion movie with clay chickens did very well at the box office.

3. The directors, Nick Park and Peter Lord, made *Chicken Run* with a budget of forty-two million dollars.

4. In the movie world, that's a real bargain.

5. And the labor was much more intensive than in ordinary pictures.

6. The five hundred shots of a regular live-action film became one hundred thousand shots for this movie.

7. The stop-motion method of filmmaking requires twenty-four changes in sets and characters' features for each second of film.

8. Therefore, *Chicken Run,* with its intricate prisonlike set and its lifelike poultry inmates, took three years to complete.

9. Nick Park made other shorter films before *Chicken Run.*

10. His *Creature Comforts* won an Academy Award in 1989 and led to *The Wrong Trousers,* now a classic in animation.

Source: Time, 19 June 2000

Exercise 3

1. John Zweifel is a big name in the world of miniatures.

2. His miniature replica of the White House impresses people around the country with its painstaking attention to detail.

3. Zweifel officially started the project during President Ford's administration.

4. Zweifel used the scale of one inch to one foot for his model of the capital's mansion.

5. Within the model's walls are tiny reproductions of all of the furnishings and personal effects of the current president and his family.

6. During Ronald Reagan's tenure, Zweifel put a tiny jar of jelly beans on the president's desk.

7. There were Amy Carter's roller-skate marks on the wooden floor of the East Room.

8. Zweifel keeps the model up-to-date through bimonthly visits to the actual White House in Washington, D.C.

9. As governor of Arkansas, Bill Clinton first saw Zweifel's amazing replica in 1979.

10. Under its realistic spell, Clinton foresaw his future as a resident of the White House and shared his premonition with Zweifel.

Source: People, 26 June 2000

Exercise 4

1. At 2 A.M. on the first Sunday in April, something happens to nearly everyone in America: Daylight Saving Time.

2. But few people are awake at two in the morning.

3. So we set the hands or digits of our clocks ahead one hour on Saturday night in preparation for it.

4. And before bed on the last Saturday in October, we turn them back again.

5. For days after both events, I have trouble with my sleep patterns and my mood.

6. In spring, the feeling is one of loss.

7. That Saturday-night sleep into Sunday is one hour shorter than usual.

8. But in fall, I gain a false sense of security about time.

9. That endless Sunday morning quickly melts into the start of a hectic week like the other fifty-one in the year.

10. All of this upheaval is due to the Uniform Time Act of 1966.

Exercise 5

1. Many Americans still shop in stores for holiday gifts.

2. With the increase in ease and access to merchandise over the Internet, more people and stores do business on computer.

3. This increase was gradual at first but rose dramatically in 1999.

4. In 1998, people ordered only one percent of their holiday purchases over the Internet.

5. However, Americans gained confidence in on-line shopping just in time for the holidays of 1999.

6. The number of Internet purchases tripled within one year.

7. Most businesses were not ready for the increase in on-line sales.

8. Some big names in toys, electronics, and pet supplies originally promised deliveries by Christmas morning, for example.

9. But by late December, the volume of orders overloaded both suppliers and shipping companies.

10. Back-ordered items and late packages spoiled lots of holiday moments.

Source: *Newsweek*, 10 Jan. 2000

PARAGRAPH EXERCISE

Put parentheses around the prepositional phrases in this paragraph from *A Golden Guide: Weather*, by Paul E. Lehr, R. William Burnett, and Herbert S. Zim.

Water Storage

Lakes and ponds obviously store a great deal of water. Not so obvious is the immense reservoir of water stored in the polar ice caps, in glaciers, and in snow on mountains and on the cold northern plains during winter. Winter snows in the mountains determine the water supply for irrigation and for power use. This snow melts with the spring thaw and fills the rivers.

SENTENCE WRITING

Write ten sentences on the topic of your favorite place to relax or hide away—or choose any topic you like. When you go back over your sentences, put parentheses around your prepositional phrases and underline your subjects once and your verbs twice.

Understanding Dependent Clauses

All clauses contain a subject and a verb; however, there are two kinds of clauses: independent and dependent. An independent clause has a subject and a verb and can stand alone as a sentence. A dependent clause has a subject and a verb but can't stand alone because it begins with a dependent word (or words) such as

after	since	where
although	so that	whereas
as	than	wherever
as if	that	whether
because	though	which
before	unless	whichever

even if	until	while
even though	what	who
ever since	whatever	whom
how	when	whose
if	whenever	why

Whenever a clause begins with one of these dependent words, it is a dependent clause (unless it's a question, which would be followed by a question mark). If we take an independent clause such as

<u>We ate dinner together.</u>

and put one of the dependent words in front of it, it becomes a dependent clause and can no longer stand alone:

After we ate dinner together . . .

Although we ate dinner together . . .

As we ate dinner together . . .

Before we ate dinner together . . .

Since we ate dinner together . . .

That we ate dinner together . . .

When we ate dinner together . . .

While we ate dinner together . . .

With the added dependent words, these do not make complete statements. They leave the reader expecting something more. Therefore, these clauses can no longer stand alone. Each would depend on another clause—an independent clause—to make a sentence. We'll place a broken line beneath the dependent clauses.

After we ate dinner together, we went to the evening seminar.

We went to the evening seminar *after* we ate dinner together.

The speaker didn't know *that* we ate dinner together.

While we ate dinner together, the restaurant became crowded.

Note that in the preceeding examples, *when a dependent clause comes at the beginning of a sentence, it is followed by a comma.* Often the comma prevents misreading, as in the following sentence:

> *When* he returned, the video was almost over.

Without a comma after *returned,* the reader would read *When he returned the video* before realizing that this was not what the author meant. The comma prevents misreading. Sometimes if the dependent clause is short and there is no danger of misreading, the comma can be left off, but it's safer simply to follow the rule that a dependent clause at the beginning of a sentence is followed by a comma.

You'll learn more about the punctuation of dependent clauses on pages 171 and 177, but right now just remember the previous rule.

Note that sometimes the dependent word is the subject of the dependent clause:

> Theirs is the house that was remodeled last month.

> The children understood what was happening.

Sometimes the dependent clause is in the middle of the independent clause:

> The house that was remodeled last month is theirs.

> The events that followed were confusing.

And sometimes the dependent clause is the subject of the entire sentence:

> What you do also affects me.

> Whichever they choose will be best for them.

> How it looks doesn't mean anything.

Also note that sometimes the *that* of a dependent clause is omitted.

> I know *that* you can tell the difference between red and green.

I know you can tell the difference between red and green.

Did everyone get the classes *that* they wanted?

Did everyone get the classes they wanted?

The word *that* doesn't always introduce a dependent clause. It may be a pronoun and serve as the subject of the sentence.

That was a big mistake.

That is my book.

That can also be a descriptive word.

That movie makes me cry every time.

I will take him to *that* restaurant tomorrow.

E X E R C I S E S

Underline the subjects once and the verbs twice in both the independent and the dependent clauses. Then put a broken line under the dependent clauses. Some sentences may have no dependent clauses, and others may have more than one.

Exercise 1

1. Mark and Jackie Tresl live in a small cabin on two hundred acres of land in Ohio.

2. The Tresls have two pets that live in the cabin with them.

3. One is a dog, whose name is Rodent, and one is a horse, whose name is Misha.

4. The Tresls found Misha when she was about six months old and discovered that she had pneumonia.

5. While Mark and Jackie cared for the sick foal, they kept her inside the house for warmth.

6. Since a horse needs a lot of floor space, the Tresls lined all of their furniture up against the cabin walls.

7. Once Misha recovered from her illness, the Tresls decided to keep her in the house.

8. Although some adjustments were necessary, the Tresls made them and truly love their thirteen-hundred-pound house pet.

9. The Tresls used sweets as a lure during the housebreaking process.

10. Now Misha goes outside only when she needs to.

Source: People, 31 Jan. 2000

Exercise 2

1. When Barbara Mitchell ate lunch at a California restaurant in late 1997, she thought that the service was terrible.

2. The lunch that Mitchell ordered consisted of salad, soup, pasta, and iced tea.

3. She received the bill, which came to twenty-four dollars, and charged it to her credit card.

4. Because the service was so bad, Mitchell wrote in a one-cent tip.

5. But when Mitchell saw her credit-card statement, she nearly fainted.

6. The tip that was a penny turned into a charge of ten thousand dollars, in addition to the twenty-four dollars for her food.

7. The waiter told authorities that he entered the huge tip amount by mistake.

8. When the restaurant's manager learned of the error, she suspended the waiter for seven days.

9. Mitchell received a full refund, an apology, and a gift certificate from the restaurant.

10. Mitchell wishes that she paid the bill with cash.

Source: Daily News (Los Angeles), 8 Jan. 1998

Exercise 3

1. In June of 2000, there was another incident of mistaken tipping at a bar in Chicago.

2. This time, a male customer left a real ten-thousand-dollar tip for a waitress who was especially nice to him.

3. At least everyone thought that he gave her that amount until the man later denied his generosity.

4. The customer, who was a London resident on a trip to the United States, did everything to convince the people in the bar that he was serious.

5. Melanie Uczen was the waitress who served the man his drinks, which added up to nine dollars.

6. He told her that he was a doctor and wanted to help with her college plans.

7. When the bar's owner questioned the tip, the customer allowed the owner to make a copy of his passport.

8. He even signed a note that verified the tip's amount.

9. Back in London, the man said that he was not a doctor and claimed that he was drunk when he signed the note.

10. Because the big tip brought the bar so much publicity, the owners paid Melanie Uczen the ten thousand dollars themselves.

Source: Washington Post, 11 June 2000

Exercise 4

1. The happiest ending to a big-tipper story came in July of 2000.

2. It began when Karen Steinmetz, who dispatches cars for Continental Limo company, received a call for a driver and limo at 2:30 in the morning.

3. The most unusual part of the customer's request was that he wanted the driver to take him over nine hundred miles, from southern California to Oregon.

4. When Steinmetz contacted the first driver to see if he wanted the job, he told her that he wanted only sleep at that hour.

5. So Steinmetz called Major Cephas, another driver who worked for Continental.

6. Cephas took the job and picked the customer up in the city of Garden Grove.

7. The two men drove through the night but stopped in Sacramento and other spots along the way for exercise and refreshments.

8. Overall, the trip took nearly eighteen hours, which resulted in a twenty-two-hundred-dollar fare.

9. The passenger paid the fare and gave Cephas a twenty-thousand-dollar tip because Cephas was so patient with him.

10. This time, the tip was as real as the disappointment of the first driver who turned down the job.

Source: Los Angeles Times, 21 July 2000

Exercise 5

1. As Mike Bell enjoyed his flight from Washington, D.C., to San Jose, California, his dog Dakota was miserable.

2. Bell and everyone else assumed that Dakota's carrier was in the special part of the plane that warmly houses animals during flights.

3. However, halfway through the trip, the plane's captain discovered that the dog was actually in the freezing part of the cargo hold.

4. The captain knew that any animal who stayed in such an environment for the remainder of the flight could die.

5. When the crew gave Bell the news that his dog was in danger, he felt worried and helpless.

6. Because they cared about the life of a dog, the crew made a special stop at the next airport.

7. They found Dakota alive but very cold and allowed Bell to bring Dakota into the cabin for the rest of the trip.

8. The other passengers who were on board were happy for Bell and his dog.

9. Bell appreciates what the captain and crew did for Dakota after they caught the mistake.

10. But he is not sure whether he wants to fly with a pet ever again.

Source: People, 26 June 2000

PARAGRAPH EXERCISE

Underline the subjects once, the verbs twice, and put a broken line under the dependent clauses in these paragraphs from *The Chocolate Companion*, by Chantal Coady. You may notice that some verbs seem to have no subject. These are commands in which a "you" subject is understood.

Tasting

[When you taste chocolate], let a small piece gently melt on your tongue. Unless it is a particularly revolting sample, . . . do not spit out [the] chocolate because [you get] information from the "mouthfeel." . . . Although coffee goes well with chocolate, it dulls the palate in the same way as other strong flavors such as chili or peppermint. . . .

Snap

If it is a bar of chocolate that you are tasting, break it and listen to check that it snaps cleanly. . . . If you hold the chocolate for a few seconds, it should begin to melt unless it contains lots of vegetable fats or your circulation is particularly bad!

Bloom

Bloom is the term for the grayish-white appearance . . . on the surface of chocolate. There are two types of bloom which develop on chocolate. The first . . . indicates that the chocolate has become too warm at some point. . . . Much more serious is sugar bloom which occurs when moisture comes into contact with chocolate. . . . The sugar crystals [which come] to the surface dissolve in the water vapor, later recrystallizing. The process destroys the texture of the chocolate, which becomes gray and gritty and although [it is] edible will hardly delight the connoisseur.

SENTENCE WRITING

Write ten sentences about your evening routine (coming home from school or work, eating dinner, etc.). Try to write sentences that contain both independent and dependent clauses. Then underline your subjects once, your verbs twice, and put a broken line under your dependent clauses.

Correcting Fragments

Sometimes a group of words looks like a sentence—with a capital letter at the beginning and a period at the end—but it is missing a subject or a verb or both. Such incomplete sentence structures are called fragments. Here are a few examples:

Just ran around hugging everyone in sight. (no subject)

Paul and his sister with the twins. (no verb)

Nothing to do but wait. (no subject and no verb)

To change these fragments into sentences, we must make sure each has a subject and an adequate verb:

The sweepstakes winner just ran around hugging everyone in sight. (We added a subject.)

Paul and his sister with the twins reconciled. (We added a verb.)

We had nothing to do but wait. (We added a subject and a verb.)

Sometimes we can simply attach such a fragment to the sentence before or after it.

I want to find a fulfilling job. A career like teaching, for example.

I want to find a fulfilling job, a career like teaching, for example.

Or we can change a word or two in the fragment and make it into a sentence.

A teaching career is one example.

PHRASES

Phrases by definition are word groups without subjects and verbs, so whenever a phrase is punctuated as a sentence, it is a fragment. Look at this example of a sentence followed by a phrase fragment beginning with *hoping* (see p. 116 for more about verbal phrases).

I waited outside the director's office. Hoping to have a chance for an audition.

We can correct this fragment by attaching it to the previous sentence.

I waited outside the director's office, hoping to have a chance for an audition.

Or we can change it to include a subject and a real verb.

I waited outside the director's office. I hoped to have a chance for an audition.

Here's another example of a sentence followed by a phrase fragment:

The actor's profile was striking. Sketched on an envelope by a famous artist.

Here the two have been combined into one complete sentence:

The actor's striking profile was sketched on an envelope by a famous artist.

Or a better revision might be

A famous artist sketched the actor's striking profile on an envelope.

Sometimes, prepositional phrases are also incorrectly punctuated as sentences. Here a prepositional phrase follows a sentence, but the word group is a fragment—it has no subject and verb of its own. Therefore, it needs to be corrected.

I have lived a simple life so far. With my family on our farm in central California.

Here is one possible correction:

I have lived a simple life so far with my family on our farm in central California.

Or it could be corrected this way:

My family and I have lived a simple life on our farm in central California.

DEPENDENT CLAUSES

Dependent clauses punctuated as sentences are still another kind of fragment. A sentence needs a subject, a verb, *and* a complete thought. As discussed in the previous section, a dependent clause has a subject and a verb, but it begins with a word that makes its meaning incomplete, such as *after, while, because, since, although, when, if, where, who, which,* and *that* (see pp. 60–61 for a list). To correct such fragments, you need to take off the word that makes the clause dependent *or* add an independent clause.

FRAGMENT
While some of us practiced our speeches.

CORRECTED
   Some of us practiced our speeches.

or

   While some of us practiced our speeches, we heard the bell.

FRAGMENT
   Which signaled the start of class.

CORRECTED
   The bell signaled the start of class.

or

   We heard the bell, *which* signaled the start of class.

Are fragments ever permissible? Fragments are sometimes used in advertising and in other kinds of writing. But such fragments are used by professional writers who know what they're doing. These fragments are used intentionally, not in error. Until you're an experienced writer, stick with complete sentences. Especially in college writing, fragments should not be used.

E X E R C I S E S

Some—but not all—of the following word groups are sentences. The others suffer from incomplete sentence structure. Put a period after each of the sentences. Make any fragments into sentences by assuring that each has a subject and an adequate verb.

Exercise 1

1. Douglas Fairbanks, Jr., died in May of 2000 at the age of ninety

2. A move star for most of his life

3. Nearly eighty films in his long career

4. Making the first at the age of thirteen and the last at seventy-two

5. The son of another prestigious actor, Douglas Fairbanks, Senior

6. Fairbanks, Sr., starred in the swashbuckling films of the 1920s and 30s

7. Marrying the famous actress Mary Pickford and becoming one of the most powerful people in Hollywood

8. Fairbanks and Pickford called their son Doug Junior but did not want him to be an actor

9. However, he disappointed his parents and followed in their footsteps

10. *The Prisoner of Zenda,* Douglas Fairbanks, Jr's, most enduring performance

Source: The Economist, 13 May 2000

Exercise 2

1. In my psychology class, we talk about gender a lot

2. Especially ways of raising children without gender bias

3. Meaning different expectations about boys' abilities and girls' abilities

4. Experts have several suggestions for parents and teachers

5. Ask girls to work in the yard and boys to do dishes sometimes

6. Not making a big deal out of it

7. Give both girls and boys affection as well as helpful criticism

8. Encouraging physically challenging activities for both genders

9. Give girls access to tools, and praise boys for kindness

10. Most of all, value their different approaches to math and computers

Exercise 3

Correct each phrase fragment by changing or adding words or by attaching the phrase to the complete sentence nearby.

1. The ocean liner Titanic sank in April of 1912. Affecting thousands of families and inspiring books and movies around the world.

2. With three close relatives on the Titanic that April night. The Belman family remembers details of the disaster.

3. Two of the Belmans were lost after the sinking. One surviving by swimming along next to a lifeboat and eventually climbing aboard.

4. The survivor, Grandfather Belman, returned to his family in Lebanon. And told them about the terrifying events of that night.

5. He recalled the efforts of the crew and the courage of the passengers. The icy cold water and the reassuring sight of the Carpathia.

6. Anthony Belman is Grandfather Belman's descendent. Now living in the United States and working as a bartender.

7. Inspired by the stories of his grandfather's survival and the loss of his other two relatives. Belman has created a cocktail in honor of all those touched by the Titanic disaster.

8. It's called the Titanic Iceberg. Made with rum, crème de menthe, and blue Curaçao.

9. After blending the mixture with ice and transferring it to a margarita glass. Belman adds two wedges of vanilla ice cream to the sea-blue drink for icebergs.

10. And as a final touch to remind everyone of the human toll of the disaster. The cocktail calls for two white Lifesaver candies floating on top of the icy blue slush.

Source: Washington Post, 18 Mar. 1998

Exercise 4

Correct each dependent clause fragment by eliminating its dependent word or by attaching the dependent clause to the independent clause before or after it.

1. When Nathan King turned twelve. He had a heart-stopping experience.

2. Nathan was tossing a football against his bedroom wall. Which made the ball ricochet and land on his bed.

3. In a diving motion, Nathan fell on his bed to catch the ball. As it landed.

4. After he caught the ball. Nathan felt a strange sensation in his chest.

5. To his surprise, he looked down and saw the eraser end of a no. 2 pencil. That had pierced his chest and entered his heart.

6. Nathan immediately shouted for his mother. Who luckily was in the house at the time.

7. Because Nathan's mom is a nurse. She knew not to remove the pencil.

8. If she had pulled the pencil out of her son's chest. He would have died.

9. After Nathan was taken to a hospital equipped for open-heart surgery. He had the pencil carefully removed.

10. Fate may be partly responsible for Nathan's happy birthday story. Since it turned out to be his heart surgeon's birthday too.

Source: Time, 20 Mar. 2000

Exercise 5

All of the following word groups contain clauses. If the clause *does not* begin with a dependent word (such as *when, while, after, because, since, although, where, if, who, which,* or *that*), put a period after it. If the clause *does* begin with a dependent word (making it a dependent clause fragment), add an independent clause or revise the dependent clause to be a sentence. These ten clauses are not about the same topic.

1. When thunderstorms interrupt golf tournaments

2. The field trip that my architecture teacher took us on

3. Snow fell all night

4. Since trash and garbage are two different things

5. A person who has graduated from college

6. That Thomas Jefferson died on the Fourth of July

7. In the box were two frightened mice

8. The team celebrated

9. If you help us with our car wash to raise money for the club

10. Joking with friends can easily backfire

PROOFREADING EXERCISE

Correct the five fragments in the following paragraph.

If you know what E-Cyas stands for. Then you probably know who or what he is. A rock star who exists only in cyberspace. E-Cyas meaning Electronic Cybernetic Superstar. The German company responsible for E-Cyas is I-D Media. E-Cyas may be the male equivalent of Lara Croft in terms of sex appeal. Getting e-mails and marriage proposals on his own Web site and having a base of loyal fans willing to go to his "concerts." Even though he will be there as only an image on a screen. E-Cyas's first song "Are You Real?" made it to the top of the charts in Germany. Only time will tell whether the first male cyberstar's popularity will last.

SENTENCE WRITING

Write ten fragments and then revise them so that they are complete sentences. Or exchange papers with another student and turn your classmate's ten fragments into sentences.

Correcting Run-on Sentences

Any word group having a subject and a verb is a clause. As we have seen, the clause may be independent (able to stand alone) or dependent (unable to stand alone). If two independent clauses are written together without proper punctuation between them, the result is called a run-on sentence. Here are some examples.

Classical music is soothing I listen to it in the evenings.

I love the sound of piano therefore, Chopin is one of my favorites.

Run-on sentences can be corrected in one of four ways:

1. Make the two independent clauses into two sentences.

Classical music is soothing. I listen to it in the evenings.

I love the sound of piano. Therefore, Chopin is one of my favorites.

2. Connect the two independent clauses with a semicolon.

Classical music is soothing; I listen to it in the evenings.

I love the sound of piano; therefore, Chopin is one of my favorites.

When a connecting word such as

also	however	otherwise
consequently	likewise	then
finally	moreover	therefore
furthermore	nevertheless	thus

is used to join two independent clauses, the semicolon comes before the connecting word, and a comma usually comes after it.

Mobile phones are convenient; however, they are very expensive.

Earthquakes scare me; therefore, I don't live in Los Angeles.

We traveled to London; then we took the "Chunnel" to Paris.

The college recently built a large new library; thus students have more quiet study areas.

NOTE- The use of the comma after the connecting word depends on how long the connecting word is. If it is only a short word, like *then* or *thus,* no comma is needed.

3. Connect the two independent clauses with a comma and one of the following seven words (the first letters of which create the word _fanboys_): _for, and, nor, but, or, yet, so._

> Classical music is soothing, _so_ I listen to it in the evenings.

> Chopin is one of my favorites, _for_ I love the sound of piano.

Each of the _fanboys_ has its own meaning (for example, _so_ means "as a result," and _for_ means "because").

> Swans are beautiful birds, _and_ they mate for life.

> Students may register for classes by phone, _or_ they may do so in person.

> I applied for financial aid, _but_ (or _yet_) I was still working at the time.

> Beth doesn't know how to use a computer, _nor_ does she plan to learn.

But before you put a comma before a _fanboys,_ be sure there are two independent clauses. The first sentence that follows has two independent clauses. The second sentence is merely one independent clause with two verbs, so no comma should be used.

> The snow began falling at dusk, and it continued to fall through the night.

> The snow began falling at dusk and continued to fall through the night.

4. Make one of the clauses dependent by adding a dependent word (such as _since, when, as, after, while,_ or _because_—see pp. 60–61 for a full list).

> _Since_ classical music is soothing, I listen to it in the evenings.

> Chopin is one of my favorites _because_ I love the sound of piano.

WAYS TO CORRECT RUN-ON SENTENCES

They learned a new routine. They needed to practice it. (two sentences)

They learned a new routine; they needed to practice it. (semicolon)

They learned a new routine; therefore, they needed to practice it. (semicolon + transition)

They learned a new routine, so they needed to practice it. (comma + _fanboys_)

Because they learned a new routine, they needed to practice it. (dependent clause first)

They needed to practice because they learned a new routine. (dependent clause last)

Learn these ways to join two clauses, and you'll avoid run-on sentences.

Exercises 1 and 2

CORRECTING RUN-ONS WITH PUNCTUATION

Most—but not all—of the following sentences are run-ons. If the sentence has two independent clauses, separate them with correct punctuation. For the first two exercises, *don't create any dependent clauses*; use only a period, a semicolon, or a comma to separate the two independent clauses. Your answers may differ from those at the back of the book depending on how you choose to separate them. Remember that a comma may be used only before the words *for, and, nor, but, or, yet, so.*

Exercise 1

1. Many Wal-Mart stores offer a surprising service but not everyone is happy about it.

2. Campers in recreation vehicles (RVs) can spend one to three nights in most Wal-Mart parking lots for free and without making reservations.

3. Official RV parks do charge fees for overnight stays these fees pay for the upkeep of facilities and for services like water and power hookups.

4. Wal-Mart parking lots offer no facilities or services yet they attract campers anyway.

5. Even the biggest motor homes and trailers find plenty of space to make themselves comfortable in a typical Wal-Mart lot.

6. While their vehicles are parked at Wal-Marts, RV owners can shop for food and other supplies in the stores.

7. To keep up with demand, Wal-Marts order the latest in camping and recreational equipment but that's not all.

8. Wal-Mart even sells a special road atlas with the addresses of all of its nearly three thousand stores across America.

9. A few towns and other large store chains have complained about Wal-Mart's free parking policy one county in Florida has completely banned it.

10. Wal-Mart's overnight parking service does seem to benefit its stores and its RV visitors however, community businesses and RV campgrounds question its fairness.

Sources: Wall Street Journal, 9 Aug. 1999, and Trailer Life, Apr. 2000

Exercise 2

1. One day is hard for me every year that day is my birthday.

2. I don't mind getting older I just never enjoy the day of my birth.

3. For one thing, I was born in August but summer is my least favorite season.

4. I hate the heat and the sun so even traditional warm-weather activities get me down.

5. Sunblock spoils swimming smog spoils biking and crowds spoil the National Parks.

6. To most people, the beach is a summer haven to me, the beach in the summer is bright, busy, and boring.

7. I love to walk on the beach on the cold, misty days of winter or early spring I wear a big sweater and have the whole place to myself.

8. August also brings fire season to most parts of the country therefore, even television is depressing.

9. There are no holidays to brighten up August in fact, it's like a black hole in the yearly holiday calendar—after the Fourth of July but before Halloween and the other holidays.

10. I have considered moving my birthday to February even being close to Groundhog Day would cheer me up.

Exercises 3 and 4
CORRECTING RUN-ONS WITH DEPENDENT CLAUSES

Most—but not all—of the following sentences are run-ons. Correct any run-on sentences by making one of the clauses dependent. You may change the words. Use a dependent word (such as *since, when, as, after, while, because,* or the others listed on pp. 60–61) to begin the dependent clause. In some sentences, you will want to put the dependent clause first; in others, you may want to put it last (or in the middle of the sentence). Since various words can be used to start a dependent clause, your answers may differ from those suggested at the back of the book.

Exercise 3

1. Along with *Survivor,* one of the reality-based TV shows of the new millennium, was *1900 House* it was shown on public television in June of 2000.

2. *Survivor* left sixteen individuals on a remote island to fight against the elements for thirty-nine days *1900 House* took a British family back one hundred years to live like a family in 1900 for three months.

3. Contestants on *Survivor* played for a million dollars four hundred families applied to live in the *1900 House* with the experience as the only reward.

4. *1900 House* producers had to renovate an existing home there were no houses in London in original 1900 condition.

5. Luckily, they found a house it had been built before 1900 and retained its original features under a layer of modern paneling and appliances.

6. Producers were delighted they found the system of pipes used for gas lights, and it still worked perfectly.

7. The Bowler family was chosen to live in the 1900 House, unlike some of the other applicants, they were eager to learn and were happy as a family.

8. In 1900, families spent almost all of their time at home often in dark rooms without any telephone or entertainment beyond their own imaginations.

9. At first, the Bowlers were excited to wear the clothes and live the lives of their ancestors they soon discovered the daily obstacles of the time.

10. The Bowlers dressed in restrictive garments, bathed in cold water, hand-washed clothes, cooked on a wood-fired stove, and played cards in the evening for ninety days they were ready to return to the luxuries of the modern world.

Source: New York Times, 12 June 2000

Exercise 4

1. The new home of the San Francisco Giants is Pacific Bell Park it had its first season in the summer of 2000.

2. Pac Bell Park stands beside an inlet of San Francisco Bay the area has been called McCovey Cove.

3. It was named after Willie McCovey he was one of the Giants' best hitters at their old home, Candlestick Park.

4. Pac Bell Park has a few unusual features they make the place unique.

5. Stadium designers wanted to give the park a retro look they built a huge replica of a 1927 Rawlings glove above the stands in left field.

6. A twenty-five-foot wall stands between right field and the bay a home-run often clears the fence and lands in the water.

7. Tom Hoynes decided to watch an exhibition game from his ten-foot boat he started a streak of homerun ball rescues.

8. In the Giants' first season, Hoynes recovered most of the homerun balls they were hit into the waters of McCovey Cove.

9. Hoynes became a celebrity that season he usually wasn't alone in the bay.

10. There were plenty of others they were anxious to be part of the lore of a new sports stadium.

Source: Los Angeles Times, 9 Apr. 2000, and *Sports Illustrated,* 31 July 2000

Exercise 5

Correct the following run-on sentences using any of the methods studied in this section: adding a period, a semicolon, a semicolon before a transition word, a comma before a *fanboys,* or using a dependent word to create a dependent clause.

1. It's summer time there will be bugs.

2. People at picnics and backyard barbecues see bees and wasps as pests but they're just being themselves.

3. These creatures build their nests earlier in the year late summer is their vacation time too.

4. They leave their homes and look for sweets they are easy to find at picnics and barbecues.

5. The smell of a soda, for instance, attracts these insects so such drinks should be covered.

6. Also, people wear perfume these people are more likely to attract insects.

7. Even hair spray, body lotion, and soap scents interest bees, wasps, and flies.

8. The picnic location may be near a hive the hive might not be obvious.

9. It is so dangerous to upset or threaten any hive of insects people must be aware of their surroundings.

10. Insects can pose a threat to the peace and safety of summer activities therefore, the best defense is understanding.

Source: Better Homes and Gardens, Sept. 2000

REVIEW OF FRAGMENTS AND RUN-ON SENTENCES

If you remember that all clauses include a subject and a verb, but only independent clauses can be punctuated as sentences (since only they can stand alone), then you will avoid fragments in your writing. And if you memorize these six rules for the punctuation of clauses, you will be able to avoid most punctuation errors.

PUNCTUATING CLAUSES	
I am a student. I am still learning.	(two sentences)
I am a student; I am still learning.	(two independent clauses)
I am a student; therefore, I am still learning.	(two independent clauses connected by a word such as *also, consequently, finally, furthermore, however, likewise, moreover, nevertheless, otherwise, then, therefore, thus*)
I am a student, so I am still learning.	(two independent clauses connected by *for, and, nor, but, or, yet, so*)
Because I am a student, I am still learning.	(dependent clause at beginning of sentence)
I am still learning because I am a student.	(dependent clause at end of sentence) The dependent words are *after, although, as, as if, because, before, even if, even though, ever since, how, if, in order that, since, so that, than, that, though, unless, until, what, whatever, when, whenever, where, whereas, wherever, whether, which, whichever, while, who, whom, whose, why.*

It is essential that you learn the italicized words in the previous table—which ones come between independent clauses and which ones introduce dependent clauses.

PROOFREADING EXERCISE

Rewrite the following paragraph, making the necessary changes so there will be no fragments or run-on sentences.

People and animals require different amounts of sleep. People have to balance on two legs all day therefore, we need to get off our feet and sleep for about eight hours each night. Horses, however, are able to rest better standing up. Because their four legs support their bodies without a strain on any one area. When horses lie down, their large bodies press uncomfortably against the earth. Making their hearts and lungs work harder than they do in standing position. Generally speaking, horses lie on the ground for about two hours a day and they spend only a little of the remaining time drowsy or lightly sleeping while still on their feet.

Source: Illustrated Horsewatching (Knickerbocker Press, 1999)

SENTENCE WRITING

Write a sample sentence of your own to demonstrate each of the six ways a writer can use to punctuate two clauses. You may model your sentences on the examples used in the preceding review chart.

Identifying Verb Phrases

Sometimes a verb is one word, but often the whole verb includes more than one word. These are called verb phrases. Look at several of the many forms of the verb *speak*, for example. Most of them are verb phrases, made up of the main verb (*speak*) and one or more helping verbs.

speak	is speaking	had been speaking
speaks	am speaking	will have been speaking
spoke	are speaking	is spoken
will speak	was speaking	was spoken
has spoken	were speaking	will be spoken
have spoken	will be speaking	can speak
had spoken	has been speaking	must speak
will have spoken	have been speaking	should have spoken

Note that words like the following are never verbs even though they may be near a verb or in the middle of a verb phrase:

already	finally	now	probably
also	just	often	really
always	never	only	sometimes
ever	not	possibly	usually

Jason has *never* spoken to his instructor before. She *always* talks with other students.

Two verb forms—*speaking* and *to speak*—look like verbs, but neither can ever be the verb of a sentence. No *ing* word by itself can ever be the verb of a sentence; it must be helped by another verb in a verb phrase. (See the discussion of verbal phrases on p. 116)

Jeanine speaking French. (not a sentence because there is no complete verb phrase)

Jeanine is speaking French. (a sentence with a verb phrase)

And no verb with *to* in front of it can ever be the verb of a sentence.

Ted to speak in front of groups. (not a sentence because there is no real verb)

Ted hates to speak in front of groups. (a sentence with *hates* as the verb)

These two forms, *speaking* and *to speak,* may be used as subjects, or they may have other uses in the sentence.

Speaking on stage is scary. To speak on stage is scary. Ted had a *speaking* part in that play.

But neither of them alone can ever be the verb of a sentence.

E X E R C I S E S

Underline the subjects once and the verbs or verb phrases twice. It's a good idea to put parentheses around prepositional phrases first. (See p. 54 if you need help in locating prepositional phrases.) The sentences may contain independent *and* dependent clauses, so there could be several verbs and verb phrases.

Exercise 1

1. Greg Smith is a young man who has already accomplished many of his goals.
2. In 1997, Greg was a seven-year-old in elementary school.
3. By the next school year, Greg had advanced to high school.
4. In 2000, Greg Smith started college at the age of ten.
5. During his first year at college, Greg studied physics, calculus, upper-level French, and ancient warfare.
6. Greg Smith's father can remember his son's first signs of genius.
7. Greg could memorize and recite books when he was just a year old.
8. Greg was given an IQ test when he was five, and the results were exceptional.
9. On the day that Greg graduated from his Florida high school, one of his baby teeth fell out.
10. Greg has already made friends in college; for some reason, everyone wants to sit next to him.

Source: Current Science, 7 Jan. 2000

Exercise 2

1. Researchers have been tagging animals with radio devices for years.

2. After they study the animals' movements, experts can help to preserve species in their natural habitats.

3. But some animals are difficult to fit with collars or other equipment.

4. For example, wild Jamaican iguanas have become endangered but can wiggle out of most tracking devices.

5. When scientists needed a stretchy and sturdy solution to the problem, they asked Nike for help.

6. Nike designed a vest that can withstand changes in temperature and terrain.

7. The iguanas that are being studied have been born in zoos, dressed in the Nike vests, and then taken to the wilds of Jamaica.

8. In their special vests, the reptiles can grow and send their vital information back to researchers.

9. The Nike logo was added to the iguana vest just for fun.

10. Like the Jamaican iguanas, Puerto Rican crested toads have been fitted with special spandex backpacks for the same kind of research.

Sources: Science World, 13 Dec. 1999, and *Current Science,* 12 May 2000

Exercise 3

1. The largest meteorite that has ever been found on earth was recently at the center of a custody battle.

2. The American Museum of Natural History in New York has owned the Willamette meteorite since the early 1900s, and it was displayed at the Hayden Planetarium.

3. Scientists believe that the car-sized meteor landed between eight and ten thousand years ago in what is now called Oregon.

4. The Wilamette meteorite may actually be the central part of an exploded planet.

5. But to one group of Native Americans, the huge meteor has always been known as "Tomanowos," or "Sky Person."

6. In a lawsuit against the museum, Grand Ronde tribe members claimed that their ancestors had worshiped Tomanowos for thousands of years before it was sold to the museum.

7. They could support their claims with tribal songs and dances that revealed a close relationship between the Grand Ronde people and the meteorite.

8. The museum and the Grand Ronde tribes did settle the dispute in August of 2000.

9. The two sides agreed that the Willamette meteorite would remain on display at the Hayden Planetarium but would be accompanied by a plaque that described the Grand Ronde tribes' connection to the meteor.

10. The museum also agreed to give the Grand Ronde people special access to the Willamette meteorite so that they may continue their relationship with Tomanowos.

Sources: Washington Post, 23 June 2000, and *New York Times Upfront,* 27 Mar. 2000

Exercise 4

1. Endangered species are currently getting help from many sources around the world.

2. The Audubon Center for Research of Endangered Species (ACRES) is located in New Orleans.

3. Through the use of freezing techniques, scientists at ACRES have successfully moved an embryo from a threatened species of African wildcat to the body of a typical house cat.

4. In November 1999, Cayenne the house cat gave birth to an African wild-cat kitten.

5. Scientists at ACRES have named the kitten Jazz.

6. Two African wildcats are still considered the biological parents of Jazz.

7. Cayenne has acted only as his surrogate mother.

8. Jazz's birth has entered the record books as the first previously frozen embryo from one species to be born to a mother from another species.

9. Through such a process, threatened species can produce more babies with less risk to their endangered mothers.

10. Cayenne has treated Jazz just like one of her own kittens.

Source: *New Orleans Magazine,* Mar. 2000

Exercise 5

1. Prehistoric musical instruments have been found before.

2. But the ancient flutes that were recently discovered in China's Henan Province included the oldest playable instrument on record.

3. The nine-thousand-year-old flute was made from the wing bone of a bird.

4. The bone was hollowed out and pierced with seven holes that produce the notes of an ancient Chinese musical scale.

5. Because one of the holes' pitches missed the mark, an additional tiny hole was added by the flute's maker.

6. The flute is played in the vertical position.

7. People who have studied ancient instruments are hoping to learn more about the culture that produced this ancient flute.

8. Other bone flutes were found at the same time and in the same location, but they were not intact or strong enough for playing.

9. Visitors to the Brookhaven National Laboratory's Web site can listen to music from the world's oldest working flute.

10. Listeners will be taken back to 7,000 years B.C.

Source: Science News, 25 Sept. 1999

REVIEW EXERCISE

To practice finding all of the sentence structures we have studied so far, mark the following paragraphs from a student essay. First, put parentheses around prepositional phrases, then underline subjects once and verbs or verb phrases twice. Finally, put a broken line beneath dependent clauses. Begin by marking the first paragraph, then check your answers at the back of the book before going on to the next paragraph. (Remember that *ing* verbs alone and the *to* ____ forms of verbs are never real verbs in sentences. We will learn more about them on p. 116.)

My brain feels like a computer's central processing unit. Information is continually pumping into its circuits. I organize the data, format it to my individual preferences, and lay it out in my own style. As I endlessly sculpt existing formulas, they become something of my own. When I need a solution to a problem, I access the data that I have gathered from my whole existence, even my preprogrammed DNA.

Since I am a student, teachers require that I supply them with specific information in various formats. When they assign an essay, I produce several paragraphs. If they need a summary, I scan the text, find its main ideas, and put them briefly into my own words. I know that I can accomplish whatever the teachers ask so that I can obtain a bachelor's degree and continue processing ideas to make a living.

I compare my brain to a processor because right now I feel that I must work like one. As I go further into my education, my processor will be continually updated—just like a Pentium! And with any luck, I will end up with real, not artificial, intelligence.

Using Standard English Verbs

The next two discussions are for those who need practice in using Standard English verbs. Many of us grew up doing more speaking than writing. But in college and in the business and professional world, the use of Standard Written English is essential.

The following charts show the forms of four verbs as they are used in Standard Written English. These forms might differ from the way you use these verbs when you speak. Memorize the Standard English forms of these important verbs. The first verb (*talk*) is one of the regular verbs (verbs that all end the same way according to a pattern); most verbs in English are regular. The other three verbs charted here (*have, be,* and *do*) are irregular and are important because they are used not only as main verbs but also as helping verbs in verb phrases.

Don't go on to the exercises until you have memorized the forms of these Standard English verbs.

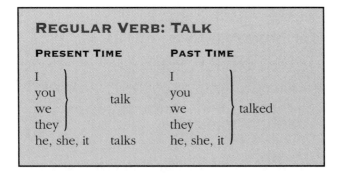

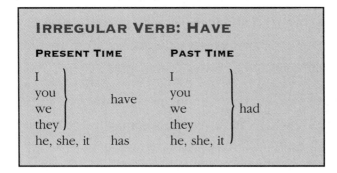

IRREGULAR VERB: BE

PRESENT TIME		PAST TIME	
I	am	I	was
you		we	
we	are	you	were
they		they	
he, she, it	is	he, she, it	was

IRREGULAR VERB: DO

PRESENT TIME		PAST TIME	
I		I	
you		you	
we	do	we	did
they		they	
he, she, it	does	he, she, it	

Sometimes you may have difficulty with the correct endings of verbs because you don't hear the words correctly. Note carefully the *s* sound and the *ed* sound at the end of words. Occasionally the *ed* is not clearly pronounced, as in *They tried to help,* but most of the time you can hear it if you listen.

Read the following sentences aloud, making sure that you say every sound.

1. He seems satisfied with his new job.

2. She likes saving money for the future.

3. It takes strength of character to control spending.

4. Todd makes salad for every potluck he attends.

5. I used to know all their names.

6. They supposed that they were right.

7. He recognized the suspect and excused himself from the jury.

8. Susan sponsored Dorothy in the school's charity event.

Now read some other sentences aloud from this text, making sure that you sound all the *s*'s and *ed*'s. Reading aloud and listening to others will help you use the correct verb endings automatically.

E X E R C I S E S

In these pairs of sentences, use the present form of the verb in the first sentence and the past form in the second. All the verbs follow the pattern of the regular verb *talk* except the irregular verbs *have*, *be*, and *do*. Keep referring to the tables if you're not sure which form to use. Correct your answers for each exercise before going to the next.

Exercise 1

1. (be)   They _____ usually late. They _____ late yesterday.

2. (have)   We _____ a new coach this week. We _____ a different coach last week.

3. (do)   She _____ her work without complaining. She _____ five pages of math last night.

4. (correct)   My son _____ his own essays now. His tutor _____ them before.

5. (have)   Tracy returned the computer; her new computer _____ a DVD player. The first one _____ only a CD drive.

6. (be)   He _____ currently an usher at the campus theater. He _____ a cashier in the box office last season.

7. (work)   Chris _____ very hard. Last week, she _____ a total of sixty hours.

8. (be)   I _____ finally happy with all of my furniture. I _____ not satisfied with my old couch.

9. (collect)   She _____ cans and bottles. She _____ newspapers last year.

10. (need)   I always _____ help with my math homework. I _____ help with English in the past.

Exercise 2

1. (be)   They _____ rich and famous now. They _____ unknown a year ago.

2. (do)   He _____ his best work in class. He _____ not do well on the take-home test.

3. (have)   She _____ a new goal. She _____ an unrealistic goal before.

4. (tag)   He _____ only the expensive items at his garage sales. In the past, he _____ all of the items.

5. (have)   I always _____ a good time with my friends. At Disneyland, I _____ the best time of all.

6. (stuff)   She _____ envelopes part time. Yesterday she _____ envelopes for five hours straight.

7. (be)   Many of us _____ allergic to milk, so we _____ unable to eat the pizza at the postgame party.

8. (do)   They _____ their best to help their parents. They _____ the grocery shopping and the dishes this week.

9. (dance)   You _____ very well now. You _____ a little awkwardly in high school.

10. (be)   At the moment, they _____ the fastest delivery people in the business. They _____ the second-fastest delivery people just six months ago.

Exercise 3

Underline the Standard English verb forms. All the verbs follow the pattern of the regular verb *talk* except the three irregular verbs *have, be,* and *do.* Keep referring to the tables if you are not sure which form to use.

1. I recently (change, changed) my career plans; now I (want, wants) to be a teacher.

2. Last year, I (have, had) my mind set on becoming a nurse.

3. I (enroll, enrolled) in nursing classes, but they (was, were) different from what I (expect, expected).

4. The classes (was, were) often too stressful, and the teachers (was, were) very demanding.

5. We (does, did) spend part of the semester working in a clinic where we (was, were) able to observe just what a nurse (do, does).

6. The nurse that I (observe, observed) (have, had) several patients to look after.

7. I (watch, watched) her as she (cares, cared) for them and (follow, followed) the doctors' orders.

8. She (have, had) her patients, their families, and the clinic's doctors and staff to worry about all the time.

9. I never (imagine, imagined) that a nurse (have, had) so many responsibilities.

10. A teacher (need, needs) to worry about the students and the school, and those (is, are) responsibilities that I (is, am) ready to take.

Exercise 4

1. My brother Ken and I (has, have) a common goal.

2. We (watch, watches) the game show *Who Wants to Be a Millionaire?* and both of us (want, wants) to be contestants.

3. Ken (like, likes) the show more than I (does, do).

4. I (is, am) better at answering the entertainment and literature questions, and Ken (is, am) better at answering the questions on history and geography.

5. Ken and I (is, are) very competitive and proud of the knowledge that we (has, have).

6. When we (play, plays) along with the show, we both (does, do) very well.

7. But the show's telephone qualification questions usually (stump, stumps) both of us.

8. One of us (call, calls) the show's toll-free contestant number every day.

9. We both (has, have) a chance to make it on the show.

10. We (love, loves) the suspense but (hope, hopes) that it (end, ends) soon.

Exercise 5

Correct any of the following sentences that do not use Standard English verb forms.

1. Last semester my drawing teacher hand us an assignment.

2. It was half of a photograph pasted onto a whole piece of paper.

3. We has to draw in the other half of the picture.

4. My picture show a woman sitting against the bottom of a tree trunk.

5. Her shoulders, hat, and umbrella was only partly there.

6. I tried to imagine what the missing parts look like.

7. The tree was easy to fill in because its shape was clear in the photo.

8. Therefore, I starts with the tree, the sky, and the ground.

9. Then I used my imagination to fill in the woman's shoulders, hat, and umbrella.

10. I receives an "A" grade for my drawing.

PROOFREADING EXERCISE

Correct any sentences in the following paragraph that do not use Standard English verb forms.

I like to lie on the floor of my room on weekend mornings. I looks out the window and watch the rays of the sun. I am free to experience the day as it start. There is nothing that can stop the sun from shining or the crisp wind from blowing. The sky is like a friend that are always there when I needs it. Its personality is changeable. It change with the weather. We never know whether the sky will be blue, gray, or white with clouds. The sky decide the way the day feels.

SENTENCE WRITING

Write ten sentences about the last party you had or attended. Check your sentences to be sure that they use Standard English verb forms. Try exchanging papers with another student if possible.

Using Regular and Irregular Verbs

All regular verbs end the same way in the past form and when used with helping verbs. Here is a table showing all the forms of some regular verbs and the various helping verbs they are used with.

REGULAR VERBS				
BASE FORM	PRESENT	PAST	PAST PARTICIPLE	*ING* FORM
(*Use after can, may, shall, will, could, might, should, would, must, do, does, did.*)			(*Use after have, has, had. Some can be used after forms of be.*)	(*Use after forms of be.*)
ask	ask (*s*)	asked	asked	asking
bake	bake (*s*)	baked	baked	baking
count	count (*s*)	counted	counted	counting
dance	dance (*s*)	danced	danced	dancing
decide	decide (*s*)	decided	decided	deciding
enjoy	enjoy (*s*)	enjoyed	enjoyed	enjoying
finish	finish (*es*)	finished	finished	finishing
happen	happen (*s*)	happened	happened	happening
learn	learn (*s*)	learned	learned	learning
like	like (*s*)	liked	liked	liking
look	look (*s*)	looked	looked	looking
mend	mend (*s*)	mended	mended	mending
need	need (*s*)	needed	needed	needing
open	open (*s*)	opened	opened	opening
start	start (*s*)	started	started	starting
suppose	suppose (*s*)	supposed	supposed	supposing
tap	tap (*s*)	tapped	tapped	tapping
walk	walk (*s*)	walked	walked	walking
want	want (*s*)	wanted	wanted	wanting

NOTE- When there are several helping verbs, the last one determines which form of the main verb should be used: they *should* finish soon; they should *have* finished an hour ago.

When do you write *ask, finish, suppose, use?* And when do you write *asked, finished, supposed, used?* Here are some rules that will help you decide.

Write *ask, finish, suppose, use* (or their *s* forms) when writing about the present time, repeated actions, or facts:

He *asks* questions whenever he is confused.

They always *finish* their projects on time.

I *suppose* you want me to help you move.

Birds *use* leaves, twigs, and feathers to build their nests.

Write *asked, finished, supposed, used*

1. When writing about the past:

He *asked* the teacher for another explanation.

She *finished* her internship last year.

They *supposed* that there were others bidding on that house.

I *used* to study piano.

2. When some form of *be* (other than the word *be* itself) comes before the word:

He was *asked* the most difficult questions.

She is *finished* with her training now.

They were *supposed* to sign at the bottom of the form.

My essay was *used* as a sample of clear narration.

3. When some form of *have* comes before the word:

The teacher has *asked* us that question before.

She will have *finished* all of her exams by the end of May.

I had *supposed* too much without any proof.

We have *used* many models in my drawing class this semester.

All the verbs in the chart on page 96 are regular. That is, they're all formed in the same way—with an *ed* ending on the past form and on the past participle. But many verbs are irregular. Their past and past participle forms change spelling instead of just adding an *ed*. Here's a chart of some irregular verbs. Notice that the base, present, and *ing* forms end the same as regular verbs. Refer to this list when you aren't sure which verb form to use. Memorize all the forms you don't know.

IRREGULAR VERBS				
BASE FORM	**PRESENT**	**PAST**	**PAST PARTICIPLE**	***ING* FORM**
(*Use after can, may, shall, will, could, might, should, would, must, do, does, did.*)			(*Use after have, has, had. Some can be used after forms of be.*)	(*Use after forms of be.*)
be	is, am, are	was, were	been	being
become	become (*s*)	became	become	becoming
begin	begin (*s*)	began	begun	beginning
break	break (*s*)	broke	broken	breaking
bring	bring (*s*)	brought	brought	bringing
build	build (*s*)	built	built	building
buy	buy (*s*)	bought	bought	buying
catch	catch (*es*)	caught	caught	catching
choose	choose (*s*)	chose	chosen	choosing
come	come (*s*)	came	come	coming
do	do (*es*)	did	done	doing
draw	draw (*s*)	drew	drawn	drawing
drink	drink (*s*)	drank	drunk	drinking
drive	drive (*s*)	drove	driven	driving
eat	eat (*s*)	ate	eaten	eating
fall	fall (*s*)	fell	fallen	falling
feel	feel (*s*)	felt	felt	feeling
fight	fight (*s*)	fought	fought	fighting
find	find (*s*)	found	found	finding
forget	forget (*s*)	forgot	forgotten	forgetting
forgive	forgive (*s*)	forgave	forgiven	forgiving
freeze	freeze (*s*)	froze	frozen	freezing
get	get (*s*)	got	got *or* gotten	getting
give	give (*s*)	gave	given	giving
go	go (*es*)	went	gone	going
grow	grow (*s*)	grew	grown	growing
have	have *or* has	had	had	having
hear	hear (*s*)	heard	heard	hearing
hold	hold (*s*)	held	held	holding
keep	keep (*s*)	kept	kept	keeping

BASE FORM	PRESENT	PAST	PAST PARTICIPLE	*ING* FORM
know	know (*s*)	knew	known	knowing
lay (to put)	lay (*s*)	laid	laid	laying
lead (like "bead")	lead (*s*)	led	led	leading
leave	leave (*s*)	left	left	leaving
lie (to rest)	lie (*s*)	lay	lain	lying
lose	lose (*s*)	lost	lost	losing
make	make (*s*)	made	made	making
meet	meet (*s*)	met	met	meeting
pay	pay (*s*)	paid	paid	paying
read (pron. "reed")	read (*s*)	read (pron. "red")	read (pron. "red")	reading
ride	ride (*s*)	rode	ridden	riding
ring	ring (*s*)	rang	rung	ringing
rise	rise (*s*)	rose	risen	rising
run	run (*s*)	ran	run	running
say	say (*s*)	said	said	saying
see	see (*s*)	saw	seen	seeing
sell	sell (*s*)	sold	sold	selling
shake	shake (*s*)	shook	shaken	shaking
shine (give light)	shine (*s*)	shone	shone	shining
shine (polish)	shine (*s*)	shined	shined	shining
sing	sing (*s*)	sang	sung	singing
sleep	sleep (*s*)	slept	slept	sleeping
speak	speak (*s*)	spoke	spoken	speaking
spend	spend (*s*)	spent	spent	spending
stand	stand (*s*)	stood	stood	standing
steal	steal (*s*)	stole	stolen	stealing
strike	strike (*s*)	struck	struck	striking
swim	swim (*s*)	swam	swum	swimming
swing	swing (*s*)	swung	swung	swinging
take	take (*s*)	took	taken	taking
teach	teach (*es*)	taught	taught	teaching
tear	tear (*s*)	tore	torn	tearing
tell	tell (*s*)	told	told	telling
think	think (*s*)	thought	thought	thinking
throw	throw (*s*)	threw	thrown	throwing
wear	wear (*s*)	wore	worn	wearing
win	win (*s*)	won	won	winning
write	write (*s*)	wrote	written	writing

Sometimes verbs from the past participle column are used after some form of the verb *be* (or verbs that take the place of *be*, like *appear, seem, look, feel, get, act, become*) to describe the subject or to say something in a passive, rather than active, way.

She is contented.

You appear pleased. (You are pleased.)

He seems delighted. (He is delighted.)

She looked surprised. (She was surprised.)

I feel shaken. (I am shaken.)

They get bored easily. (They are bored easily.)

You acted concerned. (You were concerned.)

He was thrown out of the game. (Active: *The referee threw him out of the game.*)

They were disappointed by the news. (Active: *The news disappointed them.*)

Often these verb forms become words that describe the subject; other times they still act as part of the verb of the sentence. What you call them doesn't matter. The only important thing is to be sure you use the correct form from the past participle column.

E X E R C I S E S

Write the correct form of the verb. Refer to the tables and explanations on the preceding pages if you aren't sure which form to use after a certain helping verb. Check your answers after each exercise.

Exercise 1

1. (work)   I currently _____ in my family's grocery store.

2. (work)   After I have _____ there for a year or so, I will get a new job.

3. (work)   Sometimes when I am _____ with my dad, he acts like a real boss.

4. (work)   Once, after I had _____ for over four hours, he told me to take a break.

5. (work)   But I can _____ for a long time without needing a break.

6. (work)   My dad says that he feels the same way when he _____.

7. (work)   I guess all employees don't _____ in the same way.

8. (work)   One of our employees who _____ in the produce section always wants to take a break.

9. (work)   If he _____ as hard as my dad and I do, the business would run more smoothly.

10. (work)   That is why I will always _____ as hard as I can while I'm there.

Exercise 2

1. (get)   I just _____ a new pet rat named Ginger. She has strawberry-blond fur and curly whiskers. If I don't play with her, then she _____ depressed.

2. (buy)   I _____ Ginger with the money from my last paycheck even though I usually _____ new shoes or something for school.

3. (be)   I _____ really surprised that Ginger _____ such a great pet.

4. (think)   My mom _____ that I will get tired of Ginger, but I don't _____ so.

5. (grow)   Ginger has _____ a lot since I got her. And I've _____ more responsible by taking care of her.

6. (leave)   Before I _____ for school each day, I give Ginger fresh food, treats, and water. Once I _____ her cage open by mistake and found her sleeping on my pillow when I came back.

7. (watch)   Rats love to climb and dig, so I often sit by her cage and just _____ her. She sits on my shoulder while I am _____ television in the evening.

8. (hear)   When Ginger _____ her name, she comes to the front of her cage and waits for me to open it. Then I _____ a little humming noise that means she's happy to see me.

9. (do)   Sometimes Ginger _____ really funny things, and I am _____ my best to teach her tricks.

10. (be)   At first, I _____ not sure I could love a rat, but now Ginger _____ my favorite pet so far.

Exercise 3

1. (take, suppose) My brother Jeff _____ me to the movies last Tuesday afternoon even though I was _____ to be in school.

2. (be, go) It _____ the only time that Jeff could _____ to the movies with me.

3. (call, leave, feel) So I _____ my teacher and _____ a message that I didn't _____ well enough to go to class.

4. (imagine, be) I never _____ that I would get caught, but I _____ wrong.

5. (buy, drive, see) Just as Jeff and I were _____ our tickets, my teacher _____ by and _____ us.

6. (feel, know, be) I _____ such panic because I _____ that my teacher would _____ disappointed in me.

7. (try, go) I _____ to explain myself when I _____ back to school the next day.

8. (be, undo) The damage had _____ done, however, and nothing could _____ it.

9. (wish, take) Now I _____ that I could _____ back that day.

10. (do, be) I _____ not have much fun with Jeff, and the movie _____ not even good.

Exercise 4

1. (use, have) Many people _____ cell phones that _____ voice-recognition capabilities.

2. (do, speak, dial) With such a system, callers _____ not have to dial phone numbers by hand. Instead, they just _____ into the phone, and the phone _____ the number.

3. (be, be) When driving a car, callers _____ then free to watch the road and steer the car without distraction. These phones _____ much safer.

4. (be, like, start)

Voice dialing _____ almost always optional, but so many people _____ the system that most people have _____ to use it.

5. (do, want)

My mom _____ not trust such systems; she _____ to have complete control over her own dialing.

6. (trust, be)

She barely even _____ cell phones, so she _____ definitely suspicious of voice dialing.

7. (imagine, dial)

I can _____ her as a teenager in the sixties. In my mind, she is _____ one of those rotary-operated princess phones.

8. (ask, tell, be)

I was _____ my mom about phones the other day, and I _____ her how old-fashioned she _____.

9. (look, smile)

She just _____ at me and _____.

10. (have)

My mom _____ a way of saying a lot with just a smile.

Exercise 5

1. (lie, fall)

I was _____ in the hammock last Sunday, and I _____ asleep.

2. (sleep, wake, look)

I must have _____ there for three hours before I _____ up and _____ at my watch.

3. (feel, begin, need)

At first, I _____ guilty for sleeping so long, but then I _____ to understand how much I had _____ a rest.

4. (pass, ease)

As the hours _____, the pressure on my mind _____.

5. (describe, look, see)

I can't even _____ how much better I _____ when I _____ myself in the mirror later that day.

6. (appear, be)

Before my long nap, I _____ several years older than I really _____.

7. (return, disappear)   After it, the sparkle _____ to my eyes, and a few wrinkles even _____.

8. (ache, be)   My neck and shoulders no longer _____, and my tension headache _____ gone.

9. (be, do)   That long rest in the hammock _____ the best thing I could have _____ for myself.

10. (need, challenge)   I _____ a break from my crazy life, which _____ me every single day.

PROGRESS TEST

This test covers everything you've learned in the Sentence Structure section so far. One sentence in each pair is correct. The other is incorrect. Read both sentences carefully before you decide. Then write the letter of the incorrect sentence in the blank. Try to name the error and correct it if you can.

1. ___ **A.** My roommates had already put up all of the balloons by the time I arrived.

   B. I was looking forward to a night of decorating so I was disappointed.

2. ___ **A.** Summer school goes by very quickly.

   B. Leaving us only a little time to do our assignments.

3. ___ **A.** Chris works at a home improvement center.

   B. He use to work at a pet store.

4. ___ **A.** We looked everywhere for the theater tickets before I found them.

   B. They were laying on the floor beside the couch.

5. ___ **A.** After eating a snack in the afternoon.

   B. I was able to work for several hours before dinner.

6. ___ **A.** We have took many classes together.

   B. Last semester, we enrolled in three of the same classes.

7. ___ **A.** Laverne likes every kind of restaurant.

   B. Whenever we go out to dinner.

8. ___ **A.** Their field trip took them far into the desert.

   B. Their teacher was driving he knew the road well.

9. ___ **A.** We are learning about dependent clauses in my English class.

   B. Especially how they can be fragments if they are used alone.

10. ___ **A.** I was suppose to pick up my sister after school.

    B. But she forgot and started walking home.

Maintaining Subject/Verb Agreement

As we have seen, the subject and verb in a sentence work together, so they must always agree. Different subjects need different forms of verbs. When the correct verb follows a subject, we call it subject/verb agreement.

The sentences below illustrate the rule that *s* verbs follow most singular subjects but not plural subjects.

One turtle walks.   Three turtles walk.

The baby cries.   The babies cry.

A democracy listens to the people.   Democracies listen to the people.

One child plays.   Many children play.

And the following sentences show how forms of the verb *be (is, am, are, was, were)* and helping verbs (*be, have,* and *do*) are made to agree with their subjects.

This puzzle is difficult.   These puzzles are difficult.

I am amazed.   You are amazed.

He was sleeping.   They were sleeping.

That class has been canceled.   Those classes have been canceled.

She does not want to participate.   They do not want to participate.

The following words are always singular and take an *s* verb or the irregular equivalent (*is, was, has, does*):

("ONE" WORDS)	("BODY" WORDS)	
one	anybody	each
anyone	everybody	
everyone	nobody	
no one	somebody	
someone		

Someone feeds my dog in the morning.

Everybody was at the party.

Each does her own homework.

Remember that prepositional phrases often come between subjects and verbs. You should ignore these interrupting phrases, or you may mistake the wrong word for the subject and use a verb form that doesn't agree.

Someone from the apartments feeds my dog in the morning. (*Someone* is the subject, not *apartments*.)

Everybody on the list of celebrities was at the party. (*Everybody* is the subject, not *celebrities*.)

Each of the twins does her own homework. (*Each* is the subject, not *twins*.)

However, the words *some, any, all, none,* and *most* are exceptions to this rule of ignoring prepositional phrases. These words can be singular or plural, depending on the words that follow them in prepositional phrases.

Some of the *pie* is gone.

Some of the *cookies* are gone.

Is any of the paper still in the supply cabinet?

Are any of the pencils still in the supply cabinet?

All of her work has been published.

All of her poems have been published.

None of the jewelry is missing.

None of the clothes are missing.

On July 4th, <u>most</u> of the country <u>celebrates</u>.

On July 4th, <u>most</u> of the citizens <u>celebrate</u>.

When a sentence has more than one subject joined by *and,* the subject is plural:

The <u>teacher</u> and the <u>tutors</u> <u>eat</u> lunch at noon.

A glazed <u>doughnut</u> and an onion <u>bagel</u> <u>were</u> sitting on the plate.

However, when two subjects are joined by *or,* then the subject closest to the verb determines the verb form:

Either the <u>teacher</u> *or* the <u>tutors</u> <u>eat</u> lunch at noon.

Either the <u>tutors</u> *or* the <u>teacher</u> <u>eats</u> lunch at noon.

A glazed <u>donut</u> *or* an onion <u>bagel</u> <u>was</u> sitting on the plate.

In most sentences, the subject comes before the verb. However, in some cases, the subject follows the verb, and subject/verb agreement needs special attention. Study the following examples:

Over the building <u>flies</u> a solitary <u>flag</u>. (flag flies)

Over the building <u>fly</u> several <u>flags</u>. (flags fly)

There <u>is</u> a good <u>reason</u> for my actions. (reason is)

There <u>are</u> good <u>reasons</u> for my actions. (reasons are)

E X E R C I S E S

Underline the verbs that agree with the subjects of the following sentences. Remember to ignore prepositional phrases, unless the subjects are *some, any, all, none,* or *most.* Check your answers ten at a time.

Exercise 1

    1. Internet auction sites (has, have) been popular for a long time.

    2. The concept for such sites (is, are) simple.

    3. A person (has, have) something to sell, and someone (want, wants) to buy it.

4. These two people (find, finds) each other via computer.

5. The days of hunting through antique stores for a particular collectible item (is, are) over.

6. Now a collector of old postcards, for instance, (hunt, hunts) for them on line.

7. The process of bidding on auction sites (is, are) a little complicated at first.

8. Usually the site (ask, asks) for specific user information to avoid problems with fraud.

9. This part of the process (protect, protects) all of the parties involved, even the losers of the bidding wars.

10. That way, only serious bidders from around the world (participate, participates) in the auctions.

Exercise 2

1. According to *Discover* magazine's twentieth-anniversary issue, there (is, are) twenty items that will most likely be around for the next twenty years.

2. The first two (is, are) houses and pencils, for obvious reasons.

3. Another (is, are) books, which (owe, owes) their long life partly to the difficulty of pirating their contents.

4. Some of the others (is, are) cash, knives and forks, and paper clips.

5. The automobile and airplane (figure, figures) prominently in *Discover*'s list.

6. The enjoyment of travel (overshadow, overshadows) people's concerns about traffic and noise, so they will remain with us for the time being.

7. Attempts to design cars that (drive, drives) themselves (has, have) had mixed results.

8. Therefore, driving (appear, appears) to be in our future for awhile.

9. Despite changing trends and styles, *Discover*'s writers (include, includes) suits, baseball, shopping, religion, and zippers in their list of stable elements of society.

10. Finally, death and sex (make, makes) it on the list as processes so natural that they (is, are) here to stay.

Source: Discover, Oct. 2000

Exercise 3

1. In his book *Catwatching,* Desmond Morris (explain, explains) why cats (seem, seems) to be able to feel earthquakes before they (happen, happens).

2. First of all, the cat (feel, feels) sensations that we humans (doesn't, don't).

3. Earthquakes (begin, begins) with movements far under ground, and cats often (react, reacts).

4. Some of these reactions (is, are) among the reasons why cats (has, have) been thought to have magical powers.

5. Another explanation for cats' predictions (is, are) that they (sense, senses) changes in static electricity or in the earth's magnetic fields.

6. Most of us (doesn't, don't) notice such changes, but some people (get, gets) headaches before earthquakes, headaches that may be caused by the change.

7. A human being just (isn't, aren't) able to tell the difference between a pre-earthquake headache and a regular stress-related one.

8. Cats (does, do) seem to have such abilities.

9. Many people (has, have) witnessed what cats (does, do) when an earthquake (is, are) approaching.

10. Cats suddenly (look, looks) scared and (run, runs) back and forth or in and out of a house or building; research (have, has) shown that we humans should pay close attention when they (does, do).

Source: Catwatching (Three Rivers Press, 1986)

Exercise 4

1. Some of our ancestors' customs (sound, sounds) strange to us today.

2. One of those customs (was, were) button collecting, (explain, explains) Catherine Roberts in a book about buttons.

3. The first organized button collectors in America (was, were) young unmarried women living in the middle to late 1800s.

4. Their aim in collecting buttons (was, were) to make what (was, were) called Charm Strings.

5. All of the girls had the same goal, which (was, were) to gather exactly 999 buttons on a string.

6. The rules of the game (was, were) strict and known by all, and breaking the rules (was, were) severely frowned upon.

7. A girl and her friends (was, were) supposed to get each button from a different person as a gift; some button trading (was, were) allowed, but not the use of duplicates.

8. Each of the girls (was, were) expected to remember when each of her buttons (was, were) given to her and by whom.

9. During the process of acquiring their buttons, the young women (was, were) eager to hear each other tell the stories of their Charm Strings.

10. In a final note that (show, shows) how far we (has, have) come in the last century, the Victorians believed that any girl who accidentally collected a thousandth button (was, were) destined to become an "old maid."

Source: Who's Got the Button? (David McCay Co., 1962)

Exercise 5

1. Both Melanie Lamantagne and Stacey Lamoureux (has, have) a reason to be happy and proud.

2. Together these young women (is, are) responsible for a prize-winning invention.

3. All of their prize money (add, adds) up to over sixteen hundred dollars.

4. What (was, were) their idea?

5. It (was, were) simple—snowshoes for dogs.

6. There (was, were) a science fair at their high school in Canada, and Melanie and Stacey (was, were) trying to think of a project to enter in the fair.

7. Melanie's dog, a Chihuahua-dachshund mix named Kim, (has, have) short legs and used to fall straight through the snow.

8. Not everyone (was, were) enthusiastic about their project; in fact, some of their fellow students (was, were) skeptical and made fun of it.

9. But neither Melanie nor Stacey (was, were) ready to give up when people told them that the idea of snowshoes for dogs (was, were) silly.

10. One of their supporters (was, were) a science teacher named Roger Moreau, and now Kim and other dogs (walk, walks) and even (run, runs) on top of the snow instead of underneath it.

Source: Current Science 11 Feb. 2000

PROOFREADING EXERCISE

Find and correct the ten subject/verb agreement errors in the following paragraph.

With today's high food prices, you should choose your produce wisely. However, buying ripe fruits and vegetables are a tricky process. How can you tell if an apple or a bunch of bananas are ready to buy or eat? A good rule of thumb for apples, oranges, and lemons is to judge the weight of the fruit. If the fruit are heavy, then it will probably be juicy and tasty. Lightweight fruits tends to lack juice and be tasteless. A melon, on the other hand, are almost always heavy, but a good one sloshes when you shakes it. And the stem end of a ripe cantaloupe will give slightly when you presses on it. Vegetables needs to be chosen carefully, too. If there is sprouted eyes on a potato, you should pass that one by. The sprouted eyes shows a change in the chemical structure of the potato, and it is not a good idea to eat them. When in doubt, you can ask the produce clerk, who should know a lot about the merchandise.

SENTENCE WRITING

Write ten sentences in which you describe the classes you are taking right now. Use verbs in the present time. Then go back over your sentences—underline your subjects once, underline your verbs twice, and be sure they agree.

Avoiding Shifts in Time

People often worry about using different time frames in writing. Let common sense guide you. If you begin writing a paper in past time, don't shift back and forth to the present unnecessarily; and if you begin in the present, don't shift to the past without good reason. In the following paragraph, the writer starts in the present and then shifts to the past, then shifts again to the present:

In the novel *To Kill a Mockingbird,* Jean Louise Finch is a little girl who lives in the South with her father, Atticus, and her brother, Jem. Everybody in town calls Jean Louise "Scout" as a nickname. When Atticus, a lawyer, chose to defend a black man against the charges of a white woman, some of their neighbors turned against him. Scout protected her father by appealing to the humanity of one member of the angry mob. In this chapter, five-year-old Scout turns out to be stronger than a group of adult men.

All the verbs should be in the present:

> In the novel *To Kill a Mockingbird*, Jean Louise Finch is a little girl who lives in the South with her father, Atticus, and her brother, Jem. Everybody in town calls Jean Louise "Scout" as a nickname. When Atticus, a lawyer, chooses to defend a black man against the charges of a white woman, some of their neighbors turn against him. Scout protects her father by appealing to the humanity of one member of the angry mob. In this chapter, five-year-old Scout turns out to be stronger than a group of adult men.

This sample paragraph discusses only the events that happen within the novel's plot, so it needs to maintain one time frame—the present, which we use to write about literature and repeated actions.

However, sometimes you will write about the present, the past, and even the future together. Then it may be necessary to use these different time frames within the same paragraph, each for its own reason. For example, if you were to give biographical information about Harper Lee, author of *To Kill a Mockingbird,* within a discussion of the novel and its influence, you might need to use all three time frames:

> Harper Lee grew up in Alabama, and she based elements in the book on experiences from her childhood. Like the character Atticus, Lee's father was a lawyer. She wrote the novel in his law offices. *To Kill a Mockingbird* is Harper Lee's most famous work, and it received a Pulitzer Prize for fiction in 1960. Lee's book turned forty years old in the year 2000. It will remain one of the most moving and compassionate novels in American literature.

This paragraph uses past (*grew, based, was, wrote, received, turned*), present (*is*), and future (*will remain*) in the same paragraph without committing the error of shifting. Shifting occurs when the writer changes time frames inconsistently or for no reason, confusing the reader (as in the first example given).

PROOFREADING EXERCISES

Which of the following student paragraphs shift *unnecessarily* back and forth between time frames? In those that do, change the verbs to maintain one time frame, thus making the entire paragraph read smoothly. (First, read the paragraphs to determine whether unnecessary shifting takes place. One of the paragraphs is correct.)

1. The last time I took my car in for a scheduled service, I noticed a few problems when I pick it up. I check the oil dipstick, and it has really dark oil still on it. Also, there was a screwdriver balancing on my air-filter cover. I can't believe it when I see it, but as soon as I showed the tool to the service manager, he calls the mechanic over to take my car back to the service area. After another hour, my car is ready, the dipstick has clean oil on it, and the service manager cleared the bill so that I didn't have to pay anything.

2. Richard Hatch was voted the ultimate survivor by his fellow contestants on the first "real TV" game show of the new millennium, *Survivor.* At the beginning of the island marathon, sixteen people are stranded on an island and have to compete for rewards and immunity from being kicked out of the game. The "survivors" were divided into two tribes, Tagi and Pagong. Then one by one, contestants are voted off by the other survivors. Midway through the process of eliminating players, the remaining Tagi and Pagong members merged into one tribe called Rattana. From then on, the individuals within the tribe compete against each other instead of the tribes competing in groups. It all came down to a vote for one of two people, Kelly Wiglesworth and Richard Hatch, and Hatch wins by one vote.

3. Richard Barton invented the Lapotron, which is a device used by swimmers. In 1998, Barton was a member of Quince Orchard High School's swim team. While practicing, he had trouble concentrating while keeping track of his laps. So he decided to put his knowledge of machines to work. He combined a counter, a touch sensor, a timer, and a display into one device that is positioned at the end of the swim lane. He entered the invention in several competitions and won thousands of dollars in bonds and scholarships. As a result of his Lapotron, Barton is one of the most recent inductees into the National Gallery of America's Young Inventors wing of the Inventors Hall of Fame.

Source: Washington Post, 17 Feb. 2000

Recognizing Verbal Phrases

We know (from the discussion on p. 84) that a verb phrase is made up of a main verb and at least one helping verb. But sometimes certain forms of verbs are used not as real verbs but as some other part of a sentence. Verbs put to other uses are called *verbals*.

A verbal can be a subject:

Skiing is my favorite Olympic sport. (*Skiing* is the subject, not the verb. The verb is *is*.)

A verbal can be a descriptive word:

His *bruised* ankle healed very quickly. (*Bruised* describes the subject, ankle. *Healed* is the verb.)

A verbal can be an object:

I like *to read* during the summer. (*To read* is the object. *Like* is the verb.)

Verbals link up with other words to form *verbal phrases*. To see the difference between a real verb phrase and a verbal phrase, look at these two sentences:

I was bowling with my best friends. (*Bowling* is the main verb in a verb phrase. Along with the helping verb *was*, it shows the action of the sentence.)

I enjoyed *bowling* with my best friends. (Here the real verb is *enjoyed*. *Bowling* is not the verb; it is part of a verbal phrase—*bowling with my best friends*—which is what I enjoyed.)

THERE ARE THREE KINDS OF VERBALS

1. *ing* verbs used without helping verbs (*running, thinking, baking* . . .)

2. verb forms that often end in *ed, en,* or t (*tossed, spoken, burnt* . . .)

3. verbs that follow *to* ____ (*to walk, to eat, to cause* . . .)

Look at the following sentences using the previous examples in verbal phrases:

Running two miles a day is great exercise. (real verb = is)

She spent two hours *thinking of a title for her essay*. (real verb = spent)

We had such fun *baking those cherry vanilla cupcakes*. (real verb = had)

Tossed in a salad, artichoke hearts add zesty flavor. (real verb = add)

Spoken in Spanish, the dialogue sounds even more beautiful. (real verb = sounds)

The gourmet pizza, *burnt by a careless chef,* shrunk to half its normal size. (real verb = shrunk)

I like *to walk around the zoo by myself*. (real verb = like)

To eat exotic foods takes courage. (real verb = takes)

They actually wanted *to cause an argument*. (real verb = wanted)

E X E R C I S E S

Each of the following sentences contains at least one verbal or verbal phrase. Double underline the real verbs or verb phrases, and put brackets around the verbals and verbal phrases. Remember to locate the verbal first (*running, wounded, to sleep . . .*) and include any word(s) that go with it (*running a race, wounded in the fight, to sleep all night*). Real verbs will almost never be inside verbal phrases. Complete the first set, and check your answers before going on to the next.

Exercise 1

1. It is hard to plan a successful midday office party.

2. Getting everyone in the same room at the same time is the main obstacle.

3. Employees and bosses don't normally take their breaks together, and someone needs to answer the phones.

4. It is also impossible to surprise people because everyone in an office knows each other and tells each other everything.

5. Furthermore, buying a cake to please twenty or thirty people can be frustrating.

6. It is best to choose either white cake with chocolate frosting or chocolate cake with white frosting.

7. Either of those combinations should be able to satisfy both chocolate lovers and vanilla lovers.

8. Finally, people may find it difficult to start fresh conversations with fellow employees or supervisors.

9. Office business has a way of creeping back into people's discussions.

10. At that point, it is usually time to leave the party and go back to work.

Exercise 2

1. To paraphrase Mark Twain, golfing is just a way to ruin a good walk.

2. In fact, becoming a golfer can be dangerous.

3. Golf professionals commonly suffer a couple of injuries per year resulting from long hours of practicing their swings.

4. Amateur golfers tend to injure themselves much more often.

5. Most injuries come from the twisting, squatting, and bending involved in golfing.

6. And moving the heavy bags of clubs from cars to carts can wrench the backs of potential golfers before they even begin to play.

7. Of course, there are the unfortunate incidents of people on golf courses being struck by lightning.

8. But some of the sources of golfers' ailments may be surprising.

9. Cleaning the dirt and debris off the golf balls by licking them, for instance, may have serious repercussions.

10. After swallowing the chemicals sprayed on the turf of the golf course, players can develop liver problems.

Source: I'm Afraid, You're Afraid: 448 Things to Fear and Why (Hyperion, 2000)

Exercise 3

1. Barbara Barry is trying to improve the selection of computer toys available to girls.

2. Barry works in the Media Lab at the Massachusetts Institute of Technology, thinking up alternatives to the limited pink products so far targeted at young female consumers.

3. Barry's creations, called StoryBeads, are tiny bead-shaped computers that join together as strings or necklaces.

4. StoryBeads give girls almost unlimited possibilities for playing with, communicating through, and learning about computers.

5. In its individual memory, each bead holds any messages or pictures that the girl wants to download there.

6. And the beads "talk" to each other using infrared technology.

7. An "amulet" at the center of a chain of StoryBeads acts as a screen to display the combination of messages and pictures accumulated from the whole string of beads.

8. The StoryBeads can then be rearranged to create new combinations.

9. Barry imagines that girls will want to trade beads and add to their collections.

10. Most important, she hopes that StoryBeads will inspire girls to learn more about the amazing power of computers.

Source: Discover, Sept. 2000

Exercise 4

1. Why do plumbing emergencies always happen on the weekends?

2. Toilets, sinks, and tubs seem to know when plumbers' rates go up.

3. Some emergencies—a slow-draining sink, for instance—can be tolerated for a couple of days.

4. And a dripping shower faucet may cause annoyance, but not panic.

5. However, a backed-up sewer pipe definitely can't wait until Monday.

6. No one wants to see that water rising and overflowing the rim of the bowl.

7. At that point, the only question is which "rooter" service to call.

8. Finding the main drainage line often takes more time than clearing it.

9. Once the plumber has finished fixing the problem, he or she usually eyes future potential disasters and offers to prevent them with even more work.

10. After getting the final bill, I hope that my children will grow up to be not doctors but plumbers.

Exercise 5

1. In the past, the library was the perfect place to study or to do research or homework.

2. But lately is has become a place to meet friends.

3. Things changed when students began to access the Internet.

4. Now two or three students gather near each terminal and show each other the best sites to visit on the Web.

5. Library officials have designated certain rooms as "talking areas."

6. However, such territories are hard to enforce.

7. The old image of the librarian telling everyone to be quiet is just that—an old image.

8. So people talk to each other and giggle right there in the reading room.

9. One of the librarians told me about a plan to take the Internet-access computers out of the main study room and to put them into the "talking areas."

10. I hate to read in a noisy room, so I hope that he was right.

PARAGRAPH EXERCISE

Double underline the real verbs or verb phrases and put brackets around the verbals and verbal phrases in the following paragraph from the book *The Worst-Case Scenario Survival Handbook*, by Joshua Piven and David Borgenicht.

How to Escape from a Sinking Car

As soon as you hit the water, open your window. This is your best chance of escape, because opening the door will be very difficult given the outside water pressure. (To be safe, you should drive with the windows and doors slightly open whenever you are near water or driving on ice.) Opening the windows allows water to come in and equalize the pressure. Once the water pressure inside and outside the car is equal, you'll be able to open the door.

SENTENCE WRITING

Write ten sentences that contain verbal phrases. Use the ten verbals listed here to begin your verbal phrases: *thinking, folding, skiing, marking, to take, to get, to paste, to exercise, planned, given*. The last two are particularly difficult to use as verbals. There are sample sentences listed in the Answer Section at the back of the book. But first, try to write your own so that you can compare the two.

Correcting Misplaced or Dangling Modifiers

When we modify something, we change whatever it is by adding something to it. We might modify a car, for example, by adding special tires. In English, we call words, phrases, and clauses *modifiers* when they add information to part of a sentence. To do its job properly, a modifier should be in the right spot—as close to the word it describes as possible. If we put new tires on the roof of the car instead of where they belong, they would be misplaced. In the following sentence, the modifier is too far away from the word it modifies to make sense. It is a misplaced modifier:

Swinging from tree to tree, we watched the monkeys at the zoo.

Was it *we* who were swinging from tree to tree? That's what the sentence says because the modifying phrase *Swinging from tree to tree* is next to *we*. It should be next to *monkeys*.

At the zoo, we watched the monkeys swinging from tree to tree.

The next example has no word at all for the modifier to modify:

At the age of eight, my family finally bought a dog.

Obviously the family was not eight when it bought a dog. Nor was the dog eight. The modifier *At the age of eight* is dangling there with no word to attach itself to, no word for it to modify. We can get rid of the dangling modifier by turning it into a dependent clause. (See pp. 60–61 for a discussion of dependent clauses.)

When I was eight, my family finally bought a dog.

Here the clause has its own subject and verb—*I was*—and there's no chance of misunderstanding the sentence. Here's another dangling modifier:

After a ten-minute nap, the plane landed.

Did the plane take a ten-minute nap? Who did?

After a ten-minute nap, I awoke just as the plane landed.

E X E R C I S E S

Carefully rephrase any of the following sentences that contain misplaced or dangling modifiers. Some sentences are correct.

Exercise 1

1. After waiting for an hour, my bus finally arrived.

2. Calling my parents long distance, my apology was accepted quickly.

3. I found my keys looking under the table.

4. We heard loud music walking down the street.

5. A week after returning from vacation, my car wouldn't start.

6. With a new pen, the application was easy to complete.

7. Our coach slipped and fell on the jump rope.

8. The answers are printed in the back of my math book.

9. I bought a shirt with gold buttons.

10. Sharon asked for a new car in her letter.

Exercise 2

1. Two students were chatting in the hallway.

2. The caterers served the guests drinks dressed in tuxedos.

3. Carrie, Max, and Angela campaigned for the senator at their school.

4. Sitting at my desk for three hours, my paper was finally finished.

5. The bus ended up on the curb with its blinking lights on.

6. My sisters and I ate a whole pizza waiting for the movie to start.

7. Before calling the doctor, my stomach started to feel better.

8. I ate a piece of toast watching television.

9. Wanting to verify my phone number, the police sergeant called me back.

10. After landing safely, airport security approached the plane.

Exercise 3

1. He saw a bear looking through his binoculars.

2. The nurse handed the patient a tray with a smile.

3. Learning French as a child, the trip should be a lot of fun for me.

4. Shoppers grabbed the new toys and loaded up their carts.

5. Hungry for lunch, the students lost their concentration.

6. The Glickmans danced for hours at the party without shoes.

7. You locked the door to my office by accident.

8. She sent us an invitation to her graduation from a post office in New Jersey.

9. By the age of six, Neil Armstrong had already landed on the moon.

10. The teacher will return our paragraphs on drugs.

Exercise 4

1. Taking an aspirin before my nap, my headache was gone.

2. I drove my new car home full of gas.

3. After thirteen months of planning, the reunion was a success.

4. She wrapped all the gifts in her pajamas.

5. The students watched the video in a dark room.

6. Before walking out, the bus drivers made their final offer.

7. Gathered in a bunch, the children gave the daisies to their teacher.

8. Skipping across the water, I watched the stone reach the middle of the lake.

9. Trying to look happy, his heart was breaking.

10. All along the sidewalk, we saw weeds.

Exercise 5

1. Feeling the thrill of a day at the amusement park, my blisters didn't bother me.

2. Full of touching scenes, my friends and I saw the new tearjerker.

3. My classmates and I always turned our essays in on time.

4. Practicing for an hour a day, her piano has improved.

5. Gasoline prices fluctuate with politics.

6. Sitting on a bench all day, an idea came to her.

7. On the road to their cousins' house, they discovered a new outlet mall.

8. He felt the pressure of trying to get a good job from his parents.

9. I enjoy talking to new people at parties.

10. Written in chalk, the notes on the board were hard to read.

PROOFREADING EXERCISE

Find and correct any misplaced or dangling modifiers in the following paragraph.

Walking into my neighborhood polling place during the last election, a volunteer greeted me and checked my name and address. Being misspelled slightly on their printout, he couldn't find me at first. I pointed to what I thought was my name. At least upside down, I thought it was mine. But actually, it was another person's name. Once turned toward me, I could see the printout more clearly. My name was there, but it had an extra letter stuck on the end of it. The volunteer handed me a change-of-name form with a polite smile. I filled it out and punched my ballot. Stuck on my wall at home, I have my voting receipt to remind me to check my name carefully when the next election comes around.

SENTENCE WRITING

Write five sentences that contain misplaced or dangling modifiers; then revise those sentences to put the modifiers where they belong. Use the examples in the explanations as models.

Following Sentence Patterns

Sentences are built according to a few basic patterns. For proof, rearrange each of the following sets of words to form a complete statement (not a question):

apples a ate raccoon the

the crashing beach were waves the on

your in am partner I life

been she school has to walking

you wonderful in look green

There are only one or two possible combinations for each due to English sentence patterns. Either *A raccoon ate the apples* or *The apples ate a raccoon,* and so on. But in each case, the verb or verb phrase makes its way to the middle of the statement.

To understand sentence patterns, you need to know that verbs can do three things.

1.   They can show actions:

The raccoon ate the apples.

The waves were crashing on the beach.

She has been walking to school.

2.   They can link subjects with descriptive words:

I am your partner in life.

You look wonderful in green.

3.   They can help other verbs form verb phrases:

The waves were crashing on the beach.

She has been walking to school.

Look at these sentences for more examples:

Mel grabbed a slice of pizza. (The verb *grabbed* shows Mel's action.)

His slice was the largest one in the box. (The verb *was* links *slice* with its description as *the largest one.*)

Mel had been craving pizza for a week. (The verbs *had* and *been* help the main verb *craving* in a verb phrase.)

Knowing what a verb does in a clause helps you gain an understanding of the three basic sentence patterns:

SUBJECT + ACTION VERB + OBJECT PATTERN

Some action verbs must be followed by a person or object that receives the action.

   S   **AV**   **OBJ.**

Sylvia completed the difficult math test. (*Sylvia completed* makes no sense without being followed by the object that she completed—*test.*)

SUBJECT + ACTION VERB (+ NO OBJECT) PATTERN

At other times, the action verb itself finishes the meaning and needs no object after it.

   S   **AV**

She celebrated at home with her family. (*She celebrated* makes sense alone. The two prepositional phrases—*at home* and *with her family*—are not needed to understand the meaning of the clause.)

SUBJECT + LINKING VERB + DESCRIPTION PATTERN

A special kind of verb that does not show an action but links a subject with a description is called a *linking verb*. It acts like an equal sign in a clause. Learn to recognize the most common linking verbs: *is, am, are, was, were, seem, feel, appear, become, look.*

   S   **LV**   **DESC.**

Sylvia was always an excellent student. (*Sylvia* equals *an excellent student.*)

   S   **LV**   **DESC.**

Sylvia has become very intelligent. (*Very intelligent* describes *Sylvia.*)

NOTE- We learned on page 84 that a verb phrase includes a main verb and its helping verbs. Helping verbs can be used in any of the sentence patterns.

      S   **AV**

Sylvia is going to Seattle for a vacation. (Here the verb *is* helps the main verb *going*, which is an action verb with no object followed by two prepositional phrases—*to Seattle* and *for a vacation*.)

The following chart outlines the patterns using short sentences that you should memorize:

THE THREE BASIC SENTENCE PATTERNS

S + AV + Obj.

They hit the ball.

S + AV

They ran (quickly) (around the bases).
not objects

S + LV +   Desc.

They are   state champions.
They look   professional.

These are the three basic patterns of most of the clauses used in English sentences. Knowing them can help writers control their sentences and improve their use of words.

E X E R C I S E S

First, put parentheses around any prepositional phrases. Next, underline the subjects once and the verbs or verb phrases twice. Then mark the sentence patterns above the words. Remember that the patterns never mix together. For example, unlike an action verb, a linking verb will almost never be used alone (for example, "He seems."), nor will an action verb be followed by a description of the subject (for example, "She took tall."). And if there are two independent clauses, each one may have a different pattern. Check your answers after the first set of ten.

Exercise 1

1. Wendy Hasnip lives in England.

2. She does not speak French.

3. At the age of forty-seven, Hasnip had a stroke.

4. For two weeks after the stroke, she could not talk.

5. Eventually, Hasnip regained her speaking ability.

6. But suddenly, she spoke with a distinct French accent.

7. Strangely, this condition is a known—but extremely rare—post-brain-injury symptom.

8. Doctors call it the Foreign Accent Syndrome.

9. One man in Russia recovered from a brain injury.

10. Now he can speak and understand ninety-three languages.

Sources: Moscow Times, Dec. 1999, *Salt Lake Tribune,* 13 June 2000, and *Current Science,* 6 Oct. 2000

Exercise 2

1. Local news programs are all alike.

2. They begin with the top stories of the day.

3. These stories may be local, national, or international.

4. They might include violent crimes, traffic jams, natural disasters, and political upheavals.

5. After the top stories, one of the anchors offers a quick weather update.

6. Then a sportscaster covers the latest scores and team standings.

7. At some point, a "human interest" story lightens the mood of the broadcast.

8. And then we hear the latest entertainment news.

9. Near the end of the half-hour, the weatherperson gives the full weather forecast.

10. News programs could use an update of their own.

Exercise 3

1. Scientists in West Virginia have located a sugary substance at the center of the Milky Way.

2. The Milky Way in this case is the one in outer space not the popular candy bar.

3. National Radio Astronomy Observatory personnel analyzed the makeup of a vaporous mass in the middle of the Milky Way.

4. Results of the analysis were sweet.

5. The ingredients in the cloud of gases and dust particles were particular amounts of carbon, hydrogen, and oxygen.

6. The molecular name for the compound is glycolaldehyde, a substance very similar to plain old sugar.

7. The discovery of a cloud of sugar in the middle of space doesn't surprise scientists.

8. Vaporous masses supply the foundation for planets and stars.

9. And sugars provide the basis for almost all forms of life.

10. This discovery may be important in the search for life in outer space.

Source: Current Science, 6 Oct. 2000

Exercise 4

1. One of the high points of the Clinton administration was the video spoof of his last days in the White House.

2. Clinton participated wholeheartedly in the project and demonstrated almost-professional acting abilities.

3. The brief video shows Clinton in various silly situations; all of them satirize the boredom and inactivity of the end of a presidency.

4. In one scene, Clinton runs after Hillary's limousine with her forgotten lunch sack in his hand.

5. Clinton reads a magazine and waits by a tumbling clothes dryer in another.

6. More famous people, such as actor Kevin Spacey, join the fun.

7. In the middle of a phony acceptance speech in front of a mirror, Clinton reluctantly gives the Best Actor Oscar back to Spacey.

8. In two other sections of the video, Clinton plays the kids' game Battleship with the chairman of the Joint Chiefs of Staff, General Henry Shelton, and rides a bike down White House hallways.

9. The occasion for the video was the annual White House Correspondents' Association Dinner in Washington.

10. The video entertained all of the guests, and it revealed Clinton's healthy sense of humor.

Exercise 5

1. British actor Oliver Reed died on May 2, 1999.

2. He was making *Gladiator* at the time.

3. Reed passed away before the end of filming.

4. *Gladiator* director Ridley Scott used footage from Reed's earlier takes for the film's ending.

5. Proximo is Reed's character in the film.

6. For Proximo's final scene, Scott added computer-generated prison bars to one of Reed's previously filmed close-ups.

7. In moments without close-ups, Scott used other actors for Reed's character.

8. Oliver Reed starred in many famous films before *Gladiator.*

9. He played Bill Sikes in the musical *Oliver!* and costarred in *The Three Musketeers* and *Women in Love.*

10. But *Gladiator's* Proximo was his final screen performance.

Source: People, 15 May 2000

PARAGRAPH EXERCISE

Label the sentence patterns in the following paragraph from the book *Guess Who? A Cavalcade of Famous Americans,* by Veronica Geng. It helps to surround prepositional phrases with parentheses and verbal phrases with brackets first to isolate them from the main words of the sentence patterns. Then label the subjects, the verbs, and any objects after action verbs or descriptions after linking verbs (*is, am, are, was, were, become, appear, seem,* and so on).

Thomas Alva Edison

Slow in school and poor at math, Edison quit school at twelve to work as a newsboy on a train. He used his wages to buy chemicals, for he loved experimenting. He even built a little lab in the baggage car on the train. Later he worked as a telegraph operator and learned about electricity. By 1876, he had his own lab and . . . a staggering series of inventions: a phonograph, a practical light bulb, a strip of motion picture film, and many others. By trial and error, sleepless nights, and tireless work, Edison became the most productive inventor of practical devices that America has ever seen. He was also probably the only inventor who was as well-known to every American as the most famous movie star.

SENTENCE WRITING

Write ten sentences describing the weather today and your feelings about it—make your sentences short and clear. Then go back and label the sentence patterns you have used.

Avoiding Clichés, Awkward Phrasing, and Wordiness

CLICHÉS

A cliché is an expression that has been used so often it has lost its originality and effectiveness. Whoever first said "light as a feather" had thought of an original way to express lightness, but today that expression is worn out. Most of us use an occasional cliché in speaking, but clichés have no place in writing. The good writer thinks up fresh new ways to express ideas.

Here are a few clichés. Add some more to the list.

the bottom line

older but wiser

last but not least

in this day and age

different as night and day

out of this world

white as a ghost

sick as a dog

tried and true

at the top of their lungs

the thrill of victory

one in a million

busy as a bee

easier said than done

better late than never

Clichés lack freshness because the reader always knows what's coming next. Can you complete these expressions?

the agony of . . .

breathe a sigh of . . .

lend a helping . . .

odds and . . .

raining cats and . . .

as American as . . .

been there . . .

worth its weight . . .

Clichés are expressions too many people use. Try to avoid them in your writing.

AWKWARD PHRASING

Another problem—awkward phrasing—comes from writing sentence structures that *no one* else would use because they break basic sentence patterns, omit necessary words, or use words incorrectly. Like clichés, awkward sentences might *sound* acceptable when spoken, but as polished writing, they are usually unacceptable.

AWKWARD

There should be great efforts in terms of the cooperation between coaches and their athletes.

CORRECTED

Coaches and their athletes should cooperate.

AWKWARD

During the experiment, the use of key principles was essential to ensure the success of it.

CORRECTED

The experiment was a success. *or* We did the experiment carefully.

AWKWARD

My favorite was when the guy fell all the way down the ship.

CORRECTED

In my favorite scene, a man fell all the way down the deck of the sinking ship.

WORDINESS

Good writing is concise writing. Don't say something in ten words if you can say it better in five. "In today's society" isn't as effective as "today," and it's a cliché. "At this point in time" could be "presently" or "now."

Another kind of wordiness comes from saying something twice. There's no need to write "in the month of August" or "9 A.M. in the morning" or "my personal opinion." August *is* a month, 9 A.M. *is* morning, and anyone's opinion *is* personal. All you need to write is "in August," "9 A.M.," and "my opinion."

Still another kind of wordiness comes from using expressions that add nothing to the meaning of the sentence. "The point is that we can't afford it" says no more than "We can't afford it."

Here is a sample wordy sentence:

The construction company actually worked on that particular building for a period of six months.

And here it is after eliminating wordiness:

The construction company worked on that building for six months.

WORDY WRITING	**CONCISE WRITING**
advance planning	planning
an unexpected surprise	a surprise

ask a question	ask
at a later date	later
basic fundamentals	fundamentals
but nevertheless	but (or nevertheless)
combine together	combine
completely empty	empty
down below	below
each and every	each (or every)
end result	result
fewer in number	fewer
free gift	gift
green in color	green
in order to	to
in spite of the fact that	although
just exactly	exactly
large in size	large
new innovation	innovation
on a regular basis	regularly
past history	history
rectangular in shape	rectangular
refer back	refer
repeat again	repeat
serious crisis	crisis
sufficient enough	sufficient (or enough)
there in person	there
two different kinds	two kinds
very unique	unique

E X E R C I S E S

Exercise 1

Rewrite the following sentences to eliminate clichés and awkward phrasing.

1. I believe that, when there's a will, there's a way.

2. And I've got determination a mile long and a yard wide.

3. So when I decided to learn how to juggle, there was no stopping me.

4. It was as easy as pie to get the hang of passing two beanbags from hand to hand.

5. But introducing that third bag into the mix was easier said than done.

6. I would be going along just fine, and then it would all fall apart.

7. A friend of mine who knows the ins and outs of juggling told me I was going about it all wrong.

8. He said that I needed to get the circular movement hardwired into my circuits by practicing without catching the bags before I should attempt the real thing.

9. Well, that advice was just what the doctor ordered, and I was tossing three bags like a pro before long.

10. The bottom line is I learned how to juggle with the help of some good advice.

Exercise 2

Cross out words or rewrite parts of each sentence to eliminate wordiness. Doing these exercises can almost turn into a game to see how few words you can use without changing the meaning of the sentence.

1. When they were just small young children at a Halloween party, Esther Kim and Kay Poe met each other for the very first time.

2. The Halloween party was held at the place where both girls took tae-kwondo lessons from Esther's father, Jin Won Kim.

3. Because Esther and Kay were wearing Halloween costumes, they couldn't even tell if the other was a boy or a girl since Esther wore a pirate costume and Kay wore a Ninja costume; they both just grabbed each other's hands and never let them go.

4. To make a long story short, Esther and Kay became instant best friends and stayed that way throughout the years as they trained under Esther's father's guidance to be taekwondo champions.

5. It's obvious to everyone that neither Esther nor Kay knew that, when they grew up, both of them would be in a position to fill the one final remain-

ing spot on the American taekwondo team to head for the Summer 2000 Olympics in Sydney, Australia.

6. But it turned out that the Olympic story wasn't the happier story for these two athletes; in fact, the happier story was the story about how Esther and Kay ended up face-to-face having to fight for that one final spot.

7. Kay Poe had seriously injured her knee during her previous bout with an opponent right before she was supposed to fight with Esther Kim, and only the winner of their match would be the one to go to the Olympics.

8. But when Esther Kim saw that her best friend was hurt so badly, she had a dilemma that she couldn't resolve easily; she just could not bring herself to fight against Kay Poe when she was so badly hurt.

9. So to everyone's surprise, Esther Kim decided not to fight but to forfeit the match to her injured lifelong friend.

10. Sydney, Australia, Olympic officials were so extremely impressed with Esther Kim's sacrifice in the name of sportsmanship that they provided free transportation and accommodation to Esther and her father to the Sydney Olympics, and Mr. Kim had never been prouder of his daughter than he was on the day she sacrificed her own dream for a friend's dream.

Source: Scholastic Scope, 18 Sept. 2000

Exercises 3, 4, and 5

Revise the sentences in the remaining exercises to eliminate any clichés, awkward phrasing, or wordiness.

Exercise 3

1. People tend to worry a lot about their young children and how smart or knowledgeable their children will grow up to be in the future.

2. By now, most parents have heard of the concept that kids who are exposed to great music, art, languages, and literature when they are babies or small children will grow up to be more intelligent than kids who are not exposed to such things.

3. There seems to be no definite proof that the concept is anything but another kind of experience, but most parents are ready to accept such ideas in a effort to make their kids the cream of the crop intellectually.

4. Video companies, book companies, and software companies have all been developing and selling products that help even skeptical parents to hedge their bets on their offspring's futures.

5. There are programs to help children start reading at just a few months old; these videos are full of appealing sights and sounds that include animated words, pronunciation of the words, and pictures of the meanings of the words.

6. One company was started by a mother who was looking for videos that would be appropriate for her own baby to watch and learn from.

7. Julie Aigner-Clark began a company called Baby Einstein, and her company has sold well over a million copies of videos for babies; included in the Baby Einstein line are videos titled *Baby Bach, Baby Mozart,* and *Baby Shakespeare.*

8. It seems that Clark and others have tapped into people's desire for quality and culture that they want their children to participate in.

9. Experts in the field of child development may say that children who are well-cared-for and well-fed by their parents will probably be on the same footing as kids whose parents have bought the latest video or software program to pre-educate them in the arts.

10. But the controversy all boils down to one big question: is there anything wrong with a person knowing too much Shakespeare?

Source: Washington Post, 3 Mar. 2000

Exercise 4

1. I just saw a story on the news about an animal that didn't look like anything I'd ever seen before.

2. It kind of looks like a teddy bear and a little monkey and a miniature dog all rolled into one.

3. I found out that this little guy has his own Web site and in fact was quite a celebrity in his own right.

4. The name of this odd creature is Mr. Winkle, and on his home page, even they say they don't know what he is.

5. On the Web site, a bunch of questions flash across the screen while it's loading, questions like is it an "alien?" a "stuffed animal?" a "hamster with a permanent?"

6. One thing I can say for sure is that he is pretty cute.

7. I can see why his owner stopped her car one day when she saw the strange-looking beast walking by the side of the road and took him home with her.

8. Since she found him that day, she has taken a whole bunch of pictures of him in quirky little costumes and even one of him running in a hamster wheel.

9. Of course, all of these pictures are available for purchase at the click of the mouse in the form of posters and calendars, and I must say the prices are relatively reasonable.

10. And there's no need to go hunting around for the Web address at which these products and pictures and stories can be found; just head to "mrwinkle.com."

Exercise 5

1. As with any widely used goods or services, network television must be somewhat responsive to the demands of the people who watch it.

2. One thing that one must bear in mind when judging something as widespread as television is the kind of people that watch it, namely, just about everyone.

3. To say that TV is not giving the American public the kind of programming it wants is to say that the American public all want the same kind of programming, and of course, that is not the case.

4. First of all, for TV to satisfy everyone, there would have to be a separate channel for each person that showed only those kinds of things that person wanted to see.

5. There are a couple of products that let people customize their viewing opportunities, but they have not caught on yet because there is an extra cost.

6. That brings me to my next point, network TV is free, so what more does everyone want?

7. Sure, we have to sit there and watch while some "typical" person has an experience with paper towels that changes her life.

8. But sometimes I find that the commercials are often more educational or at least more entertaining than the regular programs.

9. And what's more is that people can watch as much TV as they want at a given time.

10. The American people need different things to watch at different times, and that's the only way to make everyone happy.

PROOFREADING EXERCISE

Revise the sentences in the following paragraph to eliminate any clichés, awkward phrasing, or wordiness.

Los Angeles is a city that is mainly designed to be traveled around in by automobile. I, as a person, use my automobile as a dominant figure in my life because I need it for my work and to get to school. I deliver pizzas, and I wouldn't have even gotten the job if I didn't have my own car. Like other people in Los Angeles, I use my vehicle as a necessity to my living standards. I drive a couple of my friends to school since they don't have cars, and I am lucky I'm not like them. Automobiles are not the one and only way to get around in L.A., but they are the way that is better than taking a bus or one of the Metrolink trains. At least the subways are connecting the most popular places in L.A., and a bus will eventually get people anywhere they want to go, but it wouldn't be possible for me to deliver my pizzas by using public transportation. The toppings would be cold when I got there, and everyone would go crazy from the delicious smell of the pizzas.

SENTENCE WRITING

Go back to the sentences you wrote for the Sentence Writing exercise on page 68 or page 132 and revise them to eliminate any clichés, awkward phrasing, or wordiness.

Correcting for Parallel Structure

Your writing will be clearer and more memorable if you use parallel construction. That is, when you make any kind of list, put the items in similar form. If you write

My favorite coffee drinks are lattes, mochas, and the ones with espresso.

the sentence lacks parallel structure. The items don't all have the same form. But if you write

My favorite coffees are lattes, mochas, and espressos.

then the items are parallel. They are all single-word nouns. Or you could write

I like drinks blended with milk, flavored with chocolate, and made with espresso.

Again, the sentence has parallel structure because all three descriptions are verbal phrases. Here are some more examples. Note how much easier it is to read the sentences with parallel construction.

LACKING PARALLEL CONSTRUCTION	**HAVING PARALLEL CONSTRUCTION**
I like to hike, to ski, and going sailing.	I like to hike, to ski, and to sail. (all "to ____" verbs)
The office has run out of pens, paper, ink cartridges, and we need more toner, too.	The office needs more pens, paper, ink cartridges, and toner. (all nouns)
They decided that they needed a change, that they could afford a new house, and wanted to move to Arizona.	They decided that they needed a change, that they could afford a new house, and that they wanted to move to Arizona. (all dependent clauses)

The supporting points in an outline should always be parallel. In the following brief outlines, the supporting points in the left-hand column are not parallel in structure. Those in the right-hand column are parallel.

NOT PARALLEL

Food Irradiation
  I. How is it good?
    A. Longer shelf life
    B. Using fewer pesticides
    C. Kills bacteria
  II. Concerns
    A. Nutritional value
    B. Consumers are worried
    C. Workers' safety

PARALLEL

Food Irradiation
  I. Benefits
    A. Extends shelf life
    B. Requires fewer pesticides
    C. Kills bacteria
  II. Concerns
    A. Lowers nutritional value
    B. Alarms consumers
    C. Endangers workers

Using parallel construction will make your writing more effective. Note the effective parallelism in these well-known quotations:

A place for everything and everything in its place.

Isabella Mary Beeton

I have been poor and I have been rich. Rich is better.

Sophie Tucker

Ask not what your country can do for you; ask what you can do for your country.

John F. Kennedy

We hold these truths to be self-evident, that all men are created equal, that they are endowed by their creator with certain unalienable rights, that among these are Life, Liberty, and the pursuit of Happiness.

Thomas Jefferson

E X E R C I S E S

Most—but not all—of the following sentences lack parallel structure. In some, you will be able to cross out the part that is not parallel and write the correction above. Other sentences will need complete rephrasing.

Exercise 1

1. I started preparations for my winter vacation last week, and that's when I realized that my luggage and the coat that I use in cold weather are completely inadequate for a trip to Chicago.

2. My brother lives in "The Windy City," and he says that it gets very cold there.

3. Temperatures in San Francisco hardly ever dip below the forties, or they might get as low as the thirties.

4. The jacket I normally use is lightweight, and it does not have a liner of any kind.

5. I'll need to buy a coat made of down or maybe one of the fleece ones that skiers wear.

6. My suitcases are inadequate as well; they are soft-bodied, and they're duffel-bag style with several outer compartments closed by zippers.

7. I have taken these cases on car trips to Seattle, but it wouldn't be a good idea to travel by plane with them.

8. Anyone can access the zippered compartments while my bags are waiting in a luggage area.

9. I don't want to worry about things being stolen or that a pocket might rip or something.

10. As a result of these deficiencies, I'm currently looking for new luggage, and I need to buy a proper winter coat.

Exercise 2

1. Horses are not known to be particularly noisy, but observers have grouped the sounds horses make into eight categories.

2. One category is snorting, which horses do when they feel curious and afraid at the same time.

3. Another type of noise that horses make is squealing, which, in varying degrees of severity, can mean "Leave me alone," "I don't like that!" or that the horse needs help.

4. There are three different kinds of greeting sounds, called "nickers," but they are all similar due to their low rolling quality.

5. One nicker is used to greet another horse or when a person brings food for the horse.

6. Another lower-pitched greeting signals courtship and one horse that can be distinguished from another.

7. A mare uses the third kind of greeting sound to call her foal, and also she comforts it that way.

8. Neighing or what many people call whinnying is the most well-known of the horse's sounds.

9. Roaring and screaming are sounds made mostly by wild horses when they're fighting furiously.

10. The eighth sound, a simple blast of air, is called a "blow" and seems to be the horse's way to say "Everything's fine."

Source: Illustrated Horsewatching (Knickerbocker Press, 1999)

Exercise 3

1. Going to the new car wash in my neighborhood is like a trip to paradise.

2. It has a plush lounge that offers free coffee, cookies, and there are even pretzels for those who don't like sweets.

3. The leather furniture comforts weary customers as they wait for their cars to be cleaned.

4. Full plate-glass windows line the front wall of the lounge so that people can see their vehicles being dried, and sometimes they even check out the cars of the people around them.

5. For those who don't like to sit down, a full assortment of greeting cards lines the back wall of the lounge, as well as car accessories too.

6. To keep things interesting, every hour there is a drawing for a free car wash; I haven't ever won one of those though.

7. Whenever I am waiting in the luxurious setting of the car wash, I wonder about two things.

8. Why do people talk on cell phones when they could be resting, and how can you explain that some people stand up when they could be sitting on a nice leather sofa?

9. I will always love going to my neighborhood car wash.

10. It's the modern equivalent of going to the barbershop or to get a new hairdo at the beauty parlor.

Exercise 4

1. On June 26, 2000, scientists and their machines completed the extraordinary task of writing out the code for human life, also known as the human genome.

2. Joining the scientists were car-sized robots, and there were also massive computers that worked continuously to analyze the most basic structures of human tissues.

3. The genome project has already cost nearly four billion dollars, and ten years have gone by since it was started.

4. Now that they have our genetic code on paper, scientists will try to learn how it works.

5. The code is made up of billions of combinations of letters standing for four different chemicals: "A" for adenine, "C" for cystosine, "G" for guanine, and finally there's "T" for thymine.

6. What nobody knew before June 26, 2000, was the ordering of those four chemicals along the human genome or chain of human DNA.

7. Within DNA, genes are the smaller groupings of chemicals that instruct the different cells of the body, but the problem is that the genome includes fifty thousand genes.

8. In simpler terms, the genome is similar to a huge anthology of fifty thousand stories (genes) written so closely together that no one can tell where one ends and another begins.

9. The future of human life, disease, and how long we live may all be affected once the experts begin to identify the individual genes.

10. Some people look forward to that day optimistically, but the fear that it fills others with is just as real.

Source: Current Science, 8 Sept. 2000

Exercise 5

Make the sentences in the following list parallel.

1. To recognize a mail bomb, consider the following life-saving measures.

2. Do not touch any package or bulging letter if you sense that it is dangerous.

3. You should be wary of odd-sized or odd-looking boxes or packets.

4. It is also important to be sure that there is a preprinted return address on the package.

5. Tons of stamps instead of a clerk-issued postage label show that the package did not go through all of the checkpoints at the post office.

6. Never trust a package wrapped with any kind of rope or string.

7. Too much sealing tape is another signal that something may be wrong.

8. And greasy marks or oil spots should be looked for too.

9. Whenever any of these tell-tale signs are noted, clear the area immediately.

10. Finally, don't feel silly for being cautious.

Source: The Worst-Case Scenario Survival Handbook (Chronicle Books, 1999)

PROOFREADING EXERCISE

Proofread the following student paragraph about Clara Barton, an American hero, and revise it to correct any errors in parallel structure.

At the beginning of the American Civil War, Clara Barton heard that some of the injured soldiers were surviving without medicine and didn't have anything to eat either. So Barton took out a newspaper ad to ask for donations of medical supplies, food for the soldiers to eat, and she needed some blankets too. When the donations arrived, Barton delivered them directly to the soldiers on the battlefields. The troops could scarcely believe that Barton, a woman who stood only five feet tall, would endanger her own life and also that she would have to march through the mud just to nurse them back to health. When the war ended, Barton continued her humanitarian efforts by finding soldiers who were missing in action, and she opened an office of the International Red Cross.

Source: *Guess Who? A Cavalcade of Famous Americans* (Platt and Munk, 1969)

SENTENCE WRITING

Write ten sentences that use parallel structure. You may choose your own subject, or you may describe the process of studying for an important test. Be sure to include pairs and lists of objects, actions, locations, or ideas.

Using Pronouns

Nouns name people, places, things, and ideas—such as *students, school, computers,* and *cyberspace.* Pronouns take the place of nouns to avoid repetition and to clarify meaning. Look at the following two sentences. Nouns are needlessly repeated in the first sentence, but the second uses pronouns.

> The boy's mother felt that the children at the party were too loud, so the boy's mother told the children that the party would have to end if the children didn't calm down.

> The boy's mother felt that the children at the party were too loud, so *she* told *them* that *it* would have to end if *they* didn't calm down.

In the second sentence, *she* replaces *mother, they* and *them* replace *children,* and *it* takes the place of *party.*

Of the many kinds of pronouns, the following cause the most difficulty because they include two ways of identifying the same person (or people), but only one form is correct in a given situation:

SUBJECT GROUP	OBJECT GROUP
I	me
he	him
she	her
we	us
they	them

Use a pronoun from the Subject Group in two instances:

1. Before a verb as a subject:

> *He* is my cousin. (*He* is the subject of the verb *is.*)

> *He* is taller than *I.* (The sentence is not written out in full. It means "*He* is taller than *I* am." *I* is the subject of the verb *am.*)

Whenever you see *than* in a sentence, ask yourself whether a verb has been left off the end of the sentence. Add the verb, and then you'll automatically use the correct pronoun. In both speaking and writing, always add the verb. Instead of saying, "She's smarter than (I, me)," say, "She's smarter than I *am.*" Then you will use the correct pronoun.

2. After a linking verb (is, am, are, was, were) as a pronoun that renames the subject:

> The one who should apologize is *he*. (*He* is *the one who should apologize.* Therefore the pronoun from the Subject Group is used.)

> The winner of the lottery was *she*. (*She* was *the winner of the lottery.* Therefore the pronoun from the Subject Group is used.)

Modern usage allows some exceptions to this rule, however. For example, *It's me* or *It is her* (instead of the grammatically correct *It is I* and *It is she*) may be common in spoken English.

Use pronouns from the Object Group for all other purposes. In the following sentence, *me* is not the subject, nor does it rename the subject. It follows a preposition; therefore, it comes from the Object Group.

> My boss went to lunch with Jenny and *me*.

A good way to tell whether to use a pronoun from the Subject Group or the Object Group is to leave out any extra name (and the word *and*). By leaving out *Jenny and,* you will say, "My boss went to lunch with me." You would never say, "My boss went to lunch with I."

> My father and *I* play chess on Sundays. (*I* play chess on Sundays.)

> *She* and her friends rented a video. (*She* rented a video.)

> We saw Kevin and *them* last night. (We saw *them* last night.)

> The teacher gave *us* students certificates. (Teacher gave *us* certificates.)

> The coach asked Craig and *me* to wash the benches. (Coach asked *me* to wash the benches.)

PRONOUN AGREEMENT

Just as subjects and verbs must agree, pronouns should agree with the words they refer to. If the word referred to is singular, the pronoun should be singular. If the noun referred to is plural, the pronoun should be plural.

> Each classroom has its own chalkboard.

The pronoun *its* refers to the singular noun *classroom* and therefore is singular.

> Both classrooms have their own chalkboards.

The pronoun *their* refers to the plural noun *classrooms* and therefore is plural.

The same rules that we use to maintain the agreement of subjects and verbs also apply to pronoun agreement. For instance, ignore any prepositional phrases that come between the word and the pronoun that takes its place.

The *box* of chocolates has lost *its* label.

Boxes of chocolates often lose *their* labels.

A *player* with the best concentration usually beats *her or his* opponent.

Players with the best concentration usually beat *their* opponents.

When a pronoun refers to more than one word joined by *and,* the pronoun is plural:

The *teacher* and the *tutors* eat *their* lunches at noon.

The *salt* and *pepper* were in *their* usual spots at noon.

However, when a pronoun refers to more than one word joined by *or,* then the word closest to the pronoun determines its form:

Either the *teacher* or the *tutors* eat *their* lunches in the classroom.

Either the *tutors* or the *teacher* eats *her* lunch in the classroom.

Today many people try to avoid gender bias by writing sentences like the following:

If anyone wants help with the assignment, he or she can visit me in my office.

If anybody calls, tell him or her that I'll be back soon.

Somebody has left his or her pager in the classroom.

But those sentences are wordy and awkward. Therefore some people, especially in conversation, turn them into sentences that are not grammatically correct.

If anyone wants help with the assignment, they can visit me in my office.

If anybody calls, tell them that I'll be back soon.

Somebody has left their pager in the classroom.

Such ungrammatical sentences, however, are not necessary. It just takes a little thought to revise each sentence so that it avoids gender bias and is also grammatically correct:

Anyone who wants help with the assignment can visit me in my office.

Tell anybody who calls that I'll be back soon.

Somebody has left a pager in the classroom.

Probably the best way to avoid the awkward *he or she* and *him or her* is to make the words plural. Instead of writing, "Each actor was in his or her proper place on stage," write, "All the actors were in their proper places on stage," thus avoiding gender bias and still having a grammatically correct sentence.

PRONOUN REFERENCE

A pronoun replaces a noun to avoid repetition, but sometimes the pronoun sounds as if it refers to the wrong word in a sentence, causing confusion. Be aware that when you write a sentence, *you* know what it means, but your reader may not. What does this sentence mean?

The students tried to use the school's computers to access the Internet, but they were too slow, so they decided to go home.

Who or what was too slow, and who or what decided to go home? We don't know whether the two pronouns (both *they*) refer to the students or to the computers. One way to correct such a faulty reference is to use singular and plural nouns:

The students tried to use a school computer to access the Internet, but it was too slow, so they decided to go home.

Here's another sentence with a faulty reference:

Sharon told her mother that she needed a haircut.

Who needed the haircut—Sharon or her mother? One way to correct such a faulty reference is to use a direct quotation:

Sharon told her mother, "You need a haircut."

Sharon said, "Mom, I need a haircut."

Or you could always rephrase the sentence completely:

Sharon noticed her mother's hair was sticking out in odd places, so she told her mother to get a haircut.

Another kind of faulty reference is a *which* clause that appears to refer to a specific word, but it doesn't really.

I wasn't able to finish all the problems on the exam, which makes me worried.

The word *which* seems to replace exam, but it isn't the exam that makes me worried. The sentence should read

I am worried that I wasn't able to finish all the problems on the exam.

The pronoun *it* causes its own reference problems. Look at this sentence, for example:

When replacing the ink cartridge in my printer, it broke, and I had to call the technician to come and fix it.

Did the printer or the cartridge break? Here is one possible correction:

The new ink cartridge broke when I was putting it in my printer, and I had to call the technician for help.

E X E R C I S E S

Exercise 1

Underline the correct pronoun. Remember the trick of leaving out the extra name to help you decide which pronoun to use. Use the correct grammatical form even though an alternate form may be acceptable in conversation.

1. My brother Martin, a few friends, and (I, me) went skiing over the holidays.

2. Martin usually enjoys skiing more than (I, me).

3. This time, however, both (he and I, him and me) challenged ourselves.

4. Since Martin is less safety conscious than (I, me), he usually doesn't want to ski with my group down the gentle slopes.

5. Everytime (he and I, him and me) have been skiing before, Martin has just met my buddies and (I, me) back at the cabin at the end of the day.

6. But the one who was the most daring this time was (I, me).

7. Martin may be more of a daredevil than (I, me) most of the time, but he needed coaxing to try the steep slopes that my friends and (I, me) sailed down this time.

8. Just between (you and me, you and I), I think Martin was really scared.

9. Martin was thrilled when a ski instructor came up to (he and I, him and me) and asked, "You've been skiing for a long time, haven't you?"

10. Instead of going off on his own in the future, Martin will stay close to my friends and (I, me).

Exercise 2

Underline the pronoun that agrees with the word the pronoun replaces. If the correct answer is *his or her/her or his,* revise the sentence to eliminate the need for this awkward expression. Check your answers as you go through the exercise.

1. I live a long way from campus and don't own a car, so I carpool with my friends and rely on (his or her, their) generosity.

2. Based on my experiences, I'd say the practice of carpooling with friends has (its, their) weaknesses.

3. Each of the friends that I travel with has (his or her, their) own quirks.

4. Anna and James both want me to meet them at (his or her, their) house.

5. But Teresa and her friends meet me at (her, their) favorite hangout before driving to school.

6. One day last week, each of my rides had a problem with (his or her, their) car.

7. I went to Anna's house to wait for the auto club, but (its, their) tow truck never came, so we caught the bus at the corner.

8. As usual, everyone on the bus did (his or her, their) best to travel along without any expression on (his or her, their) face.

9. Once Anna and I reached the school stop, the driver cheerfully said "Have a nice day" to (me, us).

10. Sometimes the little moments of kindness in life make (it, them) all worthwhile.

Exercise 3

Underline the correct pronoun. Again, if the correct answer is *his or her/her or his,* revise the sentence to eliminate the need for this awkward expression.

1. When it comes to vintage postcards, no one knows more than (she, her).

2. The visiting conductor gave my fellow musicians and (I, me) a few suggestions.

3. (You and she, You and her) are different in many ways.

4. As we were discussing my crazy Uncle Jack, I discovered that my father is actually younger than (he, him).

5. Each of the shoppers at the flea market looked for (his or her, their) treasures at different speeds.

6. Cell phone companies must be very competitive in (its, their) pricing.

7. The one mentioned in the newspaper was (she, her).

8. Each of the high school students has (his or her, their) own locker in the gym.

9. The bowling leagues from each neighborhood will continue (its, their) tournament tomorrow.

10. Each citizen of the country has (his or her, their) favorite candidate and can influence the election with (his or her, their) vote.

Exercises 4 and 5

Most—but not all—of the sentences in the next two sets aren't clear because we don't know what word the pronoun refers to. Revise such sentences, making the meaning clear. Since there are more ways than one to rewrite each sentence, yours may be as good as the ones at the back of the book. Just ask yourself whether the meaning is clear.

Exercise 4

1. The school issued new student ID cards and mailed them out yesterday.

2. I finished my painting, put my supplies in my art box, and waited for it to dry.

3. Kelly told her friend that there was a backpack on top of her car.

4. We worked at the car wash this weekend, which made us all sore.

5. Trent's dad let him drive his car to the prom.

6. When I placed my key in the lock, it broke.

7. Janel told my sister that she didn't like her.

8. As we were spreading the blanket on the grass, it ripped.

9. Our teacher writes lots of comments on our essays, which helps us correct our mistakes.

10. Carl asked his new boss why he couldn't work late.

Exercise 5

1. I added the finishing touches to the wedding cake, placed the decorating tips in hot water, and moved it to the freezer.

2. When people join in campus activities, they feel more involved.

3. As we put new paper in the copier, it made a funny noise.

4. Whenever I see white clouds hugging the ridge of the mountains, it makes me happy.

5. A handmade lei from Hawaii is well-known for its beauty.

6. Hector's doctor told him to put ice on his elbow.

7. Many people use rolling backpacks for their convenience.

8. The employers interviewed the applicants in their offices.

9. The students bought new textbooks, but they were too simple for them.

10. The head nurse ordered new clipboards, and they arrived the next week.

PROOFREADING EXERCISE

The following paragraph contains errors in the use of pronouns. Find and correct the errors.

Rude drivers have one thing in common: they think that they know how to drive better than anybody else. The other day, as my friends and me were driving to school, we stopped at an intersection. A very old man who used a cane to help him walk started across it in front of my friends and I just before the light was ready to change. So we waited. But while we waited for him, a male driver behind us started to honk his horn since he couldn't see him. I wondered, "Does he want us to hit him, or what?" Finally, it was clear. He pulled his car up beside ours, opened his window, and yelled at us before it sped away. The old man reached the other side safely, but he hardly noticed.

SENTENCE WRITING

Write ten sentences about a conversation between you and someone else. Then check that your pronouns are grammatically correct, that they agree with the words they replace, and that references to specific nouns are clear.

Avoiding Shifts in Person

To understand the meaning of "person" when using pronouns, imagine a conversation between two people about a third person. The first person speaks using "I, me, my . . ."; the second person would be called "you"; and when the two of them talked of a third person, they would say "he, she, they. . . ." You should never forget the idea of "person" if you remember it as a three-part conversation.

First person—*I, me, my, we, us, our*

Second person—*you, your*

Third person—*he, him, his, she, her, hers, they, them, their, one, anyone*

You may use all three of these groups of pronouns in a paper, but don't shift from one group to another without good reason.

Wrong: Few people know how to manage *their* time. *One* need not be an efficiency expert to realize that *one* could get a lot more done if *he* budgeted *his* time. Nor do *you* need to work very hard to get more organized.

Better: *Everyone* should know how to manage *his or her* time. *One* need not be an efficiency expert to realize that *a person* could get a lot more done if *one* budgeted *one's* time. Nor does *one* need to work very hard to get more organized. (Too many *one*s in a paragraph make it sound overly formal, and they lead to the necessity of avoiding sexism by using *s/he* or *he or she,* etc. Sentences can be revised to avoid using either *you* or *one.*)

Best: Many of *us* don't know how to manage *our* time. *We* need not be efficiency experts to realize that *we* could get a lot more done if *we* budgeted *our* time. Nor do *we* need to work very hard to get more organized.

Often students write *you* in a paper when they don't really mean *you, the reader.*

You wouldn't believe how many times I saw that movie.

Such sentences are always improved by getting rid of the *you.*

I saw that movie many times.

PROOFREADING EXERCISES

Which of the following student paragraphs shift *unnecessarily* between first-, second-, and third-person pronouns? In those that do, revise the sentences to eliminate such shifting, thus making the entire paragraph read smoothly. (First, read the paragraphs to determine whether unnecessary shifting takes place. One of the paragraphs is correct.)

1. Everyone knows that, to pitch a baseball well, you need a strong arm. But it might surprise most of us to know that it also requires powerful legs. Scientists at Johns Hopkins University in Baltimore have studied pitchers and their movements. They used a specially designed pitching mound, and they wired the pitchers' joints with sensors for the experiment. Their research revealed that the energy or force of a pitch begins in the leg that the pitcher stands on, flows from there to the leg that the pitcher lands on, then travels up the body and out the end of the arm that the pitcher throws with.

Source: Current Science, 8 Sept. 2000

2. I bet you've never heard of 216 Kleopatra. It not an address or a code name but one of the thousands of asteroids that travel around our sun. Astronomers have been aware of 216 Kleopatra since the late 1800s, but it has only recently come within range of radar equipment. So nobody knew, and it might surprise you to learn, that 216 Kleopatra is most likely composed entirely of metal, is shaped almost exactly like a dumbbell or a dog bone, and is as big as the state of New Jersey.

Sources: Sky and Telescope, July 2000, and *Current Science,* 8 Oct. 2000

3. Most of us in America could use more vacation time. We hear about citizens of other countries getting several weeks—and sometimes even months—off every year to rest their bodies, recharge their energies, and lift their spirits. But in the United States, we have to fight for and often forfeit our one- or two-week vacations. In fact, if we complain too loudly about needing a break, we could be the newest person on the unemployment line. It's time for all of us to stand up for our right to sit down and take a rest.

REVIEW OF SENTENCE-STRUCTURE ERRORS

One sentence in each pair contains an error. Read both sentences carefully before you decide. Then write the letter of the *incorrect* sentence in the blank. Try to name the error and correct it if you can. You may find any of these errors:

awk	awkward phrasing
cliché	overused expression
dm	dangling modifier
frag	fragment

mm	misplaced modifier
pro	incorrect pronoun
pro agr	pronoun agreement error
pro ref	pronoun reference error
ro	run-on sentence
shift	shift in person or time
s/v agr	subject/verb agreement error
wordy	wordiness
//	not parallel

1. ___ **A.** The first one to know about the results was he.

    B. I saw a rainbow walking out of the doctor's office.

2. ___ **A.** My voice-mail password is known by only computing services and me.

    B. In today's society, passwords must be protected.

3. ___ **A.** They bought collectibles at thrift stores, sold them on auction sites, and it was a good way to make a lot of money.

    B. A person with an armload of books needs help opening doors.

4. ___ **A.** Friday was the boss's sixtieth birthday.

    B. Everyone in the office left their desks to join the party.

5. ___ **A.** At the same point in their speeches.

    B. The two students became very nervous.

6. ___ **A.** When I arrived, three trucks and a car were parked in front of the store.

    B. The row of parking spaces were almost completely filled.

7. ___ **A.** I am working on learning to write clearer essays so that people can understand exactly what I'm saying.

    B. Writers need to consider their audience.

8. ___ **A.** Either the tenants or the owner is lying about the incident.

    B. Either the tenants or the owner are lying about the incident.

9. ___ **A.** I filled out the application with a pink pen and then put it in my backpack.

   B. I should have used a blue or a black pen.

10. ___ **A.** Many community-college students plan to transfer they want to get a degree from a four-year university.

    B. Most schools require students to include a personal essay with their transfer application.

11. ___ **A.** Each of the teams' speeches were the same length.

    B. But the instructor gave Vera and me extra credit for our visual aids.

12. ___ **A.** Once the rain started coming down in buckets, stadium officials canceled the game.

    B. We returned to our cars and drove home.

13. ___ **A.** For dinner, we had lasagna, garlic bread, and a crisp green salad.

    B. One of my knees was sore after jogging all morning.

14. ___ **A.** My supervisor evaluated my work and she offered a few suggestions.

    B. Most of her suggestions were very helpful.

15. ___ **A.** People enjoy e-mailing each other because you can communicate so much faster than we could before.

    B. I haven't written a letter by hand since e-mail was introduced.

PROOFREADING EXERCISE

The following is an insightful student essay. Revise it to eliminate wordiness and to correct any errors in sentence structure.

Getting Involved

Getting involved in other people's business can be a right and a wrong thing. It all depends on the relationship you have with that person and what situation that person is going through. For example, a friend of yours is having trouble in a bad relationship and you are concerned about their well-being. Getting involved not only shows that as a friend you love them, but it can help them solve their problems.

On the other hand, some people just like to be nosey. I feel that most people who do get involved in other people's business just for fun have a boring life. They need to know about others so that their lives can be more interesting. I have been in many situations where peers have tried to learn about my life and problems so that they could show and tell. All of the things they said turned into rumors.

Since I have learned from others' mistakes about not minding your own business, I would never get involved in other people's business. If it is not going to benefit them in some way. Therefore, people should better their own lives and not worry about anyone else's. This would make the world a better place.

PART 3

Punctuation and Capital Letters

Period, Question Mark, Exclamation Point, Semicolon, Colon, Dash

Every mark of punctuation should help the reader. Here are the rules for six marks of punctuation. The first three you have known for a long time and probably have no trouble with. The one about semicolons you learned when you studied independent clauses (p. 76). The ones about the colon and the dash may be less familiar.

Put a period (.) at the end of a sentence and after most abbreviations.

> The students elected Ms. Daniels to represent the class.

> Tues.   etc.   Jan.   sq. ft.   lbs.

Put a question mark (?) after a direct question but not after an indirect one.

> Will the midterm be an open-book or a closed-book test? (direct)

> I wonder if the midterm will be an open-book or a closed-book test. (indirect)

Put an exclamation point (!) after an expression that shows strong emotion. Use it sparingly.

> I can't believe I did so well on my first exam!

Put a semicolon (;) between two independent clauses in a sentence *unless* they are joined by one of the connecting words *for, and, nor, but, or, yet, so.*

> My mother cosigned for a loan; now I have my own car.

Some careers go in and out of fashion; however, people will always need doctors.

To be sure that you are using a semicolon correctly, see if a period and capital letter can be used in its place. If they can, you are putting the semicolon in the right spot.

My mother cosigned for a loan. Now I have my own car.

Some careers go in and out of fashion. However, people will always need doctors.

Put a colon (:) after a complete statement that introduces something: one item, a list, or a quotation that follows.

The company announced its Employee-of-the-Month: Lee Jones. (The sentence before the colon introduces the name that follows.)

In London, we plan to visit the following famous sites: the Tower of London, Piccadilly Circus, and Madame Tussaud's Wax Museum. (Here, *the following famous sites* ends a complete statement and introduces the list that follows, so a colon is used.)

In London, we plan to visit the Tower of London, Piccadilly Circus, and Madame Tussaud's Wax Museum. (Here, *we plan to visit* does not end a complete statement, so no colon is used.)

Thoreau had this to say about time: "Time is but the stream I go a-fishin in." (*Thoreau had this to say about time* is a complete introductory statement. Therefore, a colon comes after it before adding the quotation.)

Thoreau said, "Time is but the stream I go a-fishin in." (*Thoreau said* is not a complete introductory statement. Therefore, a colon does not come after it.)

Use a dash (—) to indicate an abrupt change of thought or to emphasize what follows. Use it sparingly.

I found out today—or was it yesterday?—that I have inherited a fortune.

We have exciting news for you—we're moving!

E X E R C I S E S

Add to these sentences the necessary punctuation (periods, question marks, exclamation points, semicolons, colons, and dashes). The commas used within the sentences are correct and do not need to be changed.

Exercise 1

1. On July 31, 2000, Sarah George and her friend Megan Freeman climbed to the top of Table Mountain in Wyoming

2. After reaching the six-mile-high summit, George became ill she was dehydrated and unable to climb down

3. Freeman used a cell phone to call for help then she and George waited for a helicopter to rescue them

4. They had no idea that the pilot of that helicopter would be an incredibly famous movie star Harrison Ford

5. Ford volunteers as an emergency pilot when he stays at his vacation home in Jackson Hole, Wyoming

6. Taking George and Freeman to the hospital was Harrison Ford's first mission as a rescue pilot

7. George was relieved to see the helicopter bringing medical help to her and Freeman she was also impressed when the paramedic told her who was flying the chopper

8. Her enthusiasm was dampened, however, when she got airsick on the way to the hospital

9. The only conversation George and Ford had was when he asked her how she was feeling she said, "Fine"

10. Sarah George and Megan Freeman have something to tell their family and friends about for years to come

Source: People, 21 Aug. 2000

Exercise 2

1. What have spiders done for you lately

2. In the near future, a spider may save your life

3. Researchers in New York have discovered the healing power of one species in particular the Chilean Rose tarantula

4. This spider's venom includes a substance that could stop a human's heart attack once it begins

5. The substance has the ability to restore the rhythm of a heart that has stopped beating

6. A scientist in Connecticut is experimenting with the killing power of another arachnid the creature he is studying is the Australian funnel-web spider

7. Currently, pesticides that destroy insects on crops also end up killing animals accidentally

8. The funnel-web spider's venom is lethal to unwanted insects however, it's harmless to animals

9. Scientists would have to reproduce the funnel-web spider's venom artificially in order to have enough to use in fields

10. As a result of these studies into the power of spider venom, you may live longer and enjoy pesticide-free foods

Source: Discover, Sept. 2000

Exercise 3

This exercise includes titles of books that have subtitles. Use a colon to separate the main title from the subtitle.

1. The change from one millennium to another has prompted us to look back over the twentieth century and wonder what its most important elements were

2. Writers of history books whose usual topics are influential people are choosing these days to write about indispensable things

3. The twentieth century saw the rise of two particularly important objects the banana and the pointed screw

4. Virginia Scott Jenkins has written *Bananas An American History*

5. And Witold Rybczynski is the author of *One Good Turn A Natural History of the Screwdriver and the Screw*

6. Jenkins' book includes facts and stories about the banana's rise in popularity during the twentieth century in America

7. Before 1900, the banana was an unfamiliar fruit in the United States now each American consumes about seventy-five bananas per year

8. Rybczynski points out that the basic ideas for the screwdriver and the screw have been around since the ancient Greeks however, screws did not have sharpened points until the twentieth century

9. So for thousands of years, builders had to drill holes first only then could they get the screws' threads to take hold

10. Where would we be without bananas and self-starting screws

Exercise 4

1. My friend Jason and I went to the beach yesterday it was a really beautiful day

2. We had finished our homework early so that we could enjoy ourselves

3. Our English teacher had given us a special homework assignment to draw a family tree

4. I completed my drawing easily since I know my extended family very well however, I kept thinking about it after I finished it

5. I wondered how the other student's family trees would look compared to mine

6. Would theirs be as big

7. The two sides of my family tree starting at my grandparents have the same structure both sets of grandparents had seven children

8. From that level down, the two sides differ quite a bit my mom's brothers and sisters didn't have many children, but my dad's siblings did four each, to be precise

9. I had mixed feelings some good and some bad about bringing my family tree to class

10. I shouldn't have worried, however several students' families were even bigger than mine

Exercise 5

1. "Daddy, am I going to get old like Grandpa"

2. This question is typical of the ones children ask their parents about aging luckily, there are books that help parents answer them

3. Lynne S. Dumas wrote the book *Talking with Your Child about a Troubled World* in it, she discusses children's concerns and suggests ways of dealing with them

4. In response to the question about getting old "like Grandpa," Dumas stresses one main point be positive

5. Too often, Dumas says, parents pass their own fears on to children parents who focus on the negative aspects of aging will probably have children who worry about growing old

6. Other subjects homelessness, for instance require special consideration for parents

7. Dumas explains that children carefully observe how parents deal with a person asking for spare change or offering to wash windshields for money

8. The unplanned nature of these encounters often catches parents off guard therefore, they should try to prepare a uniform response to such situations

9. Dumas also suggests that parents take positive action involving children in charitable donations and activities, for example in order to illustrate their compassion for the homeless

10. The most important aspect in communicating with children is honesty the second and third most important are patience and understanding

PROOFREADING EXERCISE

Can you find the punctuation errors in this student paragraph?

The ingredients you will need for homemade brownies are—flour, butter, eggs, sugar, baking chocolate, vanilla, baking powder, and salt: nuts are optional. First, you should combine the dry ingredients then you can blend the wet ingredients in a separate bowl! Once the wet and dry ingredients are ready, you are ready to mix them? Your square baking pan needs to be greased on the bottom; so that the brownies don't stick to it. Finally, you can spread the batter into the pan and bake them for half an hour. And when they come out of the oven, be prepared to eat them right away!

SENTENCE WRITING

Write ten sentences of your own that use periods, question marks, exclamation points, semicolons, colons, and dashes correctly. Imitate the examples used in the explanations if necessary. Write about an interesting assignment you have done for a class, or choose your own topic.

Comma Rules 1, 2, and 3

Commas and other pieces of punctuation guide the reader through your sentence structures in the same way that signs guide drivers on the highway. Imagine what effects misplaced or incorrect road signs would have. Yet students often randomly place commas in their sentences. Try not to use a comma unless you know there is a need for it. Memorize this rhyme about comma use: *When in doubt, leave it out.*

Among all of the comma rules, six are most important. Learn these six rules, and your writing will be easier to read. You have already studied the first rule on page 77.

1. Put a comma before *for, and, nor, but, or, yet, so* (remember them as the *fanboys*) when they connect two independent clauses.

> The neighbors recently bought a minivan, and now they go everywhere together.

> We wrote our paragraphs in class today, but the teacher forgot to collect them.

> She was recently promoted, so she has moved to a better office.

If you use a comma alone between two independent clauses, the result is an error called a ***comma splice.***

> The ice cream looked delicious, it tasted good too. (comma splice)

> The ice cream looked delicious, and it tasted good too. (correct)

Before using a comma, be sure such words do connect two independent clauses. The following sentence is merely one independent clause with one subject and two verbs. Therefore, no comma should be used.

> The ice cream looked delicious and tasted good too.

2. Use a comma to separate three or more items in a series.

> Students in the literature class are reading short stories, poems, and plays.

> On Saturday I did my laundry, washed my car, and cleaned my room.

Occasionally, writers leave out the comma before the *and* connecting the last two items of a series, but it is more common to use it to separate all the items equally. Some words work together and don't need commas between them even though they do make up a kind of series.

> The team members wanted to wear their brand new green uniforms.

> The bright white sunlight made the room glow.

To see whether a comma is needed between words in a series, ask yourself whether *and* could be used naturally between them. It would sound all right to say *short stories and poems and plays;* therefore, commas are used. But it would not sound right to say *brand and new and green uniforms* or *bright and white sunlight;* therefore, no commas are used.

If an address or date is used in a sentence, put a comma after every item, including the last. (No comma comes between the month and day in a date.)

> My father was born on August 19, 1941, in Mesa, Arizona, and grew up there.

> She lived in St. Louis, Missouri, for two years.

When only the month and year are used in a date, no commas are needed.

> She graduated in May 1985 from Indiana University.

3. Put a comma after an introductory expression (it may be a word, a phrase, or a dependent clause) or before a comment or question that is tacked on at the end.

Finally, he was able to get through to his insurance company.

During her last performance, the actress fell and broke her foot.

Once I have finished my homework, I will call you.

He said he needed to ruminate, whatever that means.

The new chairs aren't very comfortable, are they?

E X E R C I S E S

Add commas to the following sentences according to the first three comma rules. Some sentences may not need any commas, and some may need more than one. Any other punctuation already in the sentences is correct. Check your answers after the first set.

Exercise 1

1. Chickens are the subject of riddles jokes and sayings.

2. We think of funny ways to respond to the "Why did the chicken cross the road?" question and we endlessly ponder the answer to "Which came first—the chicken or the egg?"

3. A person who runs around in a hurry is often compared to "a chicken with its head cut off."

4. Although we try not to visualize the image of the last comparison most people understand the reference to a fowl's final moments of frantic activity.

5. Anyone who has heard the story of Mike "the headless chicken" will consider the popular saying differently from that moment on for it will come to mean having a strong determination to live in spite of major setbacks.

6. On September 10 1945 a farmer in Fruita Colorado chose one of his chickens to have for dinner that night.

7. But after having his head cut off the rooster didn't die didn't seem to be in pain and continued to act "normally."

8. In fact Mike went on to become a national celebrity and his owner took him around the country so that people could see him for themselves.

9. When both *Time* and *Life* magazines ran feature stories complete with photos of Mike in October 1945 the public became fascinated by the details of Mike's ability to eat drink hear and move without a head.

10. Mike lived for eighteen months after his date with a chopping block and would have lived longer but he died by accidentally choking in 1947.

Source: The Official Mike the Headless Chicken Book (Fruita Times, 2000)

Exercise 2

1. Whenever I need advice about money I ask my friend Janice.

2. Once she hears my problem Janice knows exactly what to do.

3. The first time I needed help I had more bills than my paycheck could cover.

4. Instead of lecturing me on unwise spending as I imagined my parents would do Janice explained a strategy to avoid the same problem the next month.

5. Last month I got into trouble with money again but Janice was on a trip to Italy so I couldn't ask her for help.

6. The only people available to guide me were my parents but I didn't want to bother them at first.

7. I knew that they would worry and would ask "You can't support yourself very well can you?"

8. I didn't want to hear that lecture again so I tried to work the problem out myself.

9. Finally I asked my mom and dad for advice and they had the answer to my problem.

10. The next time I need help with money I will listen to them as much as I listen to Janice.

Exercise 3

1. As if people didn't have enough to worry about Melinda Muse has written a book called *I'm Afraid, You're Afraid: 448 Things to Fear and Why.*

2. In her book Muse points out the dangers of common places objects foods months days and activities.

3. One place that the author warns about is Las Vegas casinos and the reason is that paramedics can't get to ailing gamblers due to the crowds and huge size of the buildings.

4. Another dangerous spot is the beauty parlor where people suffer strokes caused by leaning their heads back too far into the shampoo sink.

5. New clothes need to be washed before they are worn or they may transfer dangerous chemicals to the wearers' eyes skin and lungs.

6. Grapefruit juice can interfere with certain medications' effectiveness and nutmeg contains hallucinogenic substances so these are among the foods to be avoided.

7. The month of July ranks highest in certain kinds of accidental injuries and poisonings due to Independence Day celebrations and other summer activities.

8. Mondays have two dangerous distinctions for more suicides and heart attacks occur on Mondays than on any other day of the week.

9. Even joining a large choir can permanently damage singers' ears.

10. After reading *I'm Afraid, You're Afraid* it's possible to be afraid of almost everything.

Exercise 4

1. Speaking of worst-case scenarios there is a book about how to survive them and it's called *The Worst-Case Scenario Survival Handbook.*

2. The coauthors of this self-help book are aware that most of us will never have to overpower an alligator or make an emergency landing on an airplane yet they want us to be prepared nonetheless.

3. In the "About the Authors" section of the book readers learn that Joshua Piven is a first-time writer but he has survived encounters with robbers muggers and stalled subway trains.

4. About Piven's coauthor we discover that David Borgenicht has written two other books and has had his share of worst-case scenarios especially while traveling.

5. Although the overall tone of the book is somewhat humorous because it covers such outlandish topics the information it shares is deadly serious and could save a life.

6. There are drawings in each section of the book to help the reader picture the emergency and how to survive it.

7. One of the best examples illustrates a way to avoid being attacked by a mountain lion and that is to try to appear as large as possible so the drawing shows a man holding the sides of his jacket out wide like bat wings to scare the lion away.

8. If readers wonder whether they can trust the advice on escaping from quicksand they can just flip to the list of sources consulted for each section in this case an expert on the physics of natural phenomena at the University of Sydney Australia.

9. Wisely Piven and Borgenicht begin the book by warning readers to seek professional help whenever possible instead of trying the survival techniques themselves.

10. The authors know that if people go looking for trouble they'll probably find it.

Exercise 5

1. Fish may be considered "brain food" but I've never liked it.

2. While everyone is saying how delicious a big salmon steak is or how yummy the shrimp tastes you'll find me grimacing and munching on a piece of bread and butter.

3. Part of the problem with fish is the smell but my friends who love to eat fish also love the smell of fish cooking.

4. I always thought that was strange but it makes sense doesn't it?

5. If someone hates the taste of onions that person probably also hates the smell of onions cooking.

6. Come to think of it my husband hates to eat sweets and doesn't like the smell of them either.

7. When we walk into a bakery together he practically has to hold his nose the way I would in a fish market.

8. To me that's odd but my aversion must be just as odd to someone who loves fish.

9. Our daughter loves the taste of bacon but she hates the smell of bacon frying.

10. So I guess there are exceptions to the agreement of our senses of taste and smell.

PROOFREADING EXERCISE

Apply the first three comma rules to the following paragraph.

I belong to a very large family and we have trouble keeping up with each others' birthdays. In the past we've tried to buy presents for every niece nephew uncle and cousin but we can't afford to continue or we'll go broke. Recently my extended family members and I have decided to hold a yearly birthday drawing so that each of us can plan to give and receive only one or two nice birthday gifts a year. For example my Aunt Josephine and I were chosen to exchange gifts this year. We were both born in March so our two birthdays fall close together. Of course my immediate family—mother father sisters and brothers—will buy presents for each other as usual.

SENTENCE WRITING

Combine the following sets of sentences in different ways using all of the first three comma rules. You may need to reorder the details and change the phrasing.

I am a good bowler.

I have never joined a bowling league.

The bell rings.

I leave my math class and rush to my English class.

She currently teaches dance at a local college.

She was a professional dancer in the 1970s.

She danced in several movies.

Alex and Giselle are students.

Both of them are intelligent.

They are both well-organized.

Both of them will graduate with honors.

Comma Rules 4, 5, and 6

The next three comma rules all involve using a pair of commas to enclose information that is not needed in a sentence—information that could be taken out of the sentence without affecting its meaning. Two commas are used—one before and one after—to signal unnecessary words, phrases, and clauses.

4. Put commas around the name of a person spoken to.

Did you know, Danielle, that you left your backpack at the library?

We regret to inform you, Mr. Davis, that your policy has been canceled.

5. Put commas around expressions that interrupt the flow of the sentence (such as *however, moreover, therefore, of course, by the way, on the other hand, I believe, I think*).

I know, of course, that I have missed the deadline.

They will try, however, to use the rest of their time wisely.

Today's exam, I think, is only a practice test.

Read the preceding sentences aloud, and you'll hear how those expressions interrupt the flow of the sentence. But sometimes such expressions flow smoothly into the sentence and don't need commas around them.

Of course he checked to see if their plane had been delayed.

We therefore decided to stay out of it.

I think you made the right decision.

Remember that when one of the previous words like *however* joins two independent clauses, that word needs a semicolon before it. It may also have a comma after it, especially if there seems to be a pause between the word and the rest of the sentence. (See p. 76.)

The bus was late; *however,* we still made it to the museum before it closed.

I am improving my study habits; *furthermore,* I am getting better grades.

She was interested in journalism; *therefore,* she took a job at a local newspaper.

I spent hours studying for the test; *finally,* I felt prepared.

Thus words like *however* or *therefore* may be used in three ways:

1. as an interrupter (commas around it)

2. as a word that flows into the sentence (no commas needed)

3. as a connecting word between two independent clauses (semicolon before and often a comma after)

6. Put commas around additional information that is not needed in a sentence.

Such information may be interesting, but the subject and main idea of the sentence would be clear without it. In the following sentence

Maxine Taylor, who organized the fund-raiser, will introduce the candidates.

the clause *who organized the fund-raiser* is not needed in the sentence. Without it we still know exactly who the sentence is about and what she is going to do: Maxine Taylor will introduce the candidates. Therefore, the additional information is set off from the rest of the sentence by commas to show that it could be left out. But in the following sentence

The woman who organized the fund-raiser will introduce the candidates.

The clause *who organized the fund-raiser* is needed in the sentence. Without it the sentence would read: The woman will introduce the candidates. We would have no idea which woman. The clause *who organized the fund-raiser* couldn't be left out because it tells us which woman. Therefore, commas are not used around it. In this sentence

Hamlet, Shakespeare's famous play, has been made into a movie many times.

the additional information *Shakespeare's famous play* could be left out, and we would still know the main meaning of the sentence: *Hamlet* has been made into a movie many times. Therefore, the commas surround the added material to show that it could be omitted. But in this sentence

Shakespeare's famous play *Hamlet* has been made into a movie many times.

the title of the play is necessary. Without it, the sentence would read: Shakespeare's famous play has been made into a movie many times. We would have no idea which of Shakespeare's famous plays was being discussed. Therefore, the title couldn't be left out, and commas are not used around it.

The trick in deciding whether additional information is necessary is to say, "If I don't need it, I'll put commas around it."

E X E R C I S E S

Add any necessary commas to these sentences according to Comma Rules 4, 5, and 6. Any commas already in the sentences follow Comma Rules 1, 2, and 3. Some sentences may be correct.

Exercise 1

1. This year's office party I believe was worse than last year's.

2. I believe this year's office party was worse than last year's.

3. Lee's lasagna however was better than ever.

4. However Lee's lasagna was better than ever.

5. The clerk who works in the claims division didn't bring a dessert even though he signed up for one.

6. Justin Banks who works in the claims division didn't bring a dessert even though he signed up for one.

7. And Mr. Hopkins who planned the party needed to think of a few more party games.

8. And the person who planned the party needed to think of a few more party games.

9. As usual, no one it seems had time to decorate beyond a few balloons.

10. As usual, it seems that no one had time to decorate beyond a few balloons.

Exercise 2

1. We hope of course that people will honor their summons for jury duty.

2. Of course we hope that people will honor their summons for jury duty.

3. People who serve as jurors every time they're called deserve our appreciation.

4. Thelma and Trevor Martin who serve as jurors every time they're called deserve our appreciation.

5. We should therefore be as understanding as we can be about the slow legal process.

6. Therefore we should be as understanding as we can be about the slow legal process.

7. A legal system that believes people are innocent until proven guilty must offer a trial-by-jury option.

8. The U.S. legal system which believes people are innocent until proven guilty offers a trial-by-jury option.

9. With that option, we hope that no one will receive an unfair trial.

10. With that option, no one we hope will receive an unfair trial.

Exercise 3

1. In 1998, Kevin Warwick an expert on cybernetics at the University of Reading did something that no one had ever done before.

2. He allowed doctors to implant a computer microchip in his left arm.

3. Warwick was therefore the earth's first "cyborg" a being that is part human and part computer.

4. For two decades at Reading University which is in England Professor Warwick had helped design "smart" buildings structures controlled by computer commands.

5. But Warwick turned into a walking remote-control device once he had the microchip under his skin.

6. Building doors which needed to be entered with a card key by anyone else opened by themselves as Professor Warwick approached.

7. The building's computer which recognized Warwick's signal as he walked down the halls greeted him by turning on lights and announcing the arrival of his e-mail.

8. For safety's sake, despite the small size of the device about as large as a pea Warwick had planned to and did have it removed after just nine days.

9. People in England and around the world experts and laypeople alike have reacted to Warwick's advances in a variety of ways.

10. Those who believe in taking all steps toward the future applaud his research, but others who may be wary of the dangers involved in tracking people's movements by computer remain skeptical.

Sources: Christian Science Monitor, 3 Sept. 1998, and Computerworld, 11 Jan. 1999

Exercise 4

1. The Ironman competition one of the most grueling athletic races in the world takes place in Hawaii every year.

2. The Hawaii Ironman race challenges those who enter it in three areas of physical activity.

3. They must swim over two miles, ride a bike for 112 miles, and finally run a marathon.

4. As if that race weren't enough for some fitness fanatics, it is followed soon after by the XTerra World Championship another attraction for triathletes from around the world.

5. The Xterra an obstacle course through the extreme Hawaiian landscape takes participants over ocean waves, blistering sand, dried lava, fallen tree limbs, exposed roots, and huge chunks of coral.

6. Again, the men and women who enter the race must swim, bike, and run their way to the finish line.

7. Some triathletes participate in both races Ironman and Xterra in what triathletes refer to as The Double.

8. Nobody has ever won both Ironman and Xterra in the same year.

9. Due to the short recovery time, it is possible that no one ever will.

10. However, the male and female athletes with the best times overall in both races are considered winners of The Double; they earn a thousand dollars and an invaluable title World's Toughest Athlete.

Source: Newsweek, 23 Oct. 2000

Exercise 5

1. I picked up a magazine today, and I read that scientists are anticipating the birth of an animal that they have already named Noah.

2. Cloning experts believe that Noah like his namesake with the ark has the potential to save the endangered species of the world.

3. When he's born, Noah will be the first successfully cloned endangered animal.

4. Noah's species is known as a gaur a type of wild ox.

5. Since there are relatively few gaur left, scientists turned to the reproductive techniques that produced Dolly the first mammal ever cloned by man.

6. However, Noah will be different from Dolly who was a sheep cloned from sheep DNA and born by a sheep.

7. Noah will be a rare wild ox in every way genetically, but he has been developing within the egg of a normal cow a completely different species which has been acting as his surrogate mother.

8. The future of this technology raises certain questions about the cycle of life.

9. On the horizon is another first the cloning of a bucardo an extinct mountain goat.

10. Cloning scientists have received the go-ahead to produce a clone from DNA in the remaining tissue of Celia the last living bucardo who was crushed by a tree limb, leaving her species extinct.

Source: Newsweek, 16 Oct. 2000

PROOFREADING EXERCISE

Insert the necessary commas into this paragraph according to Comma Rules 4, 5, and 6.

There are two types of punctuation internal punctuation and end punctuation. Internal punctuation is used within the sentence, and end punctuation is used at the end of the sentence. There are six main rules for the placement of commas the most important pieces of internal punctuation. Semicolons the next most important have two main functions. Their primary function separating two independent clauses is also the most widely known. A lesser-known need for semicolons to separate items in a list already containing commas occurs rarely in college writing. Colons and dashes have special uses within sentences. And of the three pieces of end punctuation—periods, question marks, and exclamation points—one is obviously the most common. That piece is the period which signals the end of the majority of English sentences.

SENTENCE WRITING

Combine the following sets of sentences in different ways using Comma Rules 4, 5, and 6. Try to combine each set in a way that needs commas and in a way that doesn't need commas. You may reorder the details and change the phrasing.

The Nutcracker ballet is just one holiday tradition.

Some people attend performances of it every year with their families.

I think.

I could learn to speak Italian fluently.

Joan is a student with black hair.

She sits in the front row.

She asks the best questions.

REVIEW OF THE COMMA

SIX COMMA RULES

1. Put a comma before *for, and, nor, but, or, yet, so* when they connect two independent clauses.

2. Put a comma between three or more items in a series.

3. Put a comma after an introductory expression or before an after-thought.

4. Put commas around the name of a person spoken to.

5. Put commas around an interrupter, like *however* or *therefore*.

6. Put commas around unnecessary additional information.

COMMA REVIEW EXERCISE

Add the missing commas, and identify which one of the six comma rules applies in the brackets at the *end* of each sentence. Each of the six sentences illustrates a different comma rule.

I'm writing this letter Mr. Hampton to ask you for a favor. [   ] I know you are

very busy but would you mind writing a letter of recommendation for me? [   ]

When I visited the financial aid office yesterday I noticed that there were many scholarships that I qualify for. [   ] All of them however require the same form of references: two letters of recommendation from current professors. [   ] Dr. Trent my math teacher is the other person that I plan to ask. [   ] I have enclosed my application my personal essay and a copy of my transcript to help you write the letter. [   ] Thank you in advance for your help.

SENTENCE WRITING

Write at least one sentence of your own to demonstrate each of the six comma rules.

Quotation Marks and Underlining/*Italics*

Put quotation marks around a direct quotation (the exact words of a speaker) but not around an indirect quotation.

The officer said, "Please show me your driver's license." (a direct quotation)

The officer asked to see my driver's license. (an indirect quotation)

If the speaker says more than one sentence, quotation marks are used before and after the entire speech.

> She said, "One of your brake lights is out. You need to take care of the problem right away."

If the quotation begins the sentence, the words telling who is speaking are set off with a comma unless, of course, a question mark or an exclamation point is needed.

> "I didn't even know it was broken," I said.

> "Do you have any questions?" she asked.

> "You mean I can go!" I yelled.

> "Yes, consider this just a warning," she said.

Each of the preceding quotations begins with a capital letter. But when a quotation is broken, the second part doesn't begin with a capital letter unless it's a new sentence.

> "If you knew how much time I spent on the essay," the student said, "you would give me an A."

> "A chef might work on a meal for days," the teacher replied. "That doesn't mean the results will taste good."

Put quotation marks around the titles of short stories, poems, songs, essays, TV program episodes, or other short works.

> I couldn't sleep after I read "The Lottery," a short story by Shirley Jackson.

> My favorite Woodie Guthrie song is "This Land Is Your Land."

> We had to read George Orwell's essay "A Hanging" for my speech class.

> Jerry Seinfeld's troubles in "The Puffy Shirt" episode are some of the funniest moments in TV history.

Underline titles of longer works such as books, newspapers, magazines, plays, record albums or CDs, movies, or the titles of TV or radio series.

> The Color Purple is a novel by Alice Walker.

> I read about the latest discovery of dinosaur footprints in Newsweek.

> Gone with the Wind was re-released in movie theaters in 1998.

> My mother listens to The Writer's Almanac on the radio every morning.

You may choose to *italicize* instead of underlining if your word processor gives you the option. Just be consistent throughout any paper in which you use underlining or italics.

The Color Purple is a novel by Alice Walker.

I read about the latest discovery of dinosaur footprints in *Newsweek*.

Gone with the Wind was re-released in movie theaters in 1998.

My mother listens to *The Writer's Almanac* on the radio every morning.

E X E R C I S E S

Punctuate quotations, and underline or put quotation marks around titles used in the following sentences. Punctuation already within the sentences is correct.

Exercise 1

1. The Andy Griffith Show is still a popular television series.

2. You make me laugh my friend Jennifer said.

3. The movie version of To Kill a Mockingbird is just as good as the book.

4. Last night we watched the movie JFK on video.

5. Sam Shepard wrote the play True West, costarred with Diane Keaton in the movie Baby Boom, and played the part of Hamlet's father's ghost in the latest film version of Hamlet.

6. Do I have to pay for all of the groceries myself my roommate asked.

7. I found her in the library reading the last issue of George magazine.

8. My teacher assigned E. B. White's essay Once More to the Lake as homework.

9. The movie can't be over said my brother I was only gone for a minute getting popcorn.

10. Some children misunderstand the words to The Pledge of Allegiance.

Exercise 2

1. Have you been to the bookstore yet Monica asked.

2. No, why I answered.

3. They've rearranged the books she said and now I can't find anything.

4. Are all of the books for one subject still together I wondered.

5. Yes, they are Monica told me but there are no markers underneath the books to say which teacher's class they're used in, so it's really confusing.

6. Why don't we just wait until the teachers show us the books and then buy them I replied.

7. That will be too late Monica shouted.

8. Calm down I told her you are worrying for nothing.

9. I guess so she said once she took a deep breath.

10. I sure hope I'm not wrong I thought to myself or Monica will really be mad at me.

Exercise 3

1. Stopping by Woods on a Snowy Evening is a poem by Robert Frost.

2. Once you finish your responses the teacher said bring your test papers up to my desk.

3. I subscribe to several periodicals, including Time and U.S. News & World Report.

4. Our country is the world William Lloyd Garrison believed our country-men are all mankind.

5. Do you know my teacher asked that there are only three ways to end a sentence?

6. Edward Young warned young people to Be wise with speed. A fool at forty is a fool indeed.

7. In Shakespeare's play Romeo and Juliet, Mercutio accidentally gets stabbed and shouts A plague on both your houses!

8. There is no such thing as a moral or an immoral book Oscar Wilde writes in his novel The Picture of Dorian Gray; Books are either well written, or badly written.

9. Molière felt that One should eat to live, and not live to eat.

10. Did you say I'm sleepy or I'm beeping?

Exercise 4

1. For my birthday, my mother gave me a copy of The Promise of a New Day, a book of quotations and inspirational discussions to get me through the year.

2. Thomas Merton believed that We must be true inside, true to ourselves, before we can know a truth that is outside us.

3. Injustice anywhere said Martin Luther King, Jr. is a threat to justice everywhere.

4. When you hold resentment toward another Catherine Ponder tells us you are bound to that person or condition by an emotional link that is stronger than steel.

5. Ellen Key feels that At every step the child should be allowed to meet the real experiences of life; the thorns should never be plucked from the roses.

6. Randall Jarrell had this to say about the effects of oppression If you have been put in your place long enough, you begin to act like the place.

7. Amelia Earhart pointed out that It is far easier to start something than it is to finish it.

8. There are two ways of spreading light: wrote Edith Wharton to be the candle or the mirror that receives it.

9. Putting a question correctly is one thing observed Anton Chekhov and finding the answer to it is something quite different.

10. Nikki Giovanni realizes that Mistakes are a fact of life. It is the response to error that counts.

Exercise 5

1. In his book Who's Buried in Grant's Tomb? A Tour of Presidential Gravesites, Brian Lamb records the final words of American presidents who have passed away.

2. Some of their goodbyes were directed at their loved ones; for example, President Zachary Taylor told those around him I regret nothing, but I am sorry that I am about to leave my friends.

3. Other presidents, such as William Henry Harrison, who died after only one month in office, addressed more political concerns; Harrison said I wish you to understand the true principles of the government. I wish them carried out. I ask for nothing more.

4. John Tyler became president due to Harrison's sudden death; Tyler served his term, lived to be seventy-one, and said Perhaps it is best when his time came.

5. At the age of eighty-three, Thomas Jefferson fought to live long enough to see the fiftieth anniversary of America's independence; on that day in 1826, Jefferson was one of only three (out of fifty-six) signers of the Declaration of Independence still living, and he asked repeatedly before he died Is it the fourth?

6. John Adams, one of the other three remaining signers, died later the same day—July 4, 1826—and his last words ironically were Thomas Jefferson still survives.

7. The third president to die on the Fourth of July (1831) was James Monroe; while he was president, people within the government got along so well that his time in office was known as the era of good feelings.

8. Doctors attempted to help James Madison live until the Fourth of July, but he put off their assistance; on June 26, 1836, when a member of his family became alarmed at his condition, Madison comforted her by saying Nothing more than a change of mind, my dear, and he passed away.

9. Grover Cleveland, who had suffered from many physical problems, was uneasy at his death; before losing consciousness, he said I have tried so hard to do right.

10. Finally, George Washington, our first president, also suffered greatly but faced death bravely; I die hard he told the people by his bedside but I am not afraid to go. 'Tis well.

PROOFREADING EXERCISE

Punctuate quotations, and underline or put quotation marks around titles used in the following paragraph.

We read Langston Hughes' essay Salvation in class the other day. It is part of his autobiography The Big Sea. In the essay, Hughes tells the story of a church meeting that he went to when he was a child. The preacher preached a wonderful rhythmical sermon Hughes explains all moans and shouts and lonely cries and dire pictures of hell. And then he sang a song about the ninety and nine safe in the fold, but one little lamb was left out in the cold. Once Hughes realizes that he is the little lamb left out in the cold, he feels that Now it was really getting late. I began to be ashamed of myself, holding everything up so long. Hughes eventually pretends to see the light to save everyone the trouble of waiting for him to have his religious experience, but afterwards he feels even worse because he lied: That night, for the last time in my life but one—for I was a big boy twelve years old—I cried. I cried, in bed alone, and couldn't stop.

SENTENCE WRITING

Write ten sentences that list and discuss your favorite songs, TV shows, characters' expressions, movies, books, and so on. Be sure to punctuate titles and quotations correctly. Refer to the rules at the beginning of this section if necessary.

Capital Letters

CAPITALIZE

1. The first word of every sentence.

Peaches taste best when they are cold.

2. The first word of every direct quotation.

She said, "I've never worked so hard before."

"I have finished most of my homework," she said, "but I still have a lot to do." (The *but* is not capitalized because it does not begin a new sentence.)

"I love my speech class," she said. "Maybe I'll change my major." (*Maybe* is capitalized because it begins a new sentence.)

3. The first, last, and every important word in a title. Don't capitalize prepositions (such as *in, of, at, with*), short connecting words, the *to* in front of a verb, or *a, an,* or *the.*

I saw a copy of Darwin's *The Origin of Species* at a yard sale.

The class enjoyed the essay "How to Write a Rotten Poem with Almost No Effort."

Shakespeare in Love is a comedy based on Shakespeare's writing of the play *Romeo and Juliet.*

4. Specific names of people, places, languages, races, and nationalities.

Rev. Jesse Jackson	China	Caesar Chavez
Ireland	Spanish	Japanese
Ryan White	Philadelphia	Main Street

5. Names of months, days of the week, and special days, but not the seasons.

March	Fourth of July	spring
Tuesday	Easter	winter
Valentine's Day	Labor Day	fall

6. A title of relationship if it takes the place of the person's name. If *my* (or *your, her, his, our, their*) is in front of the word, a capital is not used.

I think Dad wrote to her.   *but*   I think my dad wrote to her.

She visited Aunt Sophie.	*but*	She visited her aunt.
We spoke with Grandpa.	*but*	We spoke with our grandpa.

7. Names of particular people or things, but not general terms.

I admire Professor Walters.	*but*	I admire my professor.
We saw the famous Potomac River.	*but*	We saw the famous river.
Are you from the South?	*but*	Is your house south of the mountains?
I will take Philosophy 4 and English 100.	*but*	I will take philosophy and English.
She graduated from Sutter High School.	*but*	She graduated from high school.
They live at 119 Forest St.	*but*	They live on a beautiful street.
We enjoyed the Monterey Bay Aquarium.	*but*	We enjoyed the aquarium.

E X E R C I S E S

Add all of the necessary capital letters to the sentences that follow.

Exercise 1

1. robert redford's daughter is following in her father's footsteps.

2. her name is amy hart redford, and she has already been in a few movies and has played a small part on *the sopranos.*

3. robert redford, though mostly a film actor, acted on broadway in the early 1960s in the stage version of *barefoot in the park.*

4. amy hart redford has been in off-broadway productions but hopes her big break will come soon.

5. in the play *the messenger,* the younger redford starred with jane fonda's son, troy garity.

6. amy has studied at acting schools in new york, san francisco, and london.

7. amy's mother, lola, a historian, has been divorced from robert redford since 1985.

8. seeing his daughter on stage has prompted robert redford to think of trying it again himself.

9. when amy redford was growing up, she didn't always like the special treatment that a celebrity's child receives.

10. now, however, she may become a celebrated actor herself.

Source: People, 22 May 2000

Exercise 2

1. when people think of jazz, they think of *down beat* magazine.

2. *down beat's* motto may be "jazz, blues & beyond," but some people think that the magazine has gone too far "beyond" by including two guitarists in the *down beat* hall of fame.

3. the two musicians in question are jimi hendrix and frank zappa.

4. jimi hendrix was inducted into the hall of fame in 1970.

5. *down beat* added frank zappa to the list in 1994.

6. since then, readers and editors have been debating whether hendrix and zappa belong in the same group as duke ellington, john coltrane, and miles davis.

7. those who play jazz guitar have some of the strongest opinions on the subject.

8. russell malone, mark elf, and john abercrombie all agree that hendrix and zappa were great guitarists but not jazz guitarists.

9. others like steve tibbetts and bill frisell don't have any problem putting hendrix on the list, but tibbetts isn't so sure about including zappa.

10. it will be interesting to see who *down beat's* future inductees will be.

Source: Down Beat, July 1999

Exercise 3

1. i grew up watching *it's a wonderful life* once a year on tv in the winter.

2. that was before the colorized version and before every station started showing it fifteen times a week throughout the months of november and december.

3. i especially remember enjoying that holiday classic with my mother and brothers when we lived on seventh avenue.

4. "hurry up!" mom would yell, "you're going to miss the beginning!"

5. my favorite part has always been when jimmy stewart's character, george bailey, uses his own money to help the people of bedford falls and to save his father's building and loan.

6. george's disappointment turns to happiness after he and donna reed's character, mary, move into the abandoned house on their honeymoon.

7. of course, mean old mr. potter takes advantage of uncle billy's carelessness at the bank, and that starts george's breakdown.

8. in his despair, george places the petals of his daughter zuzu's flower in his pocket, leaves his house, and wants to commit suicide.

9. luckily, all of george's good deeds have added up over the years, and he is given a chance to see that thanks to a character named clarence.

10. when george feels zuzu's petals in his pocket, he knows that he's really made it home again, and the people of bedford falls come to help him.

Exercise 4

1. tracy chapman grew up in cleveland, ohio, with her sister and her mother.

2. even though they were poor enough to need food stamps at times, tracy received a scholarship and attended the private wooster school in connecticut, where her interest in music grew.

3. when tracy was a young girl, she would watch country music stars like minnie pearl and buck owens on tv.

4. their ornate guitars inspired tracy to play the instrument herself.

5. she first performed for other people during thanksgiving break when she was studying at tufts university in massachusetts.

6. on a street in boston with time to kill but no money to spend, tracy's friend urged her to play and sing for the crowd.

7. by the end of the set, chapman had made enough money to buy them both a good meal for the holiday.

8. chapman's first recording, called simply *tracy chapman,* sold ten million copies, but she wasn't ready for the pressures of fame.

9. she found the cycle of making records and then touring with the songs very unsettling; now she calls san francisco her home and tries to stay focused on what's real.

10. in 1996, tracy chapman joined lilith fair and in 2000 released her latest cd, *telling stories.*

Source: Time, 28 Feb. 2000

Exercise 5

1. helen hunt has been acting on tv and in movies since she was nine years old.

2. she portrayed the cyclone-chasing scientist named jo harding in *twister.*

3. she gave an oscar-winning performance alongside jack nicholson in *as good as it gets.*

4. her most recognizable and long-lasting tv character so far has been jamie buckman in *mad about you,* which costarred paul reiser.

5. having wanted to act with kevin spacey since she saw *american beauty,* hunt took the part of haley joel osment's mom in *pay it forward.*

6. she also worked with famous director robert altman and actor richard gere on the film *dr. t and the women.*

7. hunt played tom hanks' love interest in *cast away.*

8. she and mel gibson starred together in the romantic comedy *what women want.*

9. in addition to acting, hunt loves the olympics and even worked event tickets into her contract with nbc while she was making *mad about you.*

10. hunt has collected souvenir pins like an normal fan at the olympic games in atlanta and in sydney, australia.

Source: Los Angeles Times, 10 Sept. 2000

REVIEW OF PUNCTUATION AND CAPITAL LETTERS

Punctuate these sentences. They include all the rules for punctuation and capitalization you have learned. Compare your answers carefully with those at the back of the book. Sentences may require several pieces of punctuation or capital letters.

1. The eiffel tower is one of the most famous structures in paris

2. Have you ever read flannery o'connors short story a good man is hard to find

3. We camped out at the beach all weekend we were ready to get warm and stay dry

4. How many doughnuts can i buy with five dollars she asked

5. We received your letter mr jenkins and have forwarded your concerns to our claims department

6. The person who guesses the exact weight of the pumpkin will win first prize

7. Dr flores teaches the film class and professor duncan teaches introduction to critical theory

8. Because of the water shortage we have to take shorter showers

9. I need new pants new socks new shoes and a new coat if you want me to go to the art opening with you

10. Hamlet doesnt say the famous line something is rotten in the state of denmark but he knows it

11. My math tutor gave me the following advice dont think so much just follow the directions

12. Whenever i shop at the grocery store i pick up the tv guide and look at it but i never buy it

13. I bought two new textbooks this morning however i found out later that i didnt need either one of them

14. Is that what youre wearing to the play my father asked

15. You can lead a horse to water the old saying goes but you cant make him drink

COMPREHENSIVE TEST

In these sentences you'll find all the errors that have been discussed in the entire text. Try to name the error in the blank before each sentence, and then correct the error if you can. You may find any of these errors:

awk	awkward phrasing
apos	apostrophe
c	comma needed
cap	capitalization
cliché	overused expression
cs	comma splice
dm	dangling modifier
frag	fragment
mm	misplaced modifier
p	punctuation
pro	incorrect pronoun
pro agr	pronoun agreement
pro ref	pronoun reference
ro	run-on sentence
shift	shift in time or person
sp	misspelled word
s/v agr	subject/verb agreement
wordy	wordiness
ww	wrong word
//	not parallel

A perfect—or almost perfect—score will mean you've mastered the first part of the text.

1. _____ The scary scenes in the movie really effected me; I couldn't sleep that night.

2. _____ The police asked us what time the theft had occured.

3. _____ There are a few positive steps that can be taken toward a solution to our problems with money.

4. _____ Last semester, I took art history, spanish, and geography.

5. _____ The department store hired my friend and I as gift wrappers for the holidays.

6. _____ In just six weeks, we learned to find main ideas, to remember details, and how we can integrate new words into our vocabulary.

7. _____ The chairs should be straightened and the chalkboard should be erased before the next class.

8. _____ Hopping into the room, the students noticed a tiny frog from the biology lab.

9. _____ He tells the same joke in every speech, and people laughed.

10. _____ I bring pies to potluck parties because they are always appreciated.

11. _____ We don't know if the buses run that late at night?

12. _____ The womens' teams have their own trophy case across the hall.

13. _____ At the age of twenty-one, my mom handed me a beer.

14. _____ Their car wouldn't start the battery was dead.

15. _____ I asked the car salesman to cut to the chase and spill the beans about the price.

16. _____ In my own personal opinion, that restaurant serves terrible food.

17. _____ Everybody in the audience raised their hand.

18. _____ Because the lines were long and we couldn't find our friends.

19. _____ I plan to stay in town for spring break, it's more restful that way.

20. _____ Each of the kittens have white paws.

Writing

Aside from the basics of spelling, sentence structure, and punctuation, what else do you need to understand to write better? Just as sentences are built according to accepted patterns, so are other "structures" of English—paragraphs and essays, for example.

Think of writing as including levels of structure, beginning small with words connecting to form phrases, clauses, sentences—and then sentences connecting to form paragraphs and essays. Each level has its own set of "blueprints." Words must be spelled correctly. A sentence needs a subject, a verb, and a complete thought. Paragraphs must be indented and should contain a main idea and valid support. And an essay should explore a topic in several paragraphs, usually including an introduction, body, and conclusion. These consistent structures comfort beginning writers as patterns that they can learn to use themselves.

Not everyone approaches writing as structure, however. One can write better without thinking about structure at all. A good place to start might be to write what you care about and care about what you write. You can make an amazing amount of progress by simply being genuine, being who you are naturally. No one has to tell you to be yourself when you speak, but beginning writers often need encouragement to be themselves in their writing.

Writing is almost never done without a reason. The reason may come from an experience, such as fighting an unfair parking ticket, or from a requirement in a class. And when you are asked to write, you often receive guidance in the form of an assignment: tell a story to prove a point, paint a picture with your words, summarize an article, compare two subjects, share what you know about something, explain why you agree with or disagree with an idea.

Learning to write well is important, one of the most important things you will do in your education. Confidence is the key. The writing sections will help you build confidence, whether you are expressing your own ideas or summarizing and responding to the ideas of others. Like the sentence-structure sections, the writing sections are best taken in order. However, each one discusses an aspect of writing that can be reviewed on its own at any time.

What Is the Least You Should Know about Writing?

"Unlike medicine or the other sciences," William Zinsser points out, "writing has no new discoveries to spring on us. We're in no danger of reading in our morning newspaper that a breakthrough has been made in how to write [clearly]. . . . We may be given new technologies like the word processor to ease the burdens of composition, but on the whole we know what we need to know."

One thing we know is that we learn to write by *writing*—not by reading long discussions about writing. Therefore, the explanations and instructions in this section are as brief as they can be, followed by samples from student and professional writers.

Understanding the basic structures and learning the essential skills covered in this section will help you become a better writer.

<table>
<tr><td>**BASIC STRUCTURES**</td><td>**WRITING SKILLS**</td></tr>
<tr><td>**I.** The Paragraph</td><td>**III.** Writing in Your Own Voice</td></tr>
<tr><td>**II.** The Essay</td><td>**IV.** Finding a Topic</td></tr>
<tr><td></td><td>**V.** Organizing Ideas</td></tr>
<tr><td></td><td>**VI.** Supporting with Details</td></tr>
<tr><td></td><td>**VII.** Revising Your Papers</td></tr>
<tr><td></td><td>**VIII.** Presenting Your Work</td></tr>
<tr><td></td><td>**IX.** Writing about What You Read</td></tr>
</table>

Basic Structures

I. THE PARAGRAPH

A paragraph is unlike any other structure in English. Visually, it has its own profile: the first line is indented about five spaces, and sentences continue to fill the space between both margins until the paragraph ends (which may be in the middle of the line):

_____

_____

_____

_____

_____

_____ .

Beginning writers often forget to indent their paragraphs, or they break off in the middle of a line within a paragraph, especially when writing in class. You must remember to indent whenever you begin a new paragraph and fill the space between the margins until it ends. (Note: In business writing, paragraphs are not indented but double-spaced in between.)

Defining a Paragraph

A typical paragraph centers on one idea, usually phrased in a topic sentence from which all the other sentences in the paragraph radiate. The topic sentence does not need to begin the paragraph, but it most often does, and the other sentences support it with specific details. (For more on topic sentences and organizing paragraphs, see p. 217.) Paragraphs usually contain several sentences, though no set number is required. A paragraph can stand alone, but more commonly, paragraphs are part of a larger composition, such as an essay. There are different kinds of paragraphs, based on the jobs they are supposed to do.

Types of Paragraphs

SAMPLE PARAGRAPHS IN AN ESSAY

Introductory paragraphs begin essays. They provide background information about the essay's topic and usually include the thesis statement or main idea of the essay. (See p. 215 for information on how to write a thesis statement.) Here is the introductory paragraph of a student essay entitled "A Bit of Bad Luck":

> It's 9:45, and I'm panicking. As a student, I live a life that is almost free of misfortunes. I don't even think about bad luck. Just last week I won forty dollars in the lottery and two tickets to a concert from a radio station. So this in-class writing assignment to tell about an experience I've had with bad luck has caught me completely off guard. I don't know what to write!

In this opening paragraph, the student introduces the main idea—"I don't even think about bad luck"—and gives background information about the in-class writing assignment that has forced her to think about it.

Body paragraphs are those in the middle of essays. Each body paragraph contains a topic sentence and presents detailed information about one subtopic, stage, or idea that relates directly to the essay's thesis. (See p. 217 for more information on organizing body paragraphs.) Here are the body paragraphs of the same essay:

> I try to think of what I would call an unlucky moment. At about 9:08, we finish discussing the prompt for the assignment. "Okay," I say to myself, "this shouldn't be a problem. All I have to do is come up with a topic . . . a topic."

I can feel the class ease into deep thought as I sit and scratch my head for inspiration. By 9:15, pens are flaring all over the room. The grey shirt in front of me shifts in his chair. The guy to my left has at least a paragraph already in front of him. And the girls in front of him scribble away as if they were born to write.

At 9:37, I realize that I will soon run out of time. The minutes pass like seconds, and I find myself watching the class and wondering, "What's wrong with me?" while everyone else is making it look so easy. I'm thinking of high school, boyfriends, this morning's breakfast, and then I realize what is getting me all worked up—not knowing what to write. This has never happened to me before.

Now I glance at my teacher, and even she's writing. How hard could it be to glide ink across a white open field? Then she gets up and tells us she'll be right back. Jennifer, to my right in blue stripes, looks at me and mouths, "Are you stuck?" I nod and add, "This has never happened to me before," cursing my bad luck. Finally, I decide to write the story of the last forty-five minutes, and it rushes easily from pen to paper.

Notice that each of the three body paragraphs discusses a single stage of her experience with bad luck in the form of writer's block.

Concluding paragraphs are the final paragraphs in essays. They bring the discussion to a close and share the writer's final thoughts on the subject. (See p. 216 for more about concluding paragraphs.) Here is the conclusion of the sample essay:

It's about 10:05. Class is over; the teacher is waiting, and I'm still writing. Jennifer has gone, and the white shirt to my left is on his way out. Someone is rustling papers not caring who's around him. As I turn in my essay, I am disappointed in myself, knowing I could have done more. I will keep thinking about it when I get home. But in this misfortune, I still feel quite lucky knowing that I discovered my bit of bad luck, and the results could have been much, much worse.

In this concluding paragraph, the student finishes her story and shares her unwavering optimism even after her "bit of bad luck."

SAMPLE OF A PARAGRAPH ALONE

Single-paragraph writing assignments may be given in class or as homework. They test the beginning writer's understanding of the unique structure of a paragraph. They may ask the writer to answer a single question, perhaps following a reading, or to provide details about a limited topic. Look at this student paragraph, the result of a homework assignment asking students to report on a technological development in the news:

> I just read that scientists are trying to breed or clone an extinct animal, just the way they did in the movie *Jurassic Park*. Only this is real. A group of Japanese biologists have the idea of bringing the woolly mammoth back to life. The woolly mammoth was an elephant-like beast with huge tusks and long hair. It stood about fourteen feet high. Now thousands of years after the last mammoth walked the earth, reproductive science might allow frozen mammoth remains to be used to generate a new woolly mammoth. I think that if the scientists are doing it to be able to save current animals from becoming extinct, then it's worthwhile. But if they are just doing it to say they can, I think they should watch *Jurassic Park* again.
>
> *Source: Discover*, Apr. 1999

These shorter writing assignments help students practice presenting information within the limited structure of a paragraph.

The assignments in the upcoming Writing Skills section will sometimes ask you to write paragraphs. Remember that you may review the previous pages as often as you wish until you understand the unique structure of the paragraph.

II. THE ESSAY

Like the paragraph, an essay has its own profile, usually including a title and several paragraphs.

Title

_____

_____
_____
_____
_____ .

_____
_____
_____
_____
_____
_____ .

_____
_____
_____

_____

_____

_____

_____

_____

_____

_____

_____

_____

_____

_____

_____

_____

_____

_____

_____

_____

_____

_____

_____

_____

_____

_____

_____

While the paragraph is the single building block of text used in almost all forms of writing (letters, novels, newspaper stories, and so on), an essay is a more complex structure.

The Five-Paragraph Essay and Beyond

On pp. 201–202 you read a five-paragraph student essay illustrating the different kinds of paragraphs within essays. Many people like to include five paragraphs in an essay: an introductory paragraph, three body paragraphs, and a concluding paragraph. Three is a comfortable number of body paragraphs—it is not two, which makes an essay seem like a comparison even when it isn't; and it is not four, which may be too many subtopics for the beginning writer to organize clearly.

However, as writers become more comfortable with the flow of their ideas and gain confidence in their ability to express themselves, they are free to create essays of many different shapes and sizes. As in all things, learning about writing begins with structure and then expands to include all possibilities.

Defining an Essay

There is no such thing as a typical essay. Essays may be serious or humorous, but the best of them are thought provoking and—of course—informative. Try looking up the word *essay* in a dictionary right now. Some words used to define what an essay is might need to be explained themselves:

An essay is *prose* (meaning it is written in the ordinary language of sentences and paragraphs).

An essay is *nonfiction* (meaning it deals with real people, factual information, actual opinions and events).

An essay is a *composition* (meaning it is created in parts that make up the whole, several paragraphs that explore a single topic).

An essay is *personal* (meaning it shares the writer's unique perspective, even if only in the choice of topic, method of analysis, and details).

An essay is *analytical* and *instructive* (meaning it examines the workings of a subject and shares the results with the reader).

A Sample Essay

For an example of a piece of writing that fits the previous definition, read the following excerpt from the book *What Makes the Great Great,* by Dennis P. Kimbro.

Self-Confidence

Experts agree that all of us have deep reservoirs of ability—even genius—that we habitually fail to use. We fail to make use of our talents because we are caught up in the absurd and impossible game of imitating others who, unfortunately, are not worthy of emulation. Since there is no one on earth just like you, how can you be inferior?

Men and women who have made the greatest contributions to humanity were often scorned by ne'er-do-wells. If you find yourself bearing the wrath of others because of your dreams or beliefs, you may be wearing the mark of the achiever. In other words, don't be afraid if you are criticized—you're in good company.

. . . You're in the company of Booker T. Washington, who had the audacity to educate southern blacks. You're in the company of George Washington Carver, who was urged not to waste so much time on a tiny peanut. You're in the company of Galileo, who was criticized for postulating that the earth revolved around the sun. . . . You're walking the path blazed by Nelson Mandela, whose unquenchable thirst for freedom liberated a nation. Optimism means expecting the best, but self-confidence means knowing how to handle the worst.

Now that you have learned more about the basic structures of the paragraph and the essay, you are ready to practice the skills necessary to write them.

Writing Skills

III. WRITING IN YOUR OWN VOICE

All writing "speaks" on paper, and the person "listening" is the reader. Some beginning writers forget that writing and reading are two-way methods of communication, just like spoken conversations between two people. When you write, your reader listens; when you read, you also listen.

When speaking, you express a personality in your choice of phrases, your movements, your tone of voice. Family and friends probably recognize your voice messages on their answering machines without your having to identify yourself. Would they also be able to recognize your writing? They would if you extended your "voice" into your writing.

Writing should not sound like talking, necessarily, but it should have a "personality" that comes from the way you decide to approach a topic, to develop it with details, to say it your way.

The beginning of this book discusses the difference between spoken English (following looser patterns of speaking) and Standard Written English (following accepted patterns of writing). Don't think that the only way to add "voice" to your writing is to use the patterns of spoken English. Remember that Standard Written English does not have to be dull or sound "academic." Look at this example of Standard Written English that has a distinct voice, part of the book *How Babies Talk,* by Dr. Roberta Michnick Golinkoff and Dr. Kathy Hirsh-Pasek.

Finding a word in the language stream is much harder than you would think. Imagine yourself in a foreign country with people speaking all around you. The analogy between a language and a fast-moving body of water is quite apt. You are awash in this new language, unable to make heads or tails of it, feeling as though the new language is flooding over you and offering you no anchor point. So it is with babies. Speech is not punctuated with commas, periods, and question marks. Instead, like a continuous flow of stream water, language seems to move along quickly with no breaks in the flow.

Six-month-old Sylvia is lying in her crib, having just awakened from a nap. Delighted to see Sylvia awake, Mom notices her looking intently at the stuffed animals. She says, "HelloSylvie!DidSylviehaveanicenap?"

There are no spaces between the words when they are spoken. Someone invented the convention of spaces between words for written material. When we talk, however, words run into each other, and even the familiar words can sound somewhat different depending on how they are said. How does a baby find words in the quick-flowing stream that is speech? Perhaps he doesn't start out looking for words at all.

This excerpt illustrates Standard Written English at its best—from its solid sentence structures to its precise use of words. But more important, the writers' clear voice speaks to us and involves us in their world, in their amazement at the magic of language. Students can involve us in their writing too, when they let their own voices through. Writing does not need to be about something personal to have a voice. Here is an example of a student writing about computer hackers:

Some mischievous hackers are only out to play a joke. One of the first examples was a group who created the famous "Cookie Monster" program at Massachusetts Institute of Technology. Several hackers programmed MIT's computer to display the word "cookie" all over the screens of its users. In order for users to clear this problem, they had to "feed" the Cookie Monster by entering the word "cookie" or lose all the data on their screens.

Notice that both the professional and the student writer tell stories (narration) and paint pictures (description) in the sample paragraphs. Narration and description require practice, but once you master them, you will gain a stronger voice and will be able to add interest and clarity to even the most challenging academic writing assignments.

Narration

Narrative writing tells the reader a story, and since most of us like to tell stories, it is a good place to begin writing in your own voice. An effective narration allows readers to experience an event with the writer. Since we all see the world differently and feel unique emotions, the purpose of narration is to take readers with us through an experience. As a result, the writer gains a better understanding of what happened, and readers get to live other lives momentarily. Listen to the "voice" of this student writer telling the story of an important moment in his life.

Father's Love

When I was little, around seven years old, my father never held me in his arms. He always wrapped them around Lenny, my little brother, because Lenny's face and his were like identical twins. My mom held me because I looked like her. Every night my father would have Lenny scratch his back, and my mother would have me pull out her gray hair to keep her looking young. Like people saying prayers, we did this every night.

I never hated my father, nor was I angry with him for not holding me. I just thought he held Lenny because he wanted to even the score when my mother held me. But things changed one day when I had a horrible toothache. I was scared, not because I had to let the dentist pull my tooth, but because I had to let my father first try to do it himself, just the way he always did with Lenny. He tried wrapping a string around my painful tooth, telling me to close my eyes while he jerked it out. But it didn't work. My tooth was stronger than the string.

My father finally took me to the dentist. However, my nightmare got worse because the stupid dentist pulled the wrong tooth, and my jaw swelled to the size and shape of a cantaloupe. It was really depressing because, when my dad found out that the dentist pulled the wrong one, he wouldn't take me back again. I was left with a swollen mouth and a headache that no painkiller could get rid of.

Finally, three days after my toothache began, my pain and depression went away. My bad tooth was still with me, but my father took me in his arms for the first time after all the years of not tugging me next to him like

Lenny. I didn't expect him to do that, and it was a
feeling I will never forget. Even now I remember his
unshaved beard poking my cheeks and his callused, rough
hand petting me from my forehead to the back of my hair
over and over until my pain was gone.

I'm older now, but I still wish he had not died of
cancer and was still here. I really want him to see how
much I have accomplished after he has been gone for so
many years. I want him to take me in his arms once more
so I can tell him I love him and will always miss him.

Description

Descriptive writing paints word pictures with details that appeal to the reader's five
senses—sight, sound, touch, taste, and smell. The writer of description often uses
comparisons to help readers picture one thing by imagining something else, just as
the writer of "Father's Love" compares the shape of his swollen jaw to a canteloupe.
In the following paragraph, a student uses vivid details to bring the place she loves
best to life:

Fort Baker is located across the bay from San Francisco, almost under the
Golden Gate Bridge. When I lived there as a child, nature was all I saw. Deer
came onto our porch and nibbled the plants; raccoons dumped the trash cans
over; skunks sprayed my brother because he poked them with a stick; and little field mice jumped out of the bread drawer at my sister when she opened
it. Behind the house was a small forest of strong green trees; the dirt actually
felt soft, and tall grassy plants with bright yellow flowers grew all around. I
don't know the plant's real name, but my friend and I called it "sour grass."
When we chewed the stems, we got a mouth full of sour juice that made our
faces crinkle and our eyes water.

Here is another example, an excerpt from the book *Mysteries of Planet Earth,*
by Karl P. N. Shuker. In it, he describes a ring with unusual powers. As we read
Shuker's piece, we can visualize the ring and the events it supposedly caused.

Rudolph Valentino—Lord of the Cursed Ring?

The plain silver ring decorated only with a single semi-precious stone was decidedly commonplace. Nevertheless, on that day in 1920 . . . the great [film star] Rudolph Valentino happened to gaze into the humble San Francisco jewellery shop's window . . . and informed the shopkeeper that he wished to buy it at once.

Surprisingly, however, the shopkeeper seemed reluctant to sell it. . . . When Valentino asked why, the man informed him that the ring was cursed. . . . In Valentino's eyes, however, this made . . . him even more eager to purchase it. This he did, wearing it afterwards with great zest. He also wore it while filming . . . his last film—because shortly afterwards, with this sinister ring still on his finger, he died unexpectedly of acute peritonitis.

Following Valentino's death, the ring was given to one of his Hollywood friends, actress Pola Negri. Not long after wearing it, she too fell ill. . . .

As for the ring, she gave it to Russ Colombo, a young singer who reminded her of Valentino. . . . [H]e died soon afterwards in a shooting accident. The next owner of this jinxed jewellery was a friend of Colombo's called Joe Casino . . . [who] placed it in a glass case, but [eventually] . . . decided to wear it, which he did, until he was killed just a week later in a traffic accident.

Only one owner of this ring seemed somehow immune . . . Joe Casino's brother . . . [who] placed it inside a safe in his house, where it remained until . . . a burglar, James Willis, . . . was shot dead by a policeman alerted by the alarm. When they examined Willis's body, they found Valentino's ring in his pocket. . . .

This doom-laden finger band was returned . . . to Casino, who decided this time to seal it away from the world inside a safe deposit box in a Los Angeles Bank. . . .

You may have noticed that all of the examples in this section use both narration and description. In fact, most effective writing—even a good resume or biology lab report—calls for clear storytelling and the creation of vivid word pictures for the reader.

Writing Assignments

The following two assignments will help you develop your voice as a writer. For now, don't worry about topic sentences or thesis statements or any of the things we'll consider later. Narration and description have their own logical structures. A story has a beginning, a middle, and an end. And we describe things from top to bottom, side to side, and so on.

Assignment 1

NARRATION: FAMOUS SAYINGS

The following is a list of well-known expressions. No doubt you have had an experience that proves at least one of these to be true. Write a short essay that tells a story from your own life that relates to one of these sayings. (See if you can tell which of the sayings fits the experience narrated in the student essay "Father's Love" on p. 208.) You might want to identify the expression you have chosen in your introductory paragraph. Then tell the beginning, middle, and end of the story. Be sure to use vivid details to bring the story to life. Finish with a brief concluding paragraph in which you share your final thoughts on the experience.

When in Rome, do as the Romans do.

Familiarity breeds contempt.

Good things come to those who wait.

When the cat's away, the mice will play.

Actions speak louder than words.

Assignment 2

DESCRIPTION: A FRIEND OR RELATIVE

Describe a friend or relative who means a lot to you. You could write about someone you know now or knew when you were younger. Your goal is to make the reader visualize your chosen person and understand why the person means so much to you. Try to use details and comparisons that appeal to the reader's senses in some way. Look back at the examples for inspiration.

IV. FINDING A TOPIC

You will most often be given a topic to write about, perhaps based on a reading assignment. However, when the assignment of a paper calls for you to choose your own topic without any further assistance, try to go immediately to your interests.

Look to Your Interests

If the topic of your paper is something you know about and—more important— something you *care* about, then the whole process of writing will be smoother and more enjoyable for you. If you ski, if you are a musician, or even if you just enjoy watching a lot of television, bring that knowledge and enthusiasm into your papers.

Take a moment to think about and jot down a few of your interests now (no matter how unrelated to school they may seem), and then save the list for use later when deciding what to write about. One student's list of interests might look like this:

> surfing the Internet
>
> playing video games with friends
>
> boogie boarding in summer
>
> collecting baseball cards

Another student's list might be very different:

> playing the violin
>
> going to concerts
>
> watching old musicals on video
>
> drawing pictures of my friends

Still another student might list the following interests:

> going to the horse races
>
> reading for my book club
>
> traveling in the summer
>
> buying lottery tickets

These students have listed several worthy topics for papers. And because they are personal interests, the students have the details needed to support them.

With a general topic to start with, you can use several ways to gather the details you will need to support it in a paragraph or an essay.

Focused Free Writing (or Brainstorming)

Free writing is a good way to begin. When you are assigned a paper, try writing for ten minutes putting down all your thoughts on one subject—drawing pictures of my friends, for example. Don't stop to think about organization, sentence structures, capitalization, or spelling—just let details flow onto the page. Free writing will help you see what material you have and will help you figure out what aspects of the subject to write about.

Here is an example:

> I like to draw pictures of my friends but sometimes they dont like it when I draw them. The nose is to big they think or the hair isn't just right. Once in awhile I get it perfect, but not that often. I like to style my drawings like cartoons kind of. Its almost like you'll see little baloons like in a cartoon strip with little sayings in them. I'm not a big talker myself, so I can express myself with my friends thru my drawings of them. Again, some of them like it and some of them don't.

Now the result of this free-writing session is certainly not ready to be typed and turned in as a paragraph. But what did become clear in it was that the student could probably compare the two types of friends—those who like to be drawn and those who don't.

Clustering

Clustering is another way of thinking a topic through on paper before you begin to write. A cluster is more visual than free writing. You could cluster the topic of "book clubs," for instance, by putting it in a circle in the center of a piece of paper and then drawing lines to new circles as ideas or details occur to you. The idea is to free your mind from the limits of sentences and paragraphs to generate pure details and ideas. When you are finished clustering, you can see where you want to go with a topic.

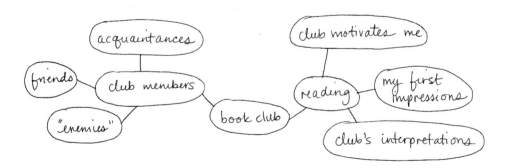

This cluster shows that the student has found two main aspects of her book club that she could write about. This cluster might lead to another where the student chooses one category—club members, for instance—and thinks of more details about them.

Talking with Other Students

It may help to talk to others when deciding on a topic. Many teachers break their classes up into groups at the beginning of an assignment. Talking with other students helps you realize that you see things just a little differently. Value the difference—it will help your written voice that we discussed earlier emerge.

Assignment 3

LIST YOUR INTERESTS

Make a list of four or five of your own interests. Be sure that they are as specific as the examples listed on page 212. Keep the list for later assignments.

Assignment 4

DO SOME FREE WRITING

Choose one of your interests, and do some focused free writing about it. Write for ten minutes with that topic in mind but without stopping. Don't worry about anything such as spelling or sentence structures while you are free writing. The results are meant to help you find out what you have to say about the topic *before* you start to write a paper about it. Save the results for a later assignment.

Assignment 5

TRY CLUSTERING IDEAS

Choose another of your interests. Put it in the center of a piece of paper, and draw a cluster of details and ideas relating to it following the sample on page 213. Take the cluster as far as it will go. Then choose one aspect to cluster again on its own. This way you will arrive at specific, interesting details and ideas—not just the first ones that come to mind. Save the results of all your efforts.

V. Organizing Ideas

The most important thing to keep in mind, no matter what you are writing, is the idea you want to get across to your reader. Whether you are writing a paragraph or an essay, you must have in mind a single idea that you want to express. In a paragraph, such an idea is called a topic sentence; in an essay, it's called a thesis statement, but they mean the same thing—an idea you want to get across. We will begin with a discussion of thesis statements.

Thesis Statements

Let's choose one of the students' interests listed on page 212 as a general topic. "Surfing the Internet" by itself doesn't make any point. What about it? What does it do for you? What point about surfing the Internet would you like to present to your reader? You might write

Surfing the Internet is a good way to discover new things.

But this is a vague statement, not worth developing. You might move into more specific territory and write

I have improved my reading and writing skills by surfing the Internet.

Now you have said something specific. *When you write in one sentence the point you want to present to your reader, you have written a thesis statement.*

All good writers have a thesis in mind when they begin to write, or the thesis may well evolve as they write. Whether they are writing essays, novels, poems, or plays, they eventually have in mind an idea they want to present to the reader. They may develop it in various ways, but behind whatever they write is their ruling thought, their reason for writing, their thesis.

For any writing assignment, after you have done some free writing or clustering to explore your topic, the next step is to write a thesis statement. As you write your thesis statement, keep two things in mind:

1. A thesis statement must be a sentence *with a subject and a verb* (not merely a topic).

2. A thesis statement must be *an idea that you can explain or defend* (not simply a statement of fact).

Exercise 1

THESIS OR FACT?

Which of the following are merely topics or facts, and which are thesis statements that you could explain or defend? In front of each one that could be a thesis statement, write THESIS. In front of each one that is a fact, write FACT. Check your answers with those at the back of the book.

1. _____ Gasoline prices are rising again.

2. _____ Some animals seem to be able to predict earthquakes.

3. _____ On July 20, 1969, Neil Armstrong planted an American flag on the moon.

4. _____ After I became a music major, many job opportunities opened up for me.

5. _____ Computer-generated movie characters can affect us in the same ways as "real-life" characters.

6. _____ Voice-recognition software is improving all the time.

7. _____ Home schooling has both advantages and disadvantages.

8. _____ Tiger Woods is an amazing golfer.

9. _____ Traveling to different countries makes people more open-minded.

10. _____ Vegetarians can suffer from health problems related to their diets.

Assignment 6

WRITE A THESIS STATEMENT

Use your free-writing or clustering results from Assignments 4 and 5 (p. 214) and write at least one thesis statement based on one of your interests. Be sure that the thesis you write is phrased as a complete thought that can be defended or explained in an essay.

Organizing an Essay

Once you have written a good thesis and explored your topic through discussion with others or by free writing and clustering, you are ready to organize your essay.

First, you need an introductory paragraph. It should catch your reader's interest, provide necessary background information, and either include or suggest your thesis statement. (See p. 201 and p. 208 for two examples of student writers' introductory paragraphs.) In your introductory paragraph, you may also list supporting points, but a more effective way is to let them unfold paragraph by paragraph rather than to give them all away in the beginning of the essay. Even if your supporting points don't appear in your introduction, your reader will easily spot them later if your paper is clearly organized.

Your second paragraph will present your first supporting point—everything about it and nothing more.

Your next paragraph will be about your second supporting point—all about it and nothing more.

Each additional paragraph will develop another supporting point.

Finally, you'll need a concluding paragraph. In a short paper, it isn't necessary to restate all your points. Your conclusion may be brief; even a single sentence to round out the paper may do the job. Remember that the main purpose of a concluding paragraph is to bring the paper to a close by sharing your final thoughts on the subject. (See p. 202 and p. 209 for two examples of concluding paragraphs.)

Learning to write this kind of paper will teach you to distinguish between the parts of an essay. Then, when you're ready to write a longer paper, you'll be able to organize it clearly and elaborate on its design and content.

Topic Sentences

A topic sentence does for a paragraph what a thesis statement does for an essay—it states the main idea. Like thesis statements, topic sentences must be phrased as complete thoughts to be proven or developed through the presentation of details. But the topic sentence introduces an idea or subtopic that is the right size to cover in a paragraph. The topic sentence doesn't have to be the first sentence in a paragraph. It may come at the end or even in the middle, but putting it first is most common.

Each body paragraph should contain only one main idea, and no detail or example should be allowed to creep into the paragraph if it doesn't support the topic sentence. (See pages 201–203 for more examples of body paragraphs within essays and of paragraphs alone.)

Organizing Body Paragraphs (or Single Paragraphs)

A single paragraph or a body paragraph within an essay is organized in the same way as an entire essay, only on a smaller scale. Here's the way you learned to organize an essay:

Thesis: stated or suggested in introductory paragraph

First supporting paragraph

Second supporting paragraph

Additional supporting paragraphs

Concluding paragraph

And here's the way to organize a paragraph:

Topic sentence

First supporting detail or example

Second supporting detail or example

Additional supporting details or examples

Concluding or transitional sentence

You should have several details to support each topic sentence. If you find that you have little to say after writing the topic sentence, ask yourself what details or examples will make your reader believe that the topic sentence is true for you.

Transitional Expressions

Transitional expressions within a paragraph and between paragraphs in an essay help the reader move from one detail or example to the next and from one supporting point to the next. When first learning to organize an essay, you might start each supporting paragraph in a paper with a transitional expression.

There are transitions to show addition:

Also

Furthermore

Another (example, point, step, etc.)

In addition

There are transitions to show sequence:

First	One reason	One example
Second	Another reason	Another example
Finally	Most important	In conclusion

There are transitions to show contrast:

However	On the other hand	In contrast

Exercise 2

ADDING TRANSITIONAL EXPRESSIONS

Place the appropriate transitional expressions into the blanks in the following paragraph to make it read smoothly. Check your answers with those in the back of the book.

> however   first   then   finally   previously   in addition

This year, my family and I decided to celebrate the Fourth of July in a whole new way. _____, we always attended a fireworks show at the sports stadium near our house. The firework shows got better every year; _____, we were getting tired of the crowds and the noise. _____, we were starting to feel bad about our own lack of creativity. The goal this time was to have each family member think of a craft project, recipe, or game related to the Fourth. The result was a day full of fun activities and good things to eat—all created by us! _____, my sister Helen taught us to make seltzer rockets from an idea she found on the Internet. We used the fireless "firecrackers" as table decorations until late afternoon when we set them off. _____, we ate dinner. Mom and Dad's contribution was "Fourth of July Franks," which were hot dogs topped with ketchup, onions, and a sprinkling of blue-corn chips. For dessert, my brother Leon assembled tall parfaits made with layers of red and blue Jello cubes divided by ridges of whipped cream. _____, we played a game of charades in which all of the answers had something to do with the American flag, the Declaration of Independence, Paul Revere's ride, and other such topics. We all enjoyed the Fourth so much that the events will probably become our new tradition.

Assignment 7

A CHIP ON THE OLD BLOCK?

Animal-care professionals are using a computer chip to keep track of dogs, cats, and other animals. The chip is surgically placed under the skin and can hold all sorts of information about the animal, as well as help authorities find the pet in case it gets lost. What do you think about this new way of identifying and tracking animals? Write a long paragraph or a short essay in which you answer this question. Your answer will be your main idea, and the reasons and details that support it should be your own opinions. Be sure to say whether any of your own animals have the chip or not. Try free writing, clustering, or discussing the subject with others to find out how you feel about the topic before you begin to write.

VI. SUPPORTING WITH DETAILS

Now you're ready to support your main ideas with subtopics and specific details. That is, you'll think of ways to convince your reader that what you say in your thesis is true. How could you convince your reader that surfing the Internet has improved your reading and writing skills? You might write

> My reading and writing skills have improved since I began surfing the Internet. (because)

1. The computer won't respond to sloppy spelling and punctuation.

2. I read much more on screen than I ever did on paper, and much faster.

3. I write e-mail to friends and family, but I never wrote real letters to them before.

NOTE- Sometimes if you imagine a *because* at the end of your thesis statement, it will help you write your reasons or subtopics clearly and in parallel form.

Types of Support

The subtopics developing a thesis and the details presented in a paragraph are not always reasons. Supporting points may take many forms based on the purpose of the essay or paragraph. They may be

> *examples* (in an illustration)
>
> *steps* (in a how-to or process paper)
>
> *types or kinds* (in a classification)
>
> *meanings* (in a definition)

similarities and/or differences (in a comparison/contrast)

effects (in a cause-and-effect analysis)

Whatever they are, supporting points should develop the main idea expressed in the thesis or topic sentence and prove it to be true.

Here is the final draft of a student essay about an embarrassing experience. Notice how the body paragraphs follow the stages of the experience. And all of the details within the body paragraphs bring the experience to life.

Super Salad?

About a year ago, I had a really embarrassing experience. It happened at a restaurant in Arcadia. I had moved to California three days before, so everything was new to me. Since I didn't have any relatives or friends in California, I had to move, unpack, and explore the neighborhood on my own. That day, I decided to treat myself to dinner as a reward, but I needed some courage because I had never dined out alone before.

As I opened the door of the restaurant, everybody looked at me, and the attention made me nervous. The manager greeted me with several menus in his hands and asked how many people were in my party. I said, "Just me." He led me over to a square table right in the middle of the restaurant. It had four chairs around it and was set with four sets of napkins and silverware. The manager pulled out one of the chairs for me, and a busboy cleared away the three extra place settings.

A waitress arrived to take my order, and I tried to keep it simple. I asked for steak and a baked potato. Truthfully speaking, before I went to the restaurant, I had practiced ordering, but as she was speaking to me, I got flustered. She said, "Super salad?" as if it were a specialty of the house, so I said, "Okay, that sounds good." Suddenly, her eyebrows went up, and she asked again, "Super salad?" And again I answered, "Yes." Her

---

face turned the color of a red leaf in fall. "You wanna a super salad?" she asked in a louder voice this time, and I answered with certainty, "Yes, that will be fine." From her reaction, I knew that something was wrong.

When the waitress returned, she had the manager with her. He asked, "Do you want *soup* or a *salad?* You can't have both." I finally realized the stupid mistake I had been making. But the way the waitress had said "Soup or salad?" sounded just like "Super salad?" to my flustered ears. I clarified that I wanted a salad and eventually finished my meal without incident. I don't remember how the steak tasted or whether I had sour cream on my potato. I just kept going over my moment of confusion in my head while trying to look like a normal person eating dinner.

At the time, I felt embarrassed and ashamed. Going out for a meal isn't usually such a traumatic experience. Of course, whenever I tell the story, instead of sympathy, I get uncontrollable laughter as a response. I guess it is pretty funny. Now whenever I order a meal alone, I use a drive-thru. That way I can blame any misunderstandings on the microphones in the drive-thru lane.

(Note: See p. 222 for a rough draft of the above essay, before its final revisions.)

Learning to support your main ideas with vivid details is perhaps the most important thing you can accomplish in this course. Many writing problems are not really *writing* problems but *thinking* problems. Whether you're writing a term paper or merely an answer to a test question, if you take enough time to think, you'll be able to write a clear thesis statement and support it with paragraphs loaded with meaningful details.

Assignment 8

WRITE AN ESSAY ON ONE OF YOUR INTERESTS

Return to the thesis statement you wrote about one of your interests for Assignment 6 on page 216. Now write a short essay to support it. You can explain the allure of your interest, its drawbacks, or its benefits (such as the one about the Internet improving the student's reading and writing skills). Don't forget to use any free writing or clustering you may have done on the topic beforehand.

Assignment 9

AN EMBARRASSING EXPERIENCE

Like the student writer of "Super Salad?" (pp. 220–221), we have all had embarrassing moments in our lives. Write an essay about a mildly embarrassing experience that you have had or one that you witnessed someone else have. Be sure to include the details that contributed to the embarrassment. For instance, the student writer showed how being in the restaurant alone made it worse. Had he been there with friends or family members, misunderstanding the waitress might have just been humorous, not embarrassing.

VII. Revising Your Papers

Great writers don't just sit down and write a final draft. They write and revise. You may have heard the expression, "Easy writing makes hard reading." True, it is *easier* to turn in a piece of writing the first time it lands on paper. But you and your reader will be disappointed by the results. Try to think of revision as an opportunity instead of a chore, as a necessity instead of a choice.

Whenever possible, write the paper several days before the first draft is due. Let it sit for a while. When you reread it, you'll see ways to improve the organization or to add more details to a weak paragraph. After revising the paper, put it away for another day and try again to improve it. Save all of your drafts along the way to see the progress that you've made or possibly to return to an area left out in later drafts but that fits in again after revision.

Don't call any paper finished until you have worked it through several times. Revising is one of the best ways to improve your writing.

Take a look at an early draft of the student essay you read on page 220. Notice that the student has revised his rough draft by crossing out some parts, correcting word forms, and adding new phrasing or reminders for later improvement.

AS ~~When~~ I opened the door of the restaurant. I (gathered
              * clarify and correct
everybody's attention. and it made me a little nervous.)
~~Eating in a restaurant alone was very new to me.~~ The   * add details
manager asked me how many people were in my party, and I
                                        led   right
said. "Just me." He ~~walked~~ me over to a square table in
the middle ~~part~~ of the restaurant. (It had four chairs
pulled up to it. and he pulled out one for me to sit
down.) * add details
     A ~~The~~ waitress ~~came~~ to take my order. and I tried to
           arrived
keep it simple. I asked for steak and a baked potato.
Truthfully
~~Frankly~~ speaking. before I went to the restaurant. I had
                                  as
practiced ordering. but ~~by the time~~ she was speaking to
me. I got ~~all~~ flustered ~~and embarrassed. I thought~~ She
          as if that were a specialty of the restaurant,
said. "Super salad?" so I said. "Okay. that sounds good."
Suddenly. her eyebrows went up, and she asked again.
"Super salad?" and again I answered. "Yes." Her face
turned the color of a red leaf in fall. "You wanna a
super salad?" she asked. in a louder voice this time. and
          with certainty,
I answered. "Yes. that will be fine." From her reaction.
     knew that
I ~~thought~~ something was wrong.
            when
~~The next time~~ the waitress returned. she had the
manager ~~of the restaurant~~ with her. He asked. "Do you want
soup or a salad? You can't have both." I finally realized
    the
~~what~~ a stupid mistake I had been making. But I swear the
way the waitress had said "Soup or salad?" sounded just
like "Super salad?" to my flustered ears. ~~as if that were a specialty of the~~
~~restaurant.~~ * add end of meal details   * move up
     At the time. I was ~~really~~ embarrassed and ashamed ~~of~~
     * add more
~~myself.~~ But whenever I tell ~~anybody~~ the story. (they laugh
              * clarify and correct   Now
so hard that I can't get anyone to feel sorry for me.) I
(hardly ever eat alone at restaurants after my first
  disaster. I if do. I make it a drive-thru. That way I can
  always blame a misunderstanding on the microphones in the
  drive-thru lane.

         combine and clarify

Can you see why each change was made? Analyzing the reasons for the changes will help you improve your own revision skills.

Assignment 10
LUCKY CHARMS?

Karl P. N. Shuker writes about Rudolph Valentino's unlucky ring on page 210. Many people, professional athletes and performers for instance, strongly believe in "lucky" and "unlucky" objects, expressions, and even people. Do you believe in lucky or unlucky charms? You might want to do a little research into the topic before you decide. Gather a few examples, think of some of your own, and then write about them in an essay of several paragraphs.

Write a rough draft of the paper and then set it aside. A little later, reread your paper to see what improvements you can make to your rough draft. Use the following checklist to help guide you through this or any other revision.

REVISION CHECKLIST

Here's a checklist of revision questions. If the answer to any of these questions is no, revise that part of your paper until you're satisfied that the answer is yes.

1. Does the introductory paragraph introduce the topic clearly and suggest or include a thesis statement that the paper will explain or defend?

2. Does each of the other paragraphs support the thesis statement?

3. Does each body paragraph contain a clear topic sentence and focus on only one supporting point?

4. Do the body paragraphs contain enough details, and are transitional expressions well used?

5. Do the final thoughts expressed in the concluding paragraph bring the paper to a smooth close?

6. Does your (the writer's) voice come through?

7. Do the sentences read smoothly and appear to be correct?

8. Are the spelling and punctuation consistent and correct?

Exchanging Papers

This checklist could also be used when you exchange papers with another student in your class. Since you both have written a response to the same assignment, you will understand what the other writer went through and learn from the differences between the two papers.

Proofreading Aloud

Finally, read your finished paper *aloud*. If you read it silently, you will see what you *think* is there, but you are sure to miss some errors. Read your paper aloud slowly, pointing to each word as you read it to catch omissions and errors in spelling and punctuation. Reading a paper to yourself this way may take fifteen minutes to half an hour, but it will be time well spent. There are even word-processing programs that will "speak" your text in a computer's voice. Using your computer to read your paper to you can be fun as well as helpful. If you don't like the way something sounds, don't be afraid to change it! Make it a rule to read each of your papers *aloud* before handing it in.

Here are four additional writing assignments to help you practice the skills of writing and revising.

Assignment 11
ARE YOU AN OPTIMIST OR A PESSIMIST?

The old test of optimism and pessimism is to look at a glass filled with water to the midpoint. An optimist, or positive thinker, would say it was "half *full*." But a pessimist, or negative thinker, would say it was "half *empty*." Which are you—an optimist or a pessimist? Organize your thoughts into the structure of a brief essay.

Assignment 12
ARE THERE DIFFERENT WAYS TO BE SMART?

No word has just one meaning. Take, for example, the word "smart." The common definition usually involves retaining a lot of knowledge and taking tests well. If that were the only meaning, then why do we call someone "street smart"? Think about the different ways a person can be "smart," and write a long paragraph or short essay about the ways in which people in general and you in particular are smart. For further prompting before you write, read the sample reaction paragraph on p. 227 about Isaac Asimov's essay "What Is Intelligence?"

Assignment 13
THE BEST (OR WORST) DECISION

What was one of the best (or worst) decisions you ever made? Choose one that you feel comfortable sharing with others. When and why did you make the decision, and what effects has it had on your life? Organize the answers to these questions into the structure of a brief essay.

Assignment 14
A QUOTATION

Look through the quotations in Exercise 4 on page 187. Does one of them apply to you? Could you profit from following one of them? Write a short paper in which you react to or offer an explanation of one of the quotations and then support your reaction or explanation with examples from your own experiences.

VIII. PRESENTING YOUR WORK

Part of the success of a paper could depend on how it looks. The same paper written sloppily or typed neatly might even receive different grades. It is human nature to respond positively when a paper has been presented with care. Here are some general guidelines to follow.

Paper Formats

Your paper should be typed or written on a computer, double-spaced, or copied neatly in ink on 8 1/2-by-11-inch paper on one side only. A one-inch margin should be left around the text on all sides for your instructor's comments. The beginning of each paragraph should be indented five spaces.

Most instructors have a particular format for presenting your name and the course material on your papers. Always follow such instructions carefully.

Titles

Finally, spend some time thinking of a good title. Just as you're more likely to read a magazine article with an interesting title, so your readers will be more eager to read your paper if you give it a good title. Which of these titles from student papers would make you want to read further?

A Sad Experience	Of Mice and Me
Falling into "The Gap"	Buying Clothes Can Be Depressing
Hunting: The Best Sport of All?	Got Elk?

Remember these three things about titles:

1. Only the first letter of the important words in a title should be capitalized.

A Night at the Races

2. Don't put quotation marks around your own titles unless they include a quotation or title of an article, short story, or poem within them.

"To Be or Not to Be" Is Not for Me

3. Don't underline (or *italicize*) your own titles unless they include the title of a book, play, movie, or magazine within them.

Still Stuck on *Titanic*

A wise person once said, "Haste is the assassin of elegance." Instead of rushing to finish a paper and turn it in, take the time to give your writing the polish it deserves.

IX. Writing about What You Read

Reading and writing are related skills. The more you read, the better you will write. When you are asked to prepare for a writing assignment by reading a newspaper story, a magazine article, a professional essay, or part of a book, there are many ways to respond in writing. Among them, you may be asked to write your reaction to a reading assignment or a summary of a reading assignment.

Writing a Reaction

Reading assignments become writing assignments when your teacher asks you to share your opinion about the subject matter or to relate the topic to your own experiences. In a paragraph, you would have enough space to offer only the most immediate impressions about the topic. However, in an essay you could share your personal reactions, as well as your opinions on the value of the writer's ideas and support. Of course, the first step is always to read the selection carefully, looking up unfamiliar words in a dictionary.

SAMPLE REACTION PARAGRAPH

Here is a sample paragraph-length response following the class's reading of an essay called "What Is Intelligence?" by Isaac Asimov. In the essay, Asimov explains that there are other kinds of intelligence besides just knowledge of theories and facts. This student shares Asimov's ideas about intelligence, and she uses her own experiences to support her statements.

I totally agree with Isaac Asimov. Intelligence doesn't only belong to Nobel Prize winners. I define "intelligence" as being able to value that special skill that a person has been born with. Not everyone is a math genius or a brain surgeon. For example, ask a brain surgeon to rotate the engine in your car. It isn't going to happen. To be able to take that certain skill that you've inherited and push it to its farthest limits I would call "intelligence." Isaac Asimov's definition is similar to mine. He believes that academic questions are only correctly answered by academicians. He gives the example of a farmer. A farming test would only be correctly answered by a farmer. Not everyone has the same talent; we are all different. When I attend my math classes, I must always pay attention. If I don't, I end up struggling with what I missed. On the other hand, when I'm in my singing class, I really do not have to struggle because the musical notes come to me with ease. This is just one example of how skills and talents differ from each other. I would rather sing a song than do math any day. We are all made differently. Some people are athletic, and some people are brainy. Some people can sing, and some can cook. It really doesn't matter what other people can do. If they have a talent—that's a form of intelligence.

If this had been an essay-length response, the student would have included more details about her own and other people's types of intelligence. And she may have wanted to quote and discuss Asimov's most important points.

Assignment 15

WRITE A REACTION PARAGRAPH

The following is an excerpt from the book *BAD TV,* by Craig Nelson, in which he calls for a thorough analysis of "bad" television. Write a paragraph in which you respond to Nelson's topic and the details he uses to support it.

```
         Television . . . The Mysteries of the Universe
               . . . and the Secret of Life
```

Many have asked: "Sure, BAD TV is fun and all, but how can it make me a better person? How will it improve my life?" The new science of "garbology" says we can understand a great deal about a culture by studying its trash—and we couldn't agree more. BAD is wonderful as an educational device. If you want to learn about something, and you try to study its best moments, there are lots of problems because you get distracted by what makes it good. The writing, the acting, the imagination, the good camerawork, the dramatic power, the funny jokes, all detract from serious analysis. The BAD, however, strips everything naked. . . .

BAD television should be explored in great depth because its very existence raises such profound philosophical questions, and the shows themselves frequently explore deep mysteries—of both the human spirit, and the universe. . . . Why do we love things that are beyond terrible? Why will people publicly humiliate themselves in front of the entire nation . . . ?

The people who make TV really only want one thing in all the world: your happiness. To that end they are constantly trying to create programming that piques your interest, embodies your dreams, and shares your concerns. When they succeed in doing so, the programs explicitly reveal America's hidden and not-so-hidden needs and desires. . . . While regular television must be deeply analyzed, . . . on BAD TV those hidden daydreams, longings, themes, and philosophies rise to the surface like grease on a pizza.

What television answers for us better than anything else is this: Who are we, as Americans? . . . TV also shows us what we'd like to be, featuring the families, the jobs, or the loved ones we wish we had.

Before starting your reaction paragraph, *read the selection again carefully*. Be sure to use a dictionary to look up any words you don't know. You can also use the free-writing and clustering techniques explained on pages 212–213. Or your instructor may want you to discuss the reading in groups.

Coming to Your Own Conclusions

Often you will be asked to come to your own conclusions based on a reading that simply reports information. In other words, you have to think about and write about what it all means.

Read the following "Police and Sheriff's Log," reprinted from the April 28, 2000, issue of *The Carmel Pine Cone* in Carmel, California. These are *real* police-log entries, recorded by the Carmel-by-the-Sea Police Department and the Monterey County Sheriff's Department, which the *Pine Cone* publishes once a week as a service to the community.

Sunday, April 16

Carmel-by-the-Sea: Vehicle found parked blocking a driveway to the Presbyterian church at Junipero and Ocean. Unable to locate owner. Vehicle cited, towed and stored by Carmel Chevron.

Carmel-by-the-Sea: Report of three intoxicated men in the area of San Carlos and Sixth. Area check made—unable to locate.

Carmel-by-the-Sea: Report of a tree limb on fire at Lincoln and Fifth. CFD notified. Cause of fire: power line. . . .

Big Sur: Gorda resident reported a cabin was damaged by an overnight guest, a San Francisco Resident.

Big Sur: Sacramento resident turned in a backpack found alongside Highway 1, above Fuller's Beach.

Carmel area: Sheriff's Dive Team responded to a report of a SCUBA diver who had failed to surface while diving with two other divers. The diver eventually surfaced and was OK.

Carmel Valley: Paso Hondo resident reported receiving idle death threats from his stepdaughter over the past several years.

Carmel Valley: Report of someone stealing a Weber barbecue kit from behind a village restaurant. . . .

Carmel area: Unknown person(s) vandalized a car on Rio Road. Damage estimated at $6,000.

Carmel Valley: Terra Grande resident reported someone smashed her mailbox.

Carmel area: Unknown person(s) stole two necklaces from a crossroads store. The total value of the necklaces was $450.

Monday, April 17

Carmel-by-the-Sea: Report of vandalism of two mission businesses. Pinkish lipliner used to scribble non-meaningful message design on windows of both businesses. No damage.

Carmel-by-the-Sea: Report of an umbrella blocking a stairway in Hazeltine Court. Item removed. Carmel Foundation notified.

Carmel-by-the-Sea: Citizen assist requested in regards to a female whose dentures fell out and became lodged underneath a bed. Officers assisted by moving the bed and retrieving the woman's dentures.

Carmel-by-the-Sea: Dolores resident thought a person was missing. During the course of the interview, the person arrived home. Apparently the person went for a walk. . . .

Pebble Beach: Deputies responded to a report of a burglary in progress at a Forest Lodge Road residence. Deputies found a 27-year-old Bonita resident inside the residence. He was arrested and booked into county jail for burglary and possession of stolen property.

Carmel Valley: Loma Del Rey resident reported receiving several calls that she believed were threatening.

Carmel area: Observed a male juvenile spray painting the Carmel River Bridge. After a short foot pursuit the juvenile was apprehended.

Carmel Valley: Calle De Este resident reported someone threw a rock into his back yard and broke his glass patio table.

Pebble Beach: Sloat Road residents found arguing about whether or not items could be removed from the residence during their divorce. In the absence of a court order, the couple was directed to their lawyers.

Tuesday, April 18

Carmel-by-the-Sea: Report of wine being consumed on the sidewalk in front of a Dolores Street restaurant. Warning given.

Carmel-by-the-Sea: Report of the sound of broken glass in Forest Hill Park. Area check made, unable to locate any broken glass, or people.

Carmel-by-the-Sea: Woman reported she lost her son in the area of Lincoln and Ocean. He apparently wandered away in a crowd. Four feet tall, dark hair, red cap, black sweats, blue windbreaker. Located by a community services officer at Ocean and Dolores and returned to mother.

Carmel-by-the-Sea: Complaint of loud music at Guadalupe and Second. Contacted someone there who advised the practice was finished for the day. Advised of city ordinance and the complaint.

Carmel-by-the-Sea: Person advised that sometime prior to 04/12/00 in the afternoon, person(s) unknown placed fish under the driver's seat and underneath the floor covering in the trunk. The vehicle was either parked in the business area or at home. The vehicle is always locked with the alarm activated and only his brother has a key. Unknown where or who committed this offense. Information only.

Carmel-by-the-Sea: Report of fire crackers ignited at Casanova and Ninth. An area check revealed debris in the back yard of the home. Attempted to make contact with the resident, but no one was home.

Carmel-by-the-Sea: Report of fireworks being ignited within Mission Trails Park. Area check made, suspects gone upon arrival. . . .

Wednesday, April 19

Carmel-by-the-Sea: Person reported seeing a white, full-size van driving around the area, possibly casing. Last seen at Rio and Santa Lucia. Area check made, no further description.

Carmel-by-the-Sea: Report of forced entry into a locked vehicle parked in an underground parking garage at Dolores and Fifth. Taken was $200 worth of TV/stereo equipment.

Carmel-by-the-Sea: Vehicle parked at Monte Verde and Ocean found to have $985 in outstanding parking citations. Towed by Carmel Chevron. Registered owner went and got a cashier's check for the full amount and mailed it in. Vehicle released.

Carmel-by-the-Sea: Vehicle found parked at San Carlos and Ninth with registration expired over six months. Towed and stored by Carmel Chevron.

Carmel-by-the-Sea: Report of an infant left in car at Scenic and 12th. Check made, turned out to be a doll in the child seat.

Carmel-by-the-Sea: Man who came in yesterday to report fish being placed inside his vehicle today advised that while parked at Casanova and Ocean, someone moved his car four spaces. He advised that he has the only key. Information only.

Carmel Valley: Mid Valley resident reported her 10-year-old daughter was chased by unknown male at the Mid Valley Shopping Center. It was found that the male was a 12-year-old playing in the area. . . .

Thursday, April 20

Carmel-by-the-Sea: Report of a dead "bear cub" in the back yard of a Torres residence. Animal was found to be a cat and alive, resting in her yard. Unfounded.

Carmel-by-the-Sea: Monte Verde Inn employee reported she received several obscene phone calls during the last few days on their 800 number. She will provide a list of the calls for a report.

Carmel-by-the-Sea: Scenic Road resident reported his car was egged last evening. Suspects unknown.

Carmel-by-the-Sea: Report of vandalism to the men's restroom and a display window at the Carmel Plaza. Suspects unknown. Information only.

Carmel-by-the-Sea: Report of a tour bus in the area of San Antonio and Seventh. Upon arrival noted the vehicle was actually a large RV.

Friday, April 21

Carmel-by-the-Sea: Man became separated from his friends and didn't remember which hotel [they were staying in]. An area check of local hotels and inns failed to reunite the lost tourists. He was allowed to sleep in the back seat of his vehicle.

Carmel-by-the-Sea: Citizen reported leaving the balcony door open at an Eighth Avenue residence. Entrance to the residence gained and door was shut. Residence secured.

Carmel-by-the-Sea: During the past three nights someone has been stealing recently planted plants. Possible suspect identified. Close patrol information completed for evening and morning watch.

Carmel-by-the-Sea: Person asked for information regarding a $10,000 bad check he received from his brother-in-law. Advised to contact the sheriff's department. . . .

Pebble Beach: Dispatched to an alarm and found an open window and unlocked door at a Riata Drive residence. No signs of forced entry. Large cat inside but owner stated the alarm company assured her the 17-pound cat won't set off alarm. Some drawers found open. . . . Nothing further. Case suspended at this time.

Saturday, April 22

Carmel-by-the-Sea: Assisted CHP locate possible house of a hit-and-run suspect. Nobody home—note left.

Carmel-by-the-Sea: Report of two people sleeping on a bench at Norton Courts. They were warned to move away from the scene.

Carmel-by-the-Sea: Report of a fence damaged at Guadalupe and Third. Close patrol requested.

Carmel-by-the-Sea: Report of suspicious circumstances at two Scenic Road cottages. Both are vacant and boarded. Since the beginning of the month, the owner has been noticing strange things happening on the property. He has found numerous bottles and cans, as well as clippings from plants not on the property, trees have been cut and the plywood over the gate has been spray painted. The owner, who lives across the street, has not seen anyone on the property and requested the occurrences be documented. Close patrol requested. . . .

Source: Reprinted with permission. © *The Carmel Pine Cone.*

Assignment 16
WHAT ARE YOUR CONCLUSIONS?

After reading the Carmel Police Log, would you like to live in Carmel? Write an essay that explains your answer, using details from the police log for support.

Writing 100-Word Summaries

One of the best ways to learn to read carefully and to write concisely is to write 100-word summaries. Writing 100 words sounds easy, but actually it isn't. Writing 200- or 300- or 500-word summaries isn't too difficult, but condensing all the main ideas of an essay or article into 100 words is a time-consuming task—not to be undertaken in the last hour before class.

A summary presents only the main ideas of a reading, *without including any reactions to it*. A summary tests your ability to read, understand, and *rephrase* the ideas contained in an essay, article, or book.

If you work at writing summaries conscientiously, you'll improve both your reading and your writing. You'll improve your reading by learning to spot main ideas and your writing by learning to construct a concise, clear, smooth paragraph. Furthermore, your skills will carry over into your reading and writing for other courses.

SAMPLE 100-WORD SUMMARY
First, read the following excerpt from the book *The True History of Chocolate*, by Sophie D. Coe and Michael D. Coe. It is followed by a student's 100-word summary.

Milton Hershey and the "Good Old Hershey Bar"

Milton Snavely Hershey (1857–1945) has been aptly characterized as "the Henry Ford of Chocolate Makers." . . . [B]y the time he was 19, he had established his own candy business, . . . producing mainly caramel confections. . . . But after a trip to the chocolate centers of Europe, he sold the caramel business for one million dollars (a huge sum in those days), bought a farm in Derry Township, Pennsylvania, and built his chocolate factory on it. . . .

"Hershey, The Chocolate Town" . . . was dominated by Milton Hershey's imposing private mansion . . . [from which] the great man would sally forth each day to survey the vast domain he had built: the milk chocolate and cocoa factory, . . . the industrial school for orphan boys, . . . The Hershey Department Store, the Hershey Bank, men's and women's clubs, five churches, the free library, the Volunteer Fire Department, two schools, Hershey Park with its fine gardens, zoo, and rollercoaster, the Hershey Hotel, and a golf course. . . . [Y]et this triumph of paternalistic capitalism was a town in name only: it had no mayor nor any form of elected municipal government—it existed only at the whim of its benevolent dictator, Milton S. Hershey. . . .

There is no doubt that Hershey was a marketing genius. . . . Hershey and his chocolate bars soon commanded the American market. Everything was mechanized, with machines and conveyor belts organized into a true assembly-line operation. Hershey's best-selling bar contained almonds imported from southern Europe. . . . But even more popular than these were "Hershey's Kisses." . . . Small wonder that the streetlights of "The Chocolate Town" are the shape of Kisses.

Milton Hershey died peacefully at the age of 85, in his own hospital. His paternalistic empire lives on. . . . So many tourists flock to the wonders of Hershey, Pennsylvania, that the company no longer offers tours of its chocolate factory.

Here is a student's 100-word summary of the article:

```
    Milton Hershey is a big name in the history of
chocolate. He was an early achiever, but he wasn't
satisfied with just making money selling caramels. Once
```

> he saw the way chocolate was made overseas, he decided to become the best chocolate maker in America. The result of his passion for chocolate was a community that he designed himself and named after himself: Hershey, Pennsylvania. It was a complete community, but it wasn't a democracy. Hershey made all the decisions there. Hershey's chocolate was and still is extremely popular due to Milton Hershey's technological advances and devoted interest in chocolate.

Assignment 17
WRITE A 100-WORD SUMMARY

Your aim in writing your summary should be to give someone who has not read a piece of writing a clear idea of its content. First, read the following excerpt from the book *Catwatching,* by Desmond Morris. Then follow the instructions given after it.

Cat Lovers vs. Dog Lovers

Because of this difference between domestic cats and domestic dogs, cat lovers tend to be rather different from dog lovers. As a rule they have a stronger personality bias toward independent thought and action. Artists like cats; soldiers like dogs. The much-lauded "group loyalty" phenomenon is alien to both cats and cat lovers. . . . The ambitious Yuppie, the aspiring politician, the professional athlete, these are not typical cat owners. It is hard to picture a football player with a cat in his lap—much easier to envisage him taking his dog for a walk.

Those who have studied cat owners and dog owners as two distinct groups report that there is also a gender bias. Cat lovers show a greater tendency to be female. This is not surprising in view of the division of labor that developed during human evolution. Prehistoric males became specialized as group hunters, while the females concentrated on food-gathering and childrearing. This difference led to a human male "pack mentality" that is far less marked in females. . . . [S]o the modern dog has much more in common with the human male than with the human female. . . .

The argument will always go on—feline self-sufficiency and individualism versus canine camaraderie and good-fellowship. But it is important to stress that in making a valid point I have caricatured the two positions. In reality there are many people who enjoy equally the company of both cats and dogs. All of us, or nearly all of us, have both feline and canine elements in our personalities. We have moods when we want to be alone and thoughtful, and other times when we wish to be in the center of a crowded, noisy room.

A good way to begin the summary is to figure out the thesis statement, the main idea the author wants to get across to the reader. Write that idea down now *before reading further.*

How honest are you with yourself? Did you write that thesis statement? If you didn't, *write it now* before you read further.

You probably wrote something like this:

Certain characteristics make people prefer either cats or dogs as pets.

Using that main idea as your first sentence, summarize the article by choosing the most important points. *Be sure to put them in your own words.* Your rough draft may be 150 words or more.

Now cut it down by including only essential points and by getting rid of wordiness. Keep within the 100-word limit. You may have a few words less but not one word more. (And every word counts—even *a, and,* and *the.*) By forcing yourself to keep within 100 words, you'll get to the kernel of the author's thought and understand the article better.

When you have written the best summary you can, then and only then compare it with the summary on page 314. If you look at the model sooner, you'll cheat yourself of the opportunity to learn to write summaries because, once you read the model, it will be almost impossible not to make yours similar. So do your own thinking and writing, and then compare.

> **SUMMARY CHECKLIST**
>
> Even though your summary is different from the model, it may be just as good. If you're not sure how yours compares, answer these questions:
>
> **1.** Did you include the same main ideas?
>
> **2.** Did you leave out all unnecessary words and examples?
>
> **3.** Did you rephrase the writer's ideas, not just recopy them?
>
> **4.** Does the summary read smoothly?
>
> **5.** Would someone who had not read the article get a clear idea of it from your summary?

Assignment 18

WRITE A REACTION OR A 100-WORD SUMMARY

Respond to Carolyn Kleiner's article "Test Case: Now the Principal's Cheating" in any of the three ways we've discussed—in a reaction paragraph, an essay, or a 100-word summary. If you plan to respond with an essay, briefly summarize Kleiner's main ideas about standardized testing in your introductory paragraph. Then write about your reactions to her ideas in your body paragraphs. Save your final thoughts for your concluding paragraph.

Test Case: Now the Principal's Cheating

It's one of the most basic lessons kids learn, right up there with the ABCs and the three Rs: Cheating is wrong. But it seems a number of educators have yet to master that. Last week [June 2000], the principal of Potomac Elementary School, a top-ranked school in one of Maryland's lushest suburbs, resigned and a teacher was placed on administrative leave amid charges that they had rigged a statewide achievement test. The whistleblowers? Fifth graders, who allege that they were prompted to modify essay responses, provided correct answers, and given extra time to finish. "I can't even imagine why anyone would do this, especially at the third-highest-achieving school in the state," says Patricia O'Neill, president of the local Montgomery County Board of Education, noting Potomac Elementary's affluent, high-achieving student body. "Was it so important to be No. 1?"

The latest example of high-level cheating comes in this era of high-stakes testing, where scores are increasingly tied to everything from educators' job security and salaries to students' promotion and graduation. Such reforms are part of a nationwide movement to boost quality and to hold educators accountable for student achievement. But they have also had some unexpected consequences. "The evidence is pretty clear that there has been an increase in educators cheating on standardized exams," says Walt Haney, a senior research associate at Boston College's Center for the Study of Testing, Evaluation, and Educational Policy.

Fallen model? This spring alone, there has been a flurry of charges in schools across the country, from California to Louisiana to Florida. A Columbus, Ohio, grade school, touted as a model by the visiting President Clinton for its skyrocketing test scores—including a fourfold jump in the percentage of students who passed the reading portion of the state exam in one year—now stands accused by a teacher and three students who insist school aides prodded fourth graders to cheat, in one case actually grabbing a boy's hand and moving his pencil to the correct multiple-choice answer. The principal denies the charges and a district investigation found no conclusive evidence of wrongdoing, but a state inquiry is pending. In New York City, even a scathing December report that fingered 52 educators at 32 schools for myriad cheating infractions failed to deter such behavior: A follow-up review, released last month, charges that teachers, paraprofessionals, and librarians in five schools tampered with recent test scores.

Critics say the tests—not teachers—are to blame. "The major problem is the unreasonable, unfair, and inappropriate use of standardized exams," says Monty Neill, executive director of the National Center for Fair & Open Testing, and a staunch opponent of high-stakes tests. Twenty-eight states now use standard exams to determine graduation and 19 to govern student promotion; a growing number also dole out performance-based bonuses for schools that show progress and threaten intervention, even closure, for those that don't. In Maryland, schools that improve scores on the state standardized test, given in grades three, five, and eight, split $2.75 million each year. These sorts of incentives and the subsequent pressure-cooker climate can drive teachers to do anything and everything to boost scores, says Neill. "The only way to stop [cheating] is to return tests to their appropriate role, not as an absolute determinate of kids' progress but as one source of information, to be judged in conjunction with things like grades and teachers' judgments."

Still, the prevailing view is that standardized exams are the best way to measure achievement—and failure—and to help improve the nation's schools. "The cause [of cheating] is not the test, not the standards movement, but some character flaw," insists Jeanne Allen, president of Washington, D.C.'s Center for Education Reform. "These tests . . . are challenging, but they reflect what should be taught in various grades, and if educators are cheating, it means they don't have the ability to get these kids to learn, which means they shouldn't be teaching in the first place."

Whatever the cause, experts agree that the ones who lose most when educators tamper with tests are students. "If kids have had a teacher giving them the correct answers, or telling them when things are wrong, then it's very easy for them to justify cheating themselves," says Edward Stancik, special commissioner of investigation for the New York City public schools, who has exposed the rampant educator-assisted cheating and worries about the fallout. "It has a residual effect on the kids, who are not stupid, and who have to make up their own minds about right and wrong."

Source: Copyright June 12, 2000, *U.S. News & World Report.*
Visit us at our Web site at www.usnews.com for additional information.

Answers

SPELLING

WORDS OFTEN CONFUSED, SET 1 (PP. 8–12)

EXERCISE 1

1. effect, a
2. course
3. know
4. an, a, desserts
5. our

6. its
7. feel
8. an, accept
9. due, its
10. Conscious, chose

EXERCISE 2

1. It's, new
2. have, accepted
3. feel, an
4. chose
5. already, fourth

6. fill, except, have
7. hear, an, advice
8. are
9. course, effects
10. complemented

EXERCISE 3

1. forth
2. feel, conscious
3. chose, a
4. an, a, an
5. know, knew

6. conscious, due, already, clothes
7. all ready
8. course
9. break
10. hear

EXERCISE 4

1. already

2. clothes

3. its, brakes

4. choose, advice

5. desert

6. affected, coarse

7. here, conscious

8. It's, feel, our

9. know, have

10. forth, accept

EXERCISE 5

1. It's, hear

2. a

3. except, it's, its

4. effects

5. new

6. knew, an

7. advice, do

8. its

9. fourth, effect

10. except, no

PROOFREADING EXERCISE

During my singing recital last semester, I suddenly became very self-~~con-science~~-*conscious.* My heart started beating faster, and I didn't ~~no~~-*know* what to ~~due~~-*do.* I looked around to see if my show of nerves was having an ~~affect~~-*effect* on the audience. Of ~~coarse~~-*course,* they could ~~here~~-*hear* my voice shaking. I was the ~~forth~~-*fourth* singer in the program, and everyone else had done so well. I felt my face turn red and would ~~of~~-*have* run out the door if it had been closer. After my performance, people tried to give me ~~complements~~-*compliments,* but I ~~new~~-*knew* that they weren't sincere.

WORDS OFTEN CONFUSED, SET 2 (PP. 17–22)

EXERCISE 1

1. past

2. piece, their

3. than

4. through, to

5. led, their

6. quite, they're, two

7. you're, where, were

8. were, woman

9. then

10. lose

EXERCISE 2

1. lose
2. where
3. quiet, write
4. personnel
5. there, two, right

6. principal
7. who's
8. principal
9. whether, quiet, past
10. than

EXERCISE 3

1. past, their
2. led
3. their, passed
4. to, their
5. You're

6. You're, quite, past
7. whose
8. loose, too
9. woman, threw, through
10. write, their, personal

EXERCISE 4

1. quite, whether
2. peace
3. loose, personal
4. past, whose, passed
5. principal

6. There, lose
7. through, their
8. women
9. than, their
10. who's

EXERCISE 5

1. your
2. you're, than
3. whether
4. piece, women
5. They're, their

6. principle
7. to, than
8. principal, their
9. to, then
10. they're, through

PROOFREADING EXERCISE

Sometimes it's hard to find the ~~write~~-*right* place to study on campus. The library used ~~too~~-*to* be the ~~principle~~-*principal* location for students to do ~~they're~~-*their* difficult course work, ~~weather~~-*whether* it was preparing research papers or writing critical essays. But now most library resources are available online, ~~two~~-*too*. This change has ~~lead~~-*led* students to use campus computer labs and cafés as study halls.

There, students can go online, get up-to-date sources, write their reports, and have peace and ~~quite~~ *quiet* without the stuffy atmosphere of the library. The only problem with doing research online is that it's easier to ~~loose~~ *lose* a piece of information on the computer ~~then~~ *than* it is to lose a hard copy in the library.

CONTRACTIONS (PP. 24–28)

EXERCISE 1

1. you've, hadn't

2. that's

3. It's

4. no contractions

5. no contractions

6. couldn't

7. no contractions

8. There's

9. It's

10. Lets, don't

EXERCISE 2

1. isn't

2. It's

3. wasn't

4. could've, who'd

5. no contractions

6. didn't

7. didn't

8. wouldn't

9. no contractions

10. I'd, couldn't

EXERCISE 3

1. moon's (moon *is*)

2. it's

3. it's (it *is* covered) (Note that the second *its* is possessive and takes no apostrophe.)

4. it's

5. don't, can't

6. moon's

7. no contractions

8. no contractions

9. moon's

10. that's

EXERCISE 4

1. should've

2. didn't, I'd

3. didn't, could've, didn't

4. wasn't, don't

5. It's, I've

6. I'm, it'd

7. wouldn't, they'd

8. who's, he'd

9. might've

10. there's

EXERCISE 5

1. I'm, she's

2. We've, we've

3. aren't

4. they're

5. they're

6. that's

7. We've, can't, doesn't

8. we'd

9. that's, it's, they're

10. can't

PROOFREADING EXERCISE

If ~~youve~~-*you've* ever read any reviews of books sold on Amazon.com, ~~youre~~ *you're* probably familiar with the writings of Harriet Klausner. Klausner ~~didnt~~-*didn't* write the books; she wrote the reviews after buying and reading the books. In fact, ~~shes~~-*she's* the reviewer ~~whos~~-*who's* ranked as the most popular on the famous website. To date, ~~Klausners~~-*Klausner's* written more than five hundred reviews, but she ~~hasnt~~-*hasn't* been paid for any of them. Her responses ~~havent~~-*haven't* gone unnoticed, however, and Amazon.com fans ~~cant~~-*can't* wait to see what ~~shell~~-*she'll* recommend next.

POSSESSIVES (PP. 30–34)

EXERCISE 4

1. no possessives

2. woman's, tree's

3. Luna's (Note: *Its* is already possessive and needs no apostrophe.)

4. Luna's, earth's

5. company's, people's

6. Luna's

7. Hill's, loggers'

8. woman's, team's, Luna's

9. *The Legacy of Luna*'s, Hill's

10. Hill's

EXERCISE 5

1. ancestors'

2. families'

3. Hatfields', McCoys'

4. states'

5. reunion's

6. enemies'

7. no possessives

8. McCoys', Hatfields'

9. Hatfields'

10. family's

PROOFREADING EXERCISE

At a ski resort in Montana, residents have more than one reason to remember New *Year's* Eve, 1999. *Everyone's* worries about Y2K computer failures, money mishaps, and military glitches proved to be unfounded. But that didn't stop human beings from causing problems of their own. Just after midnight, the town of Whitefish was celebrating the arrival of the first day of the year 2000. But the party quickly turned into a riot because of four *women's* decision to run through town without wearing any clothes. The police quickly took three of the women into custody, but the *officers'* actions upset the gathering crowd. As the *crowd's* number grew to include nearly four hundred people, some of them started throwing everything from glass bottles to snowballs at the authorities. By the end of the night, three of the streakers and twelve of the protesters had been arrested; all were released the next day. The police never learned the fourth *streaker's* identity, but they did receive many eyewitness descriptions of her.

REVIEW OF CONTRACTIONS AND POSSESSIVES (PP. 35–36)

1. I've

2. Koons'

3. sculpture's

4. wasn't

5. Puppy's

6. no contractions or possessives needing apostrophes

7. don't, hasn't, Puppy's

8. Koons'

9. Puppy's, that's

10. weren't

A Journal of My Own

I've been keeping a journal ever since I was in high school. I *don't* write it for my *teachers'* sake. I *wouldn't* turn it in even if they asked me to. *It's* mine, and it helps me remember all of the changes *I've* gone through so far in my life. The way I see it, a *diary's* purpose *isn't* just to record the facts; *it's* to capture my true feelings.

When I record the *day's* events in my journal, they *aren't* written in minute-by-minute details. Instead, if *I've* been staying at a *friend's* house for the weekend, *I'll* write something like this: "*Sharon's* the only friend I have who listens to my whole sentence before starting hers. *She's* never in a hurry to end a good conversation. Today we talked for an hour or so about the pets *we'd* had when we were kids. We agreed that *we're* both 'dog people.' We *can't* imagine our lives without dogs. Her favorites are Pomeranians, and mine are golden retrievers." *That's* the kind of an entry *I'd* make in my journal. It *doesn't* mean much to anyone but me, and *that's* the way it should be.

I know that another *person's* diary would be different from mine and that most people *don't* even keep one. *I'm* glad that writing comes easily to me. I *don't* think *I'll* ever stop writing in my journal because it helps me believe in myself and value *others'* beliefs as well.

RULE FOR DOUBLING A FINAL LETTER (PP. 38–39)

EXERCISE 1

1. betting
2. milking
3. waiting
4. parking
5. skimming

6. admitting
7. slapping
8. thinking
9. tapping
10. hitting

EXERCISE 2

1. wrapping
2. ripping
3. peeling
4. referring
5. investing

6. ordering
7. profiting
8. screaming
9. slipping
10. predicting

EXERCISE 3

1. passing
2. needing
3. fearing
4. crushing
5. occurring

6. printing
7. looking
8. heating
9. potting
10. suffering

EXERCISE 4

1. previewing
2. healing
3. chugging
4. flicking
5. booking

6. frosting
7. numbing
8. rushing
9. painting
10. sending

EXERCISE 5

1. preferring
2. shouting
3. resting
4. fastening
5. holding

6. fishing
7. feeling
8. hiccuping
9. sneaking
10. pleading

PROGRESS TEST (P. 40)

1. A. complimented
2. B. where
3. A. could have
4. A. traveled
5. A. conscience

6. A. children's
7. B. already
8. B. effects
9. A. principle
10. A. You're

SENTENCE STRUCTURE

FINDING SUBJECTS AND VERBS (PP. 51–54)

EXERCISE 1

1. The summer heat causes many problems for people.

2. Food spoils more quickly in the summer.

3. Insects and other pests seek shelter inside.

4. There are power outages due to excessive use of air conditioners and fans.

5. In some areas, smog levels increase dramatically in the summer.

6. School children suffer in overheated classrooms.

7. On the worst days, everyone searches for a swimming pool or drives to the beach.

8. Sleeping comfortably becomes impossible.

9. No activity seems worth the effort.

10. But the heat of summer fades in our minds at the first real break in the weather.

EXERCISE 2

1. In 1992, Jacquelyn Barrett became the sheriff of Fulton County, Georgia.

2. She was the first African-American woman sheriff in U.S. history.

3. As sheriff of Fulton County, Barrett managed the biggest system of jails in the state of Georgia.

4. Her department had a yearly budget of sixty-five million dollars.

5. Over a thousand people worked for the Fulton County Sheriff's office.

6. Barrett definitely broke the stereotype of southern sheriffs in TV and movies.

7. By 1999, there were over eleven hundred sheriffs in the South.

8. African-American men and women represented just five percent of the total.

9. Only one percent of them were women.

10. However, of the twenty-four female sheriffs in the country, nine were from the South.

EXERCISE 3

1. Livio De Marchi lives in Venice, Italy, with its canals and romantic gondolas.

2. Unfortunately, large power boats also crowd the canals of Venice.

3. So De Marchi built a boat of his own in response to the growing traffic problem in the canals.

4. His "boat" looks exactly like a convertible Volkswagen Beetle.

5. De Marchi carved the body of his floating VW Bug completely out of wood.

6. Even the open convertible top behind the passenger seat is wooden.

7. De Marchi's car-boat has a small motor and travels at only five miles an hour.

8. With its real headlights and glass windshield, this replica gets a lot of attention.

9. De Marchi carved other wooden cars besides the VW.

10. One of them, a Fiat, is on exhibit at a Ripley's Believe It or Not! museum in Missouri.

EXERCISE 4

1. I just read the American Film Institute's list of "America's Funniest Movies."

2. The list goes all the way back to the 1920s and includes one hundred great comedies.

3. A 1924 movie, *The Navigator,* is the earliest of AFI's funniest picks.

4. That one is an unknown to me.

5. I recognize 1925's *The Gold Rush* and remember Chaplin's classic shoe-eating scene.

6. The 1998 hit *There's Something about Mary* ends the list.

7. In between, some decades produced more of the best comedies than others.

8. Filmmakers in the 1980s, for instance, created twenty-two of the funniest.

9. But there are only five films from the 1990s.

10. Maybe Y2K worries shifted the focus to sci-fi thrillers.

EXERCISE 5

1. At the Swiss Federal Institute of Technology in Lausanne, Switzerland, teams of tiny robots roam the labs.

2. They are all about the size of a lump of sugar or a single die in a pair of dice.

3. A motor and a battery from a watch power each of the teeny technological wonders.

4. They move around and navigate in mazes through the use of sensing devices.

5. And they all have the same name: Alice.

6. Yet every Alice has its own number code.

7. Upon contact, each communicates its ranking to its companion and either leads or follows the other in numerical order.

8. The Alices also send information directly back to computers in the lab.

9. Needless to say, the Alices give scientists a lot of enjoyment.

10. Even visitors to the lab's Web site play with the Alices through remote control.

PARAGRAPH EXERCISE

Stories about air travel hold many people's interest these days. Of course, there are stories with happy and unhappy endings. Some of the stories just confuse everyone. For instance, the people in charge of landings and take-offs at Chicago's O'Hare Airport have a strange story of their own. Early in 2000, the radar at O'Hare often showed false images of airplanes on the screens. The controllers took all of the necessary precautions but found no planes there at all. They called these illusions "ghosts." And no one has a good explanation for them yet.

LOCATING PREPOSITIONAL PHRASES (PP. 56–60)

EXERCISE 1

1. (For nearly thirty years), a phone <u>booth</u> <u>stood</u> (in the middle) (of the Mojave Desert) (with absolutely nothing) (around it).

2. It <u>was</u> far (from any sign) (of civilization) but originally <u>served</u> miners (in camps) far away.

3. The <u>number</u> (for this pay phone) <u>became</u> well-known (over time): 760-733-9969.

4. <u>People</u> <u>called</u> it (from around the world) and <u>traveled</u> (to it) (for fun and adventure).

5. <u>Sites</u> (on the Internet) <u>posted</u> the isolated phone's number and <u>offered</u> maps (to its remote location) (near Baker, California).

6. <u>Individuals</u> <u>camped</u> (outside the booth) and <u>waited</u> (for random calls) (from strangers).

7. <u>Callers</u> never <u>expected</u> an answer (from a phone) (in the middle) (of nowhere).

8. (On many occasions), <u>callers</u> <u>panicked</u> and <u>said</u> nothing (for a minute or two).

9. (In addition), <u>some</u> (of its visitors) <u>vandalized</u> the booth and the phone itself.

10. So phone-company <u>workers</u> <u>removed</u> the infamous Mojave phone booth (in May 2000).

EXERCISE 2

1. <u>One</u> (of the most popular movies) (of the year 2000) <u>was</u> *Chicken Run.*

2. This stop-motion <u>movie</u> (with clay chickens) <u>did</u> very well (at the box office).

3. The <u>directors</u>, Nick Park and Peter Lord, <u>made</u> *Chicken Run* (with a budget) (of forty-two million dollars).

4. (In the movie world), <u>that's</u> [that <u>is</u>] a real bargain.

5. And the <u>labor</u> <u>was</u> much more intensive than (in ordinary pictures).

6. The five hundred <u>shots</u> (of a regular live-action film) <u>became</u> one hundred thousand shots (for this movie).

7. The stop-motion <u>method</u> (of filmmaking) <u>requires</u> twenty-four changes (in sets and characters' features) (for each second) (of film).

8. Therefore, *Chicken Run,* (with its intricate prisonlike set and its lifelike poultry inmates), took three years to complete. (*To complete* is not a prepositional phrase. See "Recognizing Verbal Phrases.")

9. Nick Park made other shorter films (before *Chicken Run*).

10. His *Creature Comforts* won an Academy Award (in 1989) and led (to *The Wrong Trousers*), now a classic (in animation).

EXERCISE 3

1. John Zweifel is a big name (in the world) (of miniatures).

2. His miniature replica (of the White House) impresses people (around the country) (with its painstaking attention) (to detail).

3. Zweifel officially started the project (during President Ford's administration).

4. Zweifel used the scale (of one inch) (to one foot) (for his model) (of the capital's mansion).

5. (Within the model's walls) are tiny reproductions (of all) (of the furnishings and personal effects) (of the current president and his family).

6. (During Ronald Reagan's tenure), Zweifel put a tiny jar (of jelly beans) (on the president's desk).

7. There were Amy Carter's roller-skate marks (on the wooden floor) (of the East Room).

8. Zweifel keeps the model up-(to-date) (through bimonthly visits) (to the actual White House) (in Washington, D.C.).

9. (As governor) (of Arkansas), Bill Clinton first saw Zweifel's amazing replica (in 1979).

10. (Under its realistic spell), Clinton foresaw his future (as a resident) (of the White House) and shared his premonition (with Zweifel).

EXERCISE 4

1. (At 2 A.M.) (on the first Sunday) (in April), something happens (to nearly everyone) (in America): Daylight Saving Time.

2. But few people are awake (at two) (in the morning).

3. So we set the hands or digits (of our clocks) ahead one hour (on Saturday night) (in preparation) (for it).

4. And (before bed) (on the last Saturday) (in October), we turn them back again.

5. (For days) (after both events), I have trouble (with my sleep patterns and my mood).

6. (In spring), the feeling is one (of loss).

7. That Saturday-night sleep (into Sunday) is one hour shorter than usual.

8. But (in fall), I gain a false sense (of security) (about time).

9. That endless Sunday morning quickly melts (into the start) (of a hectic week) (like the other fifty-one) (in the year).

10. All (of this upheaval) is due (to the Uniform Time Act) (of 1966).

EXERCISE 5

1. Many Americans still shop (in stores) (for holiday gifts).

2. (With the increase) (in ease and access) (to merchandise) (over the Internet), more people and stores do business (on computer).

3. This increase was gradual (at first) but rose dramatically (in 1999).

4. (In 1998), people ordered only one percent (of their holiday purchases) (over the Internet).

5. However, Americans gained confidence (in on-line shopping) just (in time) (for the holidays) (of 1999).

6. The number (of Internet purchases) tripled (within one year).

7. Most businesses were not ready (for the increase) (in on-line sales).

8. Some big names (in toys, electronics, and pet supplies) originally promised deliveries (by Christmas morning), (for example).

9. But (by late December), the volume (of orders) overloaded both suppliers and shipping companies.

10. Back-ordered items and late packages spoiled lots (of holiday moments).

PARAGRAPH EXERCISE

Water Storage

Lakes and ponds obviously store a great deal (of water). Not so obvious is the immense reservoir (of water) stored (in the polar ice caps), (in glaciers), and (in snow) (on mountains) and (on the cold northern plains) (during winter). Winter snows (in the mountains) determine the water supply (for irrigation) and (for power use). This snow melts (with the spring thaw) and fills the rivers.

UNDERSTANDING DEPENDENT CLAUSES (PP. 63–68)

EXERCISE 1

1. Mark and Jackie Tresl live in a small cabin on two hundred acres of land in Ohio.

2. The Tresls have two pets that live in the cabin with them.

3. One is a dog, whose name is Rodent, and one is a horse, whose name is Misha.

4. The Tresls found Misha when she was about six months old and discovered that she had pneumonia.

5. While Mark and Jackie cared for the sick foal, they kept her inside the house for warmth.

6. Since a horse needs a lot of floor space, the Tresls lined all of their furniture up against the cabin walls.

7. Once Misha recovered from her illness, the Tresls decided to keep her in the house.

8. Although some adjustments were necessary, the Tresls made them and truly love their thirteen-hundred-pound house pet.

9. The Tresls used sweets as a lure during the housebreaking process.

10. Now Misha goes outside only when she needs to.

EXERCISE 2

1. When Barbara Mitchell ate lunch at a California restaurant in late 1997, she thought that the service was terrible.

2. The lunch that Mitchell ordered consisted of salad, soup, pasta, and iced tea.

3. She received the bill, which came to twenty-four dollars, and charged it to her credit card.

4. Because the service was so bad, Mitchell wrote in a one-cent tip.

5. But when Mitchell saw her credit-card statement, she nearly fainted.

6. The tip that was a penny turned into a charge of ten thousand dollars, in addition to the twenty-four dollars for her food.

7. The waiter told authorities that he entered the huge tip amount by mistake.

8. When the restaurant's manager learned of the error, she suspended the waiter for seven days.

9. Mitchell received a full refund, an apology, and a gift certificate from the restaurant.

10. Mitchell wishes that she paid the bill with cash.

EXERCISE 3

1. In June of 2000, there was another incident of mistaken tipping at a bar in Chicago.

2. This time, a male customer left a real ten thousand dollar tip for a waitress who was especially nice to him.

3. At least everyone thought that he gave her that amount until the man later denied his generosity.

4. The customer, who was a London resident on a trip to the United States, did everything to convince the people in the bar that he was serious.

5. Melanie Uczen was the waitress who served the man his drinks, which added up to nine dollars.

6. He told her that he was a doctor and wanted to help with her college plans.

7. When the bar's owner questioned the tip, the customer allowed the owner to make a copy of his passport.

8. He even signed a note that verified the tip's amount.

9. Back in London, the man said that he was not a doctor and claimed that he was drunk when he signed the note.

10. Because the big tip brought the bar so much publicity, the owners paid Melanie Uczen the ten thousand dollars themselves.

EXERCISE 4

1. The happiest ending to a big-tipper story came in July of 2000.

2. It began when Karen Steinmetz, who dispatches cars for Continental Limo company, received a call for a driver and limo at two-thirty in the morning.

3. The most unusual part of the customer's request was that he wanted the driver to take him over nine hundred miles, from Southern California to Oregon.

4. When Steinmetz contacted the first driver to see if he wanted the job, he told her that he wanted only sleep at that hour.

5. So Steinmetz called Major Cephas, another driver who worked for Continental.

6. Cephas took the job and picked the customer up in the city of Garden Grove.

7. The two men drove through the night but stopped in Sacramento and other

spots along the way for exercise and refreshments.

8. Overall, the trip took nearly eighteen hours, which resulted in a twenty-two

hundred dollar fare.

9. The passenger paid the fare and gave Cephas a twenty-thousand-dollar tip

because Cephas was so patient with him.

10. This time the tip was as real as the disappointment of the first driver who

turned down the job.

1. As Mike Bell enjoyed his flight from Washington, D.C., to San Jose, California,

his dog Dakota was miserable.

2. Bell and everyone else assumed that Dakota's carrier was in the special part

of the plane that warmly houses animals during flights.

3. However, halfway through the trip, the plane's captain discovered that the

dog was actually in the freezing part of the cargo hold.

4. The captain knew that any animal who stayed in such an environment for the

remainder of the flight could die.

5. When the crew gave Bell the news that his dog was in danger, he felt worried

and helpless.

6. Because they cared about the life of a dog, the crew made a special stop at

the next airport.

7. They found Dakota alive but very cold and allowed Bell to bring Dakota into the cabin for the rest of the trip.

8. The other passengers who were on board were happy for Bell and his dog.

9. Bell appreciates what the captain and crew did for Dakota after they caught the mistake.

10. But he is not sure whether he wants to fly with a pet ever again.

In these paragraphs, some verbs seem to have no subject. These are commands in which a "you" subject is understood.

Tasting

[When you taste chocolate], let a small piece gently melt on your tongue. Unless it is a particularly revolting sample, . . . do not spit out [the] chocolate because [you get] information from the "mouthfeel." . . . Although coffee goes well with chocolate, it dulls the palate in the same way as other strong flavors such as chili or peppermint. . . .

Snap

If it is a bar of chocolate that you are tasting, break it and listen to check that it snaps cleanly. . . . If you hold the chocolate for a few seconds, it should begin to melt unless it contains lots of vegetable fats or your circulation is particularly bad!

Bloom

Bloom is the term for the grayish-white appearance . . . on the surface of chocolate. There are two types of bloom which develop on chocolate. The

first . . . indicates that the chocolate has become too warm at some point. . . .
Much more serious is sugar bloom which occurs when moisture comes into
contact with the chocolate. . . . The sugar crystals [which come] to the surface
dissolve in the water vapor, later recrystallizing. The process destroys the texture
of the chocolate, which becomes gray and gritty and although [it is] edible will
hardly delight the connoisseur.

CORRECTING FRAGMENTS (PP. 71–75)

EXERCISE 1
Answers may vary, but here are some possible revisions.

1. Douglas Fairbanks, Jr., died in May of 2000 at the age of ninety.

2. *He was* a movie star for most of his life.

3. *He acted in* nearly eighty films in his long career.

4. *He made* the first at the age of thirteen and the last at seventy-two.

5. *He was* the son of another prestigious actor, Douglas Fairbanks, Senior.

6. Fairbanks, Sr., starred in the swashbuckling films of the 1920s and 30s.

7. *Fairbanks, Sr., married* the famous actress Mary Pickford and *became* one of the most powerful people in Hollywood.

8. Fairbanks and Pickford called their son Doug Junior but did not want him to be an actor.

9. However, he disappointed his parents and followed in their footsteps.

10. *The Prisoner of Zenda was* Douglas Fairbanks, Jr.'s, most enduring performance.

EXERCISE 2
Answers may vary, but here are some possible revisions.

1. In my psychology class, we talk about gender a lot.

2. *We discuss* ways of raising children without gender bias.

3. *Gender bias means having* different expectations about boys' abilities and girls' abilities.

4. Experts have several suggestions for parents and teachers.

5. Ask girls to work in the yard and boys to do dishes sometimes. (In numbers 5–10, the subject is an understood *You*.)

6. *Do not make* a big deal out of it.

7. Give both girls and boys affection as well as helpful criticism.

8. *Encourage* physically challenging activities for both genders.

9. Give girls access to tools, and praise boys for kindness.

10. Most of all, value their different approaches to math and computers.

EXERCISE 3
Answers may vary, but here are some possible revisions.

1. The ocean liner Titanic sank in April of 1912, affecting thousands of families and inspiring books and movies around the world.

2. With three close relatives on the Titanic that April night, the Belman family remembers details of the disaster.

3. Two of the Belmans were lost after the sinking. One *survived* by swimming along next to a lifeboat and eventually climbing aboard.

4. The survivor, Grandfather Belman, returned to his family in Lebanon and told them about the terrifying events of that night.

5. He recalled the efforts of the crew, the courage of the passengers, the icy cold water, and the reassuring sight of the Carpathia.

6. Anthony Belman is Grandfather Belman's descendent, now living in the United States and working as a bartender.

7. Inspired by the stories of his grandfather's survival and the loss of his other two relatives, Belman has created a cocktail in honor of all those touched by the Titanic disaster.

8. It's called the Titanic Iceberg, *and it's* made with rum, crème de menthe, and blue Curaçao.

9. After blending the mixture with ice and transferring it to a margarita glass, Belman adds two wedges of vanilla ice cream to the sea-blue drink for icebergs.

10. And as a final touch to remind everyone of the human toll of the disaster, the cocktail calls for two white Lifesaver candies floating on top of the icy blue slush.

EXERCISE 4
Answers may vary, but here are some possible revisions.

1. When Nathan King turned twelve, he had a heart-stopping experience.

2. Nathan was tossing a football against his bedroom wall, which made the ball ricochet and land on his bed.

3. In a diving motion, Nathan fell on his bed to catch the ball as it landed.

4. After he caught the ball, Nathan felt a strange sensation in his chest.

5. To his surprise, he looked down and saw the eraser end of a no. 2 pencil that had pierced his chest and entered his heart.

6. Nathan immediately shouted for his mother, who luckily was in the house at the time.

7. Because Nathan's mom is a nurse, she knew not to remove the pencil.

8. If she had pulled the pencil out of her son's chest, he would have died.

9. After Nathan was taken to a hospital equipped for open-heart surgery, he had the pencil carefully removed.

10. Fate may be partly responsible for Nathan's happy birthday story since it turned out to be his heart surgeon's birthday too.

EXERCISE 5
Answers may vary, but here are some possible revisions. (Changes and additions are in italics.)

1. When thunderstorms interrupt golf tournaments, *everyone gets nervous.*

2. The field trip that my architecture teacher took us on *was fun.*

3. Snow fell all night.

4. Since trash and garbage are two different things, *they should be separated.*

5. A person who has graduated from college *will usually find a better job.*

6. *Many people do not know* that Thomas Jefferson died on the Fourth of July.

7. In the box were two frightened mice.

8. The team celebrated.

9. If you help us with our car wash, *we will* raise *more* money for the club.

10. Joking with friends can easily backfire.

PROOFREADING EXERCISE
Answers may vary, but here are some possible revisions. (Changes are in italics.)

If you know what E-Cyas stands for, then you probably know who or what he is—*a* rock star who exists only in cyberspace. E-Cyas *means* Electronic Cybernetic Superstar. The German company responsible for E-Cyas is I-D Media. E-Cyas may be the male equivalent of Lara Croft in terms of sex appeal. *He gets* e-mails and marriage proposals on his own Web site. *E-Cyas also has* a base of loyal fans willing to go to his "concerts" *even though* he will be there as only an image on a screen. E-Cyas's first song "Are You Real?" made it to the top of the charts in Germany. Only time will tell whether the first male cyberstar's popularity will last.

CORRECTING RUN-ON SENTENCES (PP. 78–82)

EXERCISE 1
Your answers may differ depending on how you chose to separate the two clauses.

1. Many Wal-Mart stores offer a surprising service, but not everyone is happy about it.

2. The sentence is correct.

3. Official RV Parks do charge fees for overnight stays; these fees pay for the upkeep of facilities and for services like water and power hookups.

4. Wal-Mart parking lots offer no facilities or services, yet they attract campers anyway.

5. The sentence is correct.

6. The sentence is correct.

7. To keep up with demand, Wal-Marts order the latest in camping and recreational equipment, but that's not all.

8. The sentence is correct.

9. A few towns and other large store chains have complained about Wal-Mart's free parking policy. One county in Florida has completely banned it.

10. Wal-Mart's overnight parking service does seem to benefit its stores and its RV visitors; however, community businesses and RV campgrounds question its fairness.

EXERCISE 2
Your answers may differ depending on how you chose to separate the two clauses.

1. One day is hard for me every year. That day is my birthday.

2. I don't mind getting older; I just never enjoy the day of my birth.

3. For one thing, I was born in August, but summer is my least favorite season.

4. I hate the heat and the sun, so even traditional warm-weather activities get me down.

5. Sunblock spoils swimming; smog spoils biking, and crowds spoil the National Parks.

6. To most people, the beach is a summer haven. To me, the beach in the summer is bright, busy, and boring.

7. I love to walk on the beach on the cold, misty days of winter or early spring. I wear a big sweater and have the whole place to myself.

8. August also brings fire season to most parts of the country; therefore, even television is depressing.

9. There are no holidays to brighten up August. In fact, it's like a black hole in the yearly holiday calendar—after the Fourth of July but before Halloween and the other holidays.

10. I have considered moving my birthday to February. Even being close to Groundhog Day would cheer me up.

EXERCISE 3

Your answers may differ since various words can be used to begin dependent clauses.

1. Along with *Survivor,* one of the reality-based TV shows of the new millennium, was *1900 House,* which was shown on public television in June of 2000. (The comma before *which* indicates that the clause contains unessential information.)

2. Whereas *Survivor* left sixteen individuals on a remote island to fight against the elements for thirty-nine days, *1900 House* took a British family back one hundred years to live like a family in 1900 for three months.

3. Although contestants on *Survivor* played for a million dollars, four hundred families applied to live in the *1900 House* with the experience as the only reward.

4. *1900 House* producers had to renovate an existing home because there were no houses in London in original 1900 condition.

5. Luckily, they found a house that had been built before 1900 and retained its original features under a layer of modern paneling and appliances.

6. Producers were delighted when they found the system of pipes used for gas lights, and it still worked perfectly.

7. The Bowler family was chosen to live in the 1900 House because, unlike some of the other applicants, they were eager to learn and were happy as a family.

8. The sentence is correct.

9. Although at first the Bowlers were excited to wear the clothes and live the lives of their ancestors, they soon discovered the daily obstacles of the time.

10. After the Bowlers dressed in restrictive garments, bathed in cold water, hand-washed clothes, cooked on a wood-fired stove, and played cards in the evening for ninety days, they were ready to return to the luxuries of the modern world.

EXERCISE 4

Your answers may differ since various words can be used to begin dependent clauses.

1. The new home of the San Francisco Giants is Pacific Bell Park, which had its first season in the summer of 2000. (The comma before *which* indicates that the clause contains unessential information.)

2. Pac Bell Park stands beside an inlet of San Francisco Bay that has been called McCovey Cove.

3. It was named after Willie McCovey, who was one of the Giants' best hitters at their old home, Candlestick Park. (The comma before *who* indicates that the clause contains unessential information.)

4. Pac Bell Park has a few unusual features that make the place unique.

5. Since stadium designers wanted to give the park a retro look, they built a huge replica of a 1927 Rawlings glove above the stands in left field.

6. Although a twenty-five-foot wall stands between right field and the bay, a homerun often clears the fence and lands in the water.

7. When Tom Hoynes decided to watch an exhibition game from his ten-foot boat, he started a streak of homerun ball rescues.

8. In the Giants' first season, Hoynes recovered most of the homerun balls that were hit into the waters of McCovey Cove.

9. Even though Hoynes became a celebrity that season, he usually wasn't alone in the bay.

10. There were plenty of others who were anxious to be part of the lore of a new sports stadium. (There is no comma before *who* in this sentence because the clause contains essential information.)

EXERCISE 5

Your answers may differ depending on how you chose to separate the clauses.

1. If it's summer time, there will be bugs.

2. People at picnics and backyard barbecues see bees and wasps as pests, but they're just being themselves.

3. Since these creatures build their nests earlier in the year, late summer is their vacation time too.

4. They leave their homes and look for sweets that are easy to find at picnics and barbecues.

5. The smell of a soda, for instance, attracts these insects, so such drinks should be covered.

6. Also, people who wear perfume are more likely to attract insects.

7. The sentence is correct.

8. The picnic location may be near a hive, but the hive might not be obvious.

9. Because it is so dangerous to upset or threaten any hive of insects, people must be aware of their surroundings.

10. Insects can pose a threat to the peace and safety of summer activities; therefore, the best defense is understanding.

REVIEW OF FRAGMENTS AND RUN-ON SENTENCES (P. 83)

Your revisions may differ depending on how you chose to correct the errors.

People and animals require different amounts of sleep. People have to balance on two legs all day; therefore, we need to get off our feet and sleep for about eight hours each night. Horses, however, are able to rest better standing up because their four legs support their bodies without a strain on any one area. When horses lie down, their large bodies press uncomfortably against the earth. This pressure makes their hearts and lungs work harder than they do in standing position. Generally speaking, horses lie on the ground for about two hours a day, and they spend only a little of the remaining time drowsy or lightly sleeping while still on their feet.

IDENTIFYING VERB PHRASES (PP. 85–89)

EXERCISE 1

1. Greg Smith is a young man who has already accomplished many (of his goals).

2. (In 1997), Greg was a seven-year-old (in elementary school).

3. (By the next school year), Greg had advanced (to high school).

4. (In 2000), Greg Smith started college (at the age) (of ten).

5. (During his first year) (at college), Greg studied physics, calculus, upper-level French, and ancient warfare.

6. Greg Smith's father can remember his son's first signs (of genius).

7. Greg could memorize and recite books when he was just a year old.

8. Greg was given an IQ test when he was five, and the results were exceptional.

9. (On the day) that Greg graduated (from his Florida High School), one (of his baby teeth) fell out.

10. Greg has already made friends (in college); (for some reason), everyone wants to sit (next to him).

EXERCISE 2

1. Researchers have been tagging animals (with radio devices) (for years).

2. After they study the animals' movements, experts can help to preserve species (in their natural habitats).

3. But some animals are difficult to fit (with collars or other equipment).

4. (For example), wild Jamaican iguanas have become endangered but can wiggle (out of most tracking devices).

5. When scientists needed a stretchy and sturdy solution (to the problem), they asked Nike (for help).

6. Nike designed a vest that can withstand changes (in temperature and terrain).

7. The iguanas that are being studied have been born (in zoos), dressed (in the Nike vests), and then taken (to the wilds) (of Jamaica).

8. (In their special vests), the reptiles can grow and send their vital information back (to researchers).

9. The Nike logo was added (to the iguana vest) just (for fun).

10. (Like the Jamaican iguanas), Puerto Rican crested toads have been fitted (with special spandex backpacks) (for the same kind) (of research).

EXERCISE 3

1. The largest meteorite that has ever been found (on Earth) was recently (at the center) (of a custody battle).

2. The American Museum of Natural History (in New York) has owned the Willamette meteorite (since the early 1900s), and it was displayed (at the Hayden Planetarium).

3. Scientists believe that the car-sized meteor landed (between eight and ten thousand years ago) (in what is now called Oregon). (The last prepositional phrase includes a subject and verb because it has a dependent clause as its object.)

4. The Willamette meteorite may actually be the central part (of an exploded planet).

5. But (to one group) (of Native Americans), the huge meteor has always been known (as "Tomanowos," or "Sky Person").

6. (In a lawsuit) (against the museum), Grand Ronde tribe members claimed that their ancestors had worshipped Tomanowos (for thousands of years) before it was sold (to the museum).

7. They could support their claims (with tribal songs and dances) that revealed a close relationship (between the Grand Ronde people and the meteorite).

8. The museum and the Grand Ronde tribes did settle the dispute (in August) (of 2000).

9. The two sides agreed that the Willamette meteorite would remain (on display) (at the Hayden Planetarium) but would be accompanied (by a plaque) that described the Grand Ronde tribes' connection (to the meteor).

10. The museum also agreed to give the Grand Ronde people special access (to the Willamette meteorite) so that they may continue their relationship (with Tomanowos).

EXERCISE 4

1. Endangered species are currently getting help (from many sources) (around the world).

2. The Audubon Center for Research of Endangered Species (ACRES) is located (in New Orleans).

3. (Through the use) (of freezing techniques), scientists (at ACRES) have successfully moved an embryo (from a threatened species) (of African wildcat) (to the body) (of a typical house cat).

4. (In November 1999), Cayenne the house cat gave birth (to an African wildcat kitten).

5. Scientists (at ACRES) have named the kitten Jazz.

6. Two African wildcats are still considered the biological parents (of Jazz).

7. Cayenne has acted only (as his surrogate mother).

8. Jazz's birth has entered the record books (as the first previously frozen embryo) (from one species) to be born (to a mother) (from another species).

9. (Through such a process), threatened species can produce more babies (with less risk) (to their endangered mothers).

10. Cayenne has treated Jazz just (like one) (of her own kittens).

EXERCISE 5

1. Prehistoric musical instruments have been found before.

2. But the ancient flutes that were recently discovered (in China's Henan Province) included the oldest playable instrument (on record).

3. The nine-thousand-year-old flute was made (from the wing bone) (of a bird).

4. The bone was hollowed out and pierced (with seven holes) that produce the notes (of an ancient Chinese musical scale).

5. Because one (of the holes' pitches) missed the mark, an additional tiny hole was added (by the flute's maker).

6. The flute is played (in the vertical position).

7. People who have studied ancient instruments are hoping to learn more (about the culture) that produced this ancient flute.

8. Other bone flutes were found (at the same time) and (in the same location), but they were not intact or strong enough (for playing).

9. Visitors (to the Brookhaven National Laboratory's Web site) can listen (to music) (from the world's oldest working flute).

10. Listeners will be taken back (to 7,000 years B.C.)

REVIEW EXERCISE (P. 89)

My brain feels (like a computer's central processing unit). Information is continually pumping (into its circuits). I organize the data, format it (to my individual preferences), and lay it out (in my own style). As I endlessly sculpt existing formulas, they become something (of my own). When I need a solution (to a problem), I access the data that I have gathered (from my whole existence), even my pre-programmed DNA.

Since I am a student, teachers require that I supply them (with specific information) (in various formats). When they assign an essay, I produce several paragraphs. If they need a summary, I scan the text, find its main ideas, and put them briefly (into my own words). I know that I can accomplish whatever the teachers ask so that I can obtain a bachelor's degree and continue processing ideas to make a living.

I compare my brain (to a processor) because right now I feel that I must work (like one). As I go further (into my education), my processor will be continually updated—just (like a Pentium)! And (with any luck), I will end up (with real, not artificial, intelligence).

USING STANDARD ENGLISH VERBS (PP. 92–95)

EXERCISE 1

1. are, were
2. have, had
3. does, did
4. corrects, corrected
5. has, had

6. is, was
7. works, worked
8. am, was
9. collects, collected
10. need, needed

EXERCISE 2

1. are, were
2. does, did
3. has, had
4. tags, tagged
5. have, had

6. stuffs, stuffed
7. are, were
8. do, did
9. dance, danced
10. are, were

EXERCISE 3

1. changed, want
2. had
3. enrolled, were, expected
4. were, were
5. did, were, does

6. observed, had
7. watched, cared, followed
8. had
9. imagined, had
10. needs, are, am

EXERCISE 4

1. have
2. watch, want
3. likes, do
4. am, is
5. are, have

6. play, do
7. stump
8. calls
9. have
10. love, hope, ends

EXERCISE 5

1. Last semester my drawing teacher *handed* us an assignment.

2. The sentence is correct.

3. We *had* to draw in the other half of the picture.

4. My picture *showed* a woman sitting against the bottom of a tree trunk.

5. Her shoulders, hat, and umbrella *were* only partly there.

6. I tried to imagine what the missing parts *looked* like.

7. The sentence is correct.

8. Therefore, I *started* with the tree, the sky, and the ground.

9. The sentence is correct.

10. I *received* an "A" grade for my drawing.

PROOFREADING EXERCISE

I like to lie on the floor of my room on weekend mornings. I *look* out the window and watch the rays of the sun. I am free to experience the day as it *starts*. There is nothing that can stop the sun from shining or the crisp wind from blowing. The sky is like a friend that *is* always there when I *need* it. Its personality is changeable. It *changes* with the weather. We never know whether the sky will be blue, gray, or white with clouds. The sky *decides* the way the day feels.

USING REGULAR AND IRREGULAR VERBS (PP. 100–104)

EXERCISE 1
1. work
2. worked
3. working
4. worked
5. work

6. works
7. work
8. works
9. worked
10. work

EXERCISE 2
1. got, gets
2. bought, buy
3. was, is
4. thinks, think
5. grown, grown

6. leave, left
7. watch, watching
8. hears, hear
9. does, doing
10. was, is

EXERCISE 3
1. took, supposed
2. was, go
3. called, left, feel
4. imagined, was
5. buying, drove, saw

6. felt, knew, be
7. tried, went (or got)
8. been, undo
9. wish, take
10. did, was

EXERCISE 4
1. use, have
2. do, speak, dials
3. are, are
4. is, like, started
5. does, wants

6. trusts, is
7. imagine, dialing
8. asking, told, is
9. looked, smiled
10. has

EXERCISE 5

1. lying, fell

2. slept, woke, looked

3. felt, began, needed

4. passed, eased

5. describe, looked, saw

6. appeared, am

7. returned, disappeared

8. ached, was

9. was, done

10. needed, challenges

PROGRESS TEST (P. 105)

1. B. run-on sentence (. . . a night of decorating, so I was disappointed.)

2. B. fragment (*It leaves us only a little time . . .*)

3. B. incorrect verb form (He *used* to work . . .)

4. B. incorrect verb form (They were *lying* on the floor . . .)

5. A. fragment (Attach this phrase to the next sentence.)

6. A. incorrect verb form (have *taken*)

7. B. fragment (Attach the dependent clause to the previous sentence.)

8. B. run-on sentence (Their teacher was driving; he knew the road well.)

9. B. fragment (*We have learned that they can be fragments if they are used alone.*)

10. A. incorrect verb form (was *supposed*)

MAINTAINING SUBJECT/VERB AGREEMENT (PP. 108–112)

EXERCISE 1

1. have

2. is

3. has, wants

4. find

5. are

6. hunts

7. is

8. asks

9. protects

10. participate

EXERCISE 2

1. are

2. are

3. is, owe

4. are

5. figure

6. overshadows

7. drive, have

8. appears

9. include

10. make, are

EXERCISE 3

1. explains, seem, happen
2. feels, don't
3. begin, react
4. are, have
5. is, sense

6. don't, get
7. isn't
8. do
9. have, do, is
10. look, run, has, do

EXERCISE 4

1. sound
2. was, explains
3. were
4. was, were
5. was

6. were, was
7. were, was
8. was, was
9. were
10. shows, have, was

EXERCISE 5

1. have
2. are
3. adds
4. was
5. was

6. was, were
7. has
8. was, were
9. was, was
10. was, walk, run

PROOFREADING EXERCISE

With today's high food prices, you should choose your produce wisely. However, buying ripe fruits and vegetables *is* a tricky process. How can you tell if an apple or a bunch of bananas *is* ready to buy or eat? A good rule of thumb for apples, oranges, and lemons is to judge the weight of the fruit. If the fruit *is* heavy, then it will probably be juicy and tasty. Lightweight fruits *tend* to lack juice and be tasteless. A melon, on the other hand, *is* almost always heavy, but a good one sloshes when you *shake* it. And the stem end of a ripe cantaloupe will give slightly when you *press* on it. Vegetables *need* to be chosen carefully, too. If there *are* sprouted eyes on a potato, you should pass that one by. The sprouted eyes *show* a change in the chemical structure of the potato, and it is not a good idea to eat them. When in doubt, you can ask the produce clerk, who should know a lot about the merchandise.

AVOIDING SHIFTS IN TIME (PP. 114–115)

1. The last time I took my car in for a scheduled service, I noticed a few problems when I picked it up. I checked the oil dipstick, and it had really dark oil still on it. Also, there was a screwdriver balancing on my air-filter cover. I couldn't believe it when I saw it, but as soon as I showed the tool to the service manager, he called the mechanic over to take my car back to the service area. After another hour, my car was ready, the dipstick had clean oil on it, and the service manager cleared the bill so that I didn't have to pay anything.

2. Richard Hatch was voted the ultimate survivor by his fellow contestants on the first "real TV" game show of the new millennium, *Survivor.* At the beginning of the island marathon, sixteen people were stranded on an island and had to compete for rewards and immunity from being kicked out of the game. The "survivors" were divided into two tribes, Tagi and Pagong. Then one by one, contestants were voted off by the other survivors. Midway through the process of eliminating players, the remaining Tagi and Pagong members merged into one tribe called Rattana. From then on, the individuals within the tribe competed against each other instead of the tribes competing in groups. It all came down to a vote for one of two people, Kelly Wiglesworth and Richard Hatch, and Hatch won by one vote.

3. The paragraph is correct.

RECOGNIZING VERBAL PHRASES (PP. 117–121)

EXERCISE 1

1. It is hard [to plan a successful midday office party].

2. [Getting everyone in the same room at the same time] is the main obstacle.

3. Employees and bosses don't normally take their breaks together, and someone needs [to answer the phones].

4. It is also impossible [to surprise people] because everyone in an office knows each other and tells each other everything.

5. Furthermore, [buying a cake] [to please twenty or thirty people] can be [frustrating].

6. It is best [to choose either white cake with chocolate [frosting] or chocolate cake with white [frosting]].

7. Either of those combinations should be able [to satisfy both chocolate lovers and vanilla lovers].

8. Finally, people may find it difficult [to start fresh conversations with fellow employees or supervisors].

9. Office business <u>has</u> a way of [creeping back into people's discussions].

10. At that point, it <u>is</u> usually time [to leave the party and go back to work].

1. [To paraphrase Mark Twain], [golfing] <u>is</u> just a way [to ruin a good walk].

2. In fact, [becoming a golfer] <u>can be</u> dangerous.

3. Golf professionals commonly <u>suffer</u> a couple of injuries per year [resulting from long hours] of [practicing their swings].

4. Amateur golfers <u>tend</u> [to injure themselves] much more often.

5. Most injuries <u>come</u> from the [twisting], [squatting], and [bending] [involved in [golfing]].

6. And [moving the heavy bags of clubs] from cars to carts <u>can wrench</u> the backs of potential golfers before they even <u>begin</u> [to play].

7. Of course, there <u>are</u> the unfortunate incidents of people on golf courses [being struck by lightning].

8. But some of the sources of golfers' ailments <u>may be</u> [surprising].

9. [Cleaning the dirt and debris off the golf balls] by [licking them], for instance, <u>may have</u> serious repercussions.

10. After [swallowing the chemicals] [sprayed on the turf] of the golf course, players <u>can develop</u> liver problems.

1. Barbara Barry <u>is trying</u> [to improve the selection of computer toys] available to girls.

2. Barry <u>works</u> in the Media Lab at the Massachusetts Institute of Technology, [thinking up alternatives] to the [limited] pink products so far [targeted at young female consumers].

3. Barry's creations, [called StoryBeads], <u>are</u> tiny bead-[shaped] computers that <u>join</u> together as strings or necklaces.

4. StoryBeads <u>give</u> girls almost [unlimited] possibilities for [playing with, communicating through, and learning about computers].

5. In its individual memory, each bead holds any messages or pictures that the girl wants [to download there].

6. And the beads "talk" to each other [using infrared technology].

7. An "amulet" at the center of a chain of StoryBeads acts as a screen [to display the combination of messages and pictures] [accumulated from the whole string of beads].

8. The StoryBeads can then be rearranged [to create new combinations].

9. Barry imagines that girls will want [to trade beads and add to their collections].

10. Most important, she hopes that StoryBeads will inspire girls [to learn more about the [amazing] power of computers].

EXERCISE 4

1. Why do [plumbing] emergencies always happen on the weekends?

2. Toilets, sinks, and tubs seem [to know when plumbers' rates go up].

3. Some emergencies—a slow-[draining] sink, for instance—can be tolerated for a couple of days.

4. And a [dripping] shower faucet may cause annoyance, but not panic.

5. However, a [backed]-up sewer pipe definitely can't wait until Monday.

6. No one wants [to see that water [rising] and [overflowing] the rim of the bowl].

7. At that point, the only question is which "rooter" service [to call].

8. [Finding the main drainage line] often takes more time than [clearing it].

9. Once the plumber has finished [fixing the problem], he or she usually eyes future potential disasters and offers [to prevent them with even more work].

10. After [getting the final bill], I hope that my children will grow up [to be not doctors but plumbers].

EXERCISE 5

1. In the past, the library was the perfect place [to study] or [to do research or homework].

2. But lately it has become a place [to meet friends].

3. Things changed when students began [to access the Internet].

4. Now two or three students gather near each terminal and show each other the best sites [to visit on the Web].

5. Library officials <u>have designated</u> certain rooms as ["talking areas"].

6. However, such territories <u>are</u> hard [to enforce].

7. The old image of the librarian [telling everyone [to be quiet]] <u>is</u> just that—an old image.

8. So people <u>talk</u> to each other and <u>giggle</u> right there in the [reading] room.

9. One of the librarians <u>told</u> me about a plan [to take the Internet-access computers out of the main study room] and [to put them into the ["talking] areas"].

10. I <u>hate</u> [to read in a noisy room], so I <u>hope</u> that he <u>was</u> right.

PARAGRAPH EXERCISE

How [to Escape from a [Sinking] Car]

As soon as you <u>hit</u> the water, <u>open</u> your window. This <u>is</u> your best chance of escape, because [opening the door] <u>will be</u> very difficult [given the outside water pressure]. ([To be safe], you <u>should drive</u> with the windows and doors slightly open whenever you <u>are</u> near water or [driving on ice].) [Opening the windows] <u>allows</u> water [to come in and equalize the pressure]. Once the water pressure inside and outside the car <u>is</u> equal, you'll <u>be able</u> [to open the door].

SENTENCE WRITING

Your sentences may vary, but make sure that your verbals are not actually the main verbs of your clauses. You should be able to double underline your real verbs, as we have done here.

1. [Thinking of a good title] <u>takes</u> time.

2. We <u>spent</u> the morning [folding laundry].

3. I <u>enjoy</u> [skiing in spring] even though the snow is better in winter.

4. I <u>was taught</u> that [marking up a book] <u>is</u> wrong.

5. I <u>would love</u> [to take you to school].

6. I <u>need</u> [to get a good grade on the next quiz].

7. Yesterday, I <u>started</u> [to paste my old photos in a scrapbook].

8. He <u>doesn't have</u> the desire [to exercise regularly].

9. The school <u>canceled</u> the [planned] parking lot next to the library.

10. [Given the opportunity], my dog <u>will escape</u> from our yard.

CORRECTING MISPLACED OR DANGLING MODIFIERS (PP. 122–125)

EXERCISE 1

1. After *I waited* for an hour, my bus finally arrived.

2. *Since I called* my parents long distance, they quickly accepted my apology.

3. *Looking under the table,* I found my keys.

4. We heard loud music *while we were* walking down the street.

5. A week *after we returned from* vacation, my car wouldn't start.

6. With a new pen, *I had an easy time completing* the application.

7. Our coach *slipped on the jump rope and fell.*

8. The sentence is correct.

9. I bought a shirt *that has* gold buttons.

10. *In her letter,* Sharon asked for a new car.

EXERCISE 2

1. The sentence is correct.

2. *Dressed in tuxedos,* the caterers served the guests drinks.

3. *At their school,* Carrie, Max, and Angela campaigned for the senator.

4. Sitting at my desk for three hours, *I finally finished* my paper.

5. The sentence is correct.

6. *Waiting for the movie to start,* my sisters and I ate a whole pizza.

7. Before *I called* the doctor, my stomach started to feel better.

8. *Watching television,* I ate a piece of toast.

9. The sentence is correct.

10. *After the plane landed safely,* airport security approached it.

EXERCISE 3

1. *Looking through his binoculars,* he saw a bear.

2. *With a smile,* the nurse handed the patient a tray.

3. *Because I learned French as a child,* the trip should be a lot of fun for me.

4. The sentence is correct.

5. The sentence is correct.

6. The Glickmans *danced barefoot at the party for hours.*

7. The sentence is correct.

8. *From a post office in New Jersey,* she sent us an invitation to her graduation.

9. *By the time I was six,* Neil Armstrong had already landed on the moon.

10. The teacher will return our paragraphs *about* drugs.

EXERCISE 4

1. *Because I took an aspirin before my nap,* my headache was gone.

2. *I filled my new car's gas tank and drove home.*

3. After thirteen months of planning, *we had a successful reunion.*

4. She wrapped all the gifts *while she was still in her pajamas.*

5. The sentence is correct.

6. The sentence is correct.

7. The children gave *the bunch of daisies* to their teacher.

8. I watched the stone *as it skipped across the water and reached the middle of the lake.*

9. *As he tried to look happy,* his heart was breaking.

10. We saw *weeds all along the sidewalk.*

EXERCISE 5

1. *Because I felt the thrill of a day at the amusement park,* my blisters didn't bother me.

2. My friends and I saw the new tearjerker, *which is full of touching scenes.*

3. The sentence is correct.

4. Practicing for an hour a day, *she improved her piano playing.*

5. The sentence is correct.

6. *While she was sitting on a bench all day,* an idea came to her.

7. They discovered a new outlet mall *on the road to their cousins' house.*

8. *From his parents,* he felt the pressure of trying to get a good job.

9. The sentence is correct.

10. The sentence is correct.

PROOFREADING EXERCISE
Corrections are italicized. Yours may differ slightly.

As I walked into my neighborhood polling place during the last election, a volunteer greeted me and checked my name and address. *Because it was misspelled slightly on their printout, the volunteer couldn't find my name* at first. I pointed to what I thought was my name. At least upside down, *it looked like mine.* But actually, it was another person's name. *Once the printout was turned toward me,* I could see *it* more clearly. My name was there, but it had an extra letter stuck on the end of it. *With a polite smile,* the volunteer handed me a change-of-name form. I filled it out and punched my ballot. Stuck on my wall at home, *my voting receipt reminds me* to check my name carefully when the next election comes around.

FOLLOWING SENTENCE PATTERNS (PP. 128–132)

EXERCISE 1

       S   AV
1. Wendy Hasnip lives (in England).

     S   AV   OBJ.
2. She does not speak French.

                  S   AV   OBJ.
3. (At the age) (of forty-seven), Hasnip had a stroke.

                  S   AV
4. (For two weeks) (after the stroke), she could not talk.

        S   AV   OBJ.
5. Eventually, Hasnip regained her speaking ability.

        S AV
6. But suddenly, she spoke (with a distinct French accent).

           S   LV
7. Strangely, this condition is a known—but extremely rare—post-brain-injury
   DESC.
symptom.

        S   AV OBJ.
8. Doctors call it the Foreign Accent Syndrome.

       S   **AV**

9. One man (in Russia) recovered (from a brain injury).

      S   **AV**   **AV**   **OBJ.**

10. Now he can speak and understand ninety-three languages.

EXERCISE 2

           S   **LV**   **DESC.**

1. Local news programs are all alike.

   S   **AV**

2. They begin (with the top stories) (of the day).

          S   **LV**   **DESC.**   **DESC.**   **DESC.**

3. These stories may be local, national, or international.

    S   **AV**   **OBJ.**   **OBJ.**   **OBJ.**

4. They might include violent crimes, traffic jams, natural disasters, and political

   OBJ.

upheavals.

                   S   **AV**   **OBJ.**

5. (After the top stories), one (of the anchors) offers a quick weather update.

         S   **AV**   **OBJ.**   **OBJ.**

6. Then a sportscaster covers the latest scores and team standings.

                       S   **AV**   **OBJ.**

7. (At some point), a "human interest" story lightens the mood (of the broadcast).

      S **AV**   **OBJ.**

8. And then we hear the latest entertainment news.

                      S   **AV**

9. (Near the end) (of the half-hour), the weatherperson gives the full weather

   OBJ.

forecast.

       S   **AV**   **OBJ.**

10. News programs could use an update (of their own).

EXERCISE 3

       S   **AV**   **OBJ.**

1. Scientists (in West Virginia) have located a sugary substance (at the center) (of the Milky Way).

              S   **LV**   **DESC.**

2. The Milky Way (in this case) is the one (in outer space), not the popular candy bar.

                                 S   **AV**   **OBJ.**

3. National Radio Astronomy Observatory personnel analyzed the makeup (of a vaporous mass) (in the middle) (of the Milky Way).

       S   **LV**   **DESC.**

4. Results (of the analysis) were sweet.

        S   **LV**

5. The ingredients (in the cloud) (of gases and dust particles) were particular

    DESC.

amounts (of carbon, hydrogen, and oxygen).

             S   **LV**   **DESC.**

6. The molecular name (for the compound) is glycolaldehyde, a substance very similar (to plain old sugar).

        S   **AV**

7. The discovery (of a cloud) (of sugar) (in the middle) (of space) doesn't

    AV   **OBJ.**

surprise scientists.

             S   **AV**   **OBJ.**

8. Vaporous masses supply the foundation (for planets and stars).

          S   **AV**   **OBJ.**

9. And sugars provide the basis (for almost all forms) (of life).

          S   **LV**   **DESC.**

10. This discovery may be important (in the search) (for life) (in outer space).

EXERCISE 4

    S   **LV**   **DESC.**

1. One (of the high points) (of the Clinton administration) was the video spoof

(of his last days) (in the White House).

    S   **AV**   **AV**

2. Clinton participated wholeheartedly (in the project) and demonstrated almost

                    OBJ.

professional acting abilities.

        S   **AV**   **OBJ.**   **S**   **AV**

3. The brief video shows Clinton (in various silly situations); all (of them) satirize

    OBJ.   **OBJ.**

the boredom and inactivity (of the end) (of a presidency).

                    S   **AV**

4. (In one scene), Clinton runs (after Hillary's limousine) (with her forgotten

lunch sack) (in his hand).

    S   **AV**   **OBJ.**   **AV**

5. Clinton reads a magazine and waits (by a tumbling clothes dryer) (in another).

              S   **AV**   **OBJ.**

6. More famous people, such as actor Kevin Spacey, join the fun.

7. (In the middle) (of a phony acceptance speech) (in front) (of a mirror),

    S   **AV**   **OBJ.**

Clinton reluctantly gives the Best Actor Oscar back (to Spacey).

                                S   **AV**   **OBJ.**

8. (In two other sections) (of the video), Clinton plays the kids' game Battleship

(with the chairman) (of the Joint Chiefs) (of Staff), General Henry Shelton, and

    AV   **OBJ.**

rides a bike (down White House hallways).

          S   **LV**

9. The occasion (for the video) was the annual White House Correspondents'

               DESC.

Association Dinner (in Washington).

      S   **AV**   **OBJ.**   **S**   **AV**

10. The video entertained all (of the guests), and it revealed Clinton's healthy

    OBJ.

sense (of humor).

EXERCISE 5

             S   **AV**

1. British actor Oliver Reed died (on May 2, 1999).

     S   **AV**   **OBJ.**

2. He was making *Gladiator* (at the time).

       S   **AV**

3. Reed passed away (before the end) (of filming).

             S   **AV**   **OBJ.**

4. *Gladiator* director Ridley Scott used footage (from Reed's earlier takes) (for

the film's ending).

     S   **LV**   **DESC.**

5. Proximo is Reed's character (in the film).

                            S   **AV**   **OBJ.**

6. (For Proximo's final scene), Scott added computer-generated prison bars (to

one) (of Reed's previously filmed close-ups).

                            S   **AV**   **OBJ.**

7. (In moments) (without close-ups), Scott used other actors (for Reed's character).

       S   **AV**

8. Oliver Reed starred (in many famous films) (before *Gladiator*).

     S   **AV**   **OBJ.**   **AV**

9. He played Bill Sikes (in the musical *Oliver!*) and costarred (in *The Three*

Musketeers and *Women in Love*).

                      S   **LV**   **DESC.**

10. But *Gladiator*'s Proximo was his final screen performance.

PARAGRAPH EXERCISE

Thomas Alva Edison

                                       S   AV   OBJ.

Slow (in school) and poor (at math), Edison quit school (at twelve) [to work

                 S   AV   OBJ.   S   AV

as a newsboy (on a train)]. He used his wages [to buy chemicals], for he loved

OBJ.   S   AV   OBJ.

[experimenting]. He even built a little lab (in the baggage car) (on the train). Later

S   AV   AV   S

he worked (as a telegraph operator) and learned (about electricity). (By 1876), he

AV   OBJ.   OBJ.

had his own lab and . . . a staggering series (of inventions): a phonograph, a

practical light bulb, a strip (of motion picture film), and many others. (By trial and

                                            S   LV

error, sleepless nights, and tireless work), Edison became the most productive

DESC.

inventor (of practical devices) that America has ever seen. He was also probably

                DESC.   S LV   DESC.

the only inventor who was as well-known (to every American) as the most famous

movie star. (The word *as* in the last sentence does not begin a prepositional phrase
either time it's used.)

AVOIDING CLICHÉS, AWKWARD PHRASING, AND WORDINESS (PP. 135–141)

Your answers may differ from these possible revisions.

EXERCISE 1

1. I have a strong will and determination.

2. Combined with answer no. 1.

3. So I knew that I could learn how to juggle.

4. Passing two beanbags from hand to hand was easy.

5. But introducing a third bag was more difficult.

6. I would improve and then fail again.

7. Then a juggler friend gave me some advice.

8. He suggested that I practice the circular movement without catching the bags before I continued.

9. Soon I was juggling three bags without any difficulty.

10. I learned how to juggle with some helpful advice.

EXERCISE 2

1. Esther Kim and Kay Poe met as children at a Halloween party.

2. The party took place at the taekwondo school where they studied with Esther's father, Jin Won Kim.

3. Because Esther wore a pirate costume and Kay wore a Ninja costume, they couldn't tell if the other was a boy or a girl, but they grabbed each other's hands and never let go.

4. Esther and Kay became best friends and trained for years with Esther's father to be taekwondo champions.

5. Neither girl knew that one of them would eventually fill the last position on the American taekwondo team for the 2000 Olympics in Sydney.

6. But the Olympic story wasn't as happy as the one about fighting for that final spot.

7. Kay had seriously injured her knee in a match right before she was supposed to fight with Esther, and only the winner would go to the Olympics.

8. But when Esther saw her best friend so badly hurt, she could not fight.

9. To everyone's surprise, Esther decided to forfeit the match to her lifelong friend.

10. Olympic officials were so impressed with Esther Kim's sportsmanship that they provided a free trip for her and her father to the Sydney Olympics, and Mr. Kim had never been prouder than the day his daughter sacrificed her dream for a friend's.

EXERCISE 3

1. Parents worry about their children's development.

2. Most parents have heard that children exposed to great music, art, languages, and literature will be more intelligent than those who are not.

3. Many parents accept such ideas even without proof.

4. Video, book, and software companies have created products to help parents better their offspring's futures.

5. Some videos help children start reading at just a few months through appealing animation, pronunciation, and images of words.

6. One mother looking for educational videos for her baby started her own company.

7. Julie Aigner-Clark created Baby Einstein, a company that has sold over a million copies of *Baby Bach*, *Baby Mozart*, and *Baby Shakespeare* videos.

8. Clark and others satisfy concerned parents' desire for quality and culture in their children's lives.

9. Child development experts may say that pre-educating children in the arts will not increase their intellect.

10. But can a person really know too much Shakespeare?

EXERCISE 4

1. I just saw a news story about an unusual animal.

2. It resembles a teddy bear, a little monkey, and a miniature dog.

3. I found out that this animal is a celebrity with his own Web site.

4. His name is Mr. Winkle, and even his owner doesn't know what he is.

5. Questions flash across his loading Web page: Is it an "alien?" a "stuffed animal?" a "hamster with a permanent?"

6. Certainly, he is cute.

7. I can understand why his owner took him home after finding him by the side of the road one day.

8. Since then, she has photographed him wearing quirky costumes and even running in a hamster wheel.

9. Of course, pictures of Mr. Winkle fill posters and calendars, which can be purchased at reasonable prices.

10. His Web address is simply "mrwinkle.com."

EXERCISE 5

1. As with any widely used service, network television must respond to its viewers.

2. Nearly everyone watches some network television.

3. Such a broad audience demands a wide range of programming.

4. To satisfy everyone, TV would have to offer a separate channel for each person.

5. Products that do let people customize their viewing are expensive.

6. Network TV is free, so it is difficult to criticize.

7. Watching a "typical" person have a life-altering experience with paper towels is the price we pay for free TV.

8. In truth, the commercials are often more educational and entertaining than the regular programs.

9. And Americans can watch TV whenever they want.

10. The American people need diverse programming to satisfy most of the people most of the time.

PROOFREADING EXERCISE

Your revisions may vary, but here is one possibility:

    Los Angeles is a city designed for the automobile. My car dominates my life; I need it for work and school. I deliver pizzas, and the job requires that I have my own car. Like others in L.A., my vehicle is a necessity. I even drive friends who don't have cars to school because I feel sorry for them. Driving a car is better than taking a bus or a Metrolink train. Although the subways do connect the most popular places in L.A. and buses eventually arrive at any destination, I could never deliver my pizzas using public transportation. The toppings would get cold, and the delicious pizza smell would drive everyone crazy.

CORRECTING FOR PARALLEL STRUCTURE (PP. 143–147)

Your revisions may vary.

EXERCISE 1

1. I started preparations for my winter vacation last week and realized that my luggage and cold-weather coat are completely inadequate for a trip to Chicago.

2. The sentence is correct but could be shortened: My brother lives in "The Windy City" and says that it gets very cold there.

3. Temperatures in San Francisco hardly ever dip below the thirties or forties.

4. The jacket I normally use is lightweight and unlined.

5. I'll need to buy a coat made of down or fleece, like the ones that skiers wear.

6. My soft-bodied, duffel-bag style suitcases are inadequate as well; they have several outer compartments closed by zippers.

7. These cases may be appropriate for car trips but not for plane travel.

8. The sentence is correct.

9. I don't want to worry about things being stolen or a pocket ripping.

10. As a result of these deficiencies, I'm currently looking for new luggage and a proper winter coat.

EXERCISE 2

1. The sentence is correct.

2. The sentence is correct.

3. Another type of noise that horses make is squealing, which, in varying degrees of severity, can mean "Leave me alone," "I don't like that!" or "Help!"

4. The sentence is correct.

5. One nicker is used to greet another horse or a person bringing food.

6. Another lower-pitched greeting signals courtship and distinguishes one horse from another.

7. A mare uses the third kind of greeting sound to call and comfort her foal.

8. Neighing or whinnying is the most well known of the horse's sounds.

9. The sentence is correct.

10. The sentence is correct.

EXERCISE 3

1. The sentence is correct.

2. It has a plush lounge that offers free coffee, cookies, and even pretzels for those who don't like sweets.

3. The sentence is correct.

4. Full plate-glass windows line the front wall of the lounge so that people can see their vehicles being dried and check out the cars of the people around them.

5. For those who don't like to sit down, a full assortment of greeting cards and car accessories lines the back wall of the lounge.

6. To keep things interesting, every hour there is a drawing for a free car wash, but I have never won one.

7. The sentence is correct.

8. Why do people talk on cell phones when they could be resting, and why do some people stand up when they could be sitting on a nice leather sofa?

9. The sentence is correct.

10. It's the modern equivalent of going to the barbershop or getting a new hairdo at the beauty parlor.

EXERCISE 4

1. The sentence is correct.

2. Joining the scientists were car-sized robots and massive computers that worked continuously to analyze the most basic structures of human tissues.

3. The genome project has already cost nearly four billion dollars and has taken ten years to complete.

4. The sentence is correct.

5. The code is made up of billions of combinations of letters standing for four different chemicals: "A" for adenine, "C" for cystosine, "G" for guanine, and "T" for thymine.

6. The sentence is correct.

7. Within DNA, genes are the smaller groupings of chemicals that instruct the different cells of the body, but the genome includes fifty thousand genes.

8. The sentence is correct.

9. The future of human life, disease, and longevity may all be affected once the experts begin to identify the individual genes.

10. Some people look forward to that day optimistically, but others fear it.

EXERCISE 5

Correct sentences are unchanged.

1. To recognize a mail bomb, consider the following life-saving measures.

2. Do not touch any package or bulging letter if you sense that it is dangerous.

3. Be wary of odd-sized or odd-looking boxes or packets.

4. Be sure there is a preprinted return address on the package.

5. Check for tons of stamps instead of a clerk-issued label; such self-postage shows that the package did not go through all of the checkpoints at the post office.

6. Never trust a package wrapped with any kind of rope or string.

7. Beware of too much sealing tape, which is another signal that something may be wrong.

8. And look for greasy marks or oil spots.

9. Clear the area immediately whenever any of these tell-tale signs are noted.

10. Finally, don't feel silly for being cautious.

PROOFREADING EXERCISE

At the beginning of the American Civil War, Clara Barton heard that some of the injured soldiers were surviving without medicine or anything to eat. So Barton took out a newspaper ad to ask for donations of medical supplies, food, and blankets. When the donations arrived, Barton delivered them directly to the soldiers on the battlefields. The troops could scarcely believe that Barton, a woman who stood only five feet tall, would endanger her own life and march through the mud just to nurse them back to health. When the war ended, Barton continued her humanitarian efforts by locating soldiers who were missing in action and by opening an office of the International Red Cross.

USING PRONOUNS (PP. 152–156)

EXERCISE 1
1. I

2. I

3. he and I

4. I

5. he and I, me

6. I

7. I, I

8. you and me

9. him and me

10. me

EXERCISE 2
1. their

2. its

3. *All* of the friends that I travel with *have their* own quirks.

4. their

5. their

6. One day last week, *all* of my rides had *problems* with *their cars*.

7. its

8. As usual, *people* on the bus did *their* best to travel along without any expression on *their faces*.

9. us

10. it

EXERCISE 3

 1. she

 2. me

 3. You and she

 4. he

 5. *Shoppers* at the flea market looked for *their* treasures at different speeds.

 6. their

 7. she

 8. *All* of the high school students *have their* own *lockers* in the gym.

 9. their

10. *Citizens* of the country *have their* favorite candidates and can influence the election with *their votes.*

EXERCISE 4

 1. The sentence is correct.

 2. I finished my painting, put my supplies in my art box, and waited for the painting to dry.

 3. Kelly told her friend, "There is a backpack on top of your car."

 4. Working at the car wash this weekend made us all sore.

 5. Trent drove his car to the prom with his father's permission.

 6. When I placed my key in the lock, my key broke.

 7. Janel didn't like my sister and told her so.

 8. As we were spreading the blanket on the grass, the blanket ripped.

 9. Our teacher writes lots of comments on our essays to help us correct our mistakes.

10. Carl asked his new boss, "Why can't I work late?"

EXERCISE 5

 1. I added the finishing touches to the wedding cake, placed the decorating tips in hot water, and moved the cake to the freezer.

 2. People who join in campus activities feel more involved.

 3. As we added new paper, the copier made a funny noise.

4. Whenever I see white clouds hugging the ridge of the mountains, I feel happy.

5. Handmade leis from Hawaii are beautiful.

6. The doctor told Hector to put ice on his elbow.

7. Many people use rolling backpacks because they are so convenient.

8. In their offices, the employers interviewed the applicants.

9. The students bought new textbooks, but the books were too simple for them.

10. The sentence is correct.

PROOFREADING EXERCISE (CORRECTIONS ARE ITALICIZED)

    Rude drivers have one thing in common: they think that they know how to drive better than anybody else. The other day, as my friends and *I* were driving to school, we stopped at an intersection. A very old man who used a cane to help him walk started across *the intersection* in front of my friends and *me* just before the light was ready to change. So we waited. But while we waited for him, a male driver behind us started to honk his horn since he couldn't see *the old man.* I wondered, "Does *this driver* want us to hit *that man,* or what?" Finally, *the intersection* was clear. *The rude driver* pulled his car up beside ours, opened his window, and yelled at us before *his car* sped away. The old man reached the other side safely, but the *rude driver* hardly noticed.

AVOIDING SHIFTS IN PERSON (PP. 157–158)

1. To pitch a baseball well requires not only a strong arm but also powerful legs. Scientists at Johns Hopkins University in Baltimore have studied pitchers and their movements. They used a specially designed pitching mound, and they wired the pitchers' joints with sensors for the experiment. Their research revealed that the energy or force of a pitch begins in the leg that the pitcher stands on, flows from there to the leg that the pitcher lands on, then travels up the body and out the end of the arm that the pitcher throws with.

2. 216 Kleopatra is not an address or a code name but one of the thousands of asteroids that travel around our sun. Astronomers have been aware of 216 Kleopatra since the late 1800s, but it has only recently come within range of radar equipment. So they did not know that 216 Kleopatra is most likely composed entirely of metal, is shaped almost exactly like a dumbbell or a dog bone, and is as big as the state of New Jersey.

3. The paragraph is correct.

REVIEW OF SENTENCE STRUCTURE ERRORS (PP. 158–161)

1. B. mm (*As I was walking out of the doctor's office,* I saw a rainbow.)

2. B. cliché (Today, passwords must be protected.)

3. A. // (They bought collectibles at thrift stores, sold them on auction sites, and made a lot of money.)

4. B. pro agr (Everyone in the office *stopped working* to join the party.)

5. A. frag (*At the same point in their speeches,* the two students became very nervous.)

6. B. s/v agr (The row of parking spaces *was* almost completely filled.)

7. A. wordy (I am learning to write clearer essays.)

8. B. s/v agr (Either the tenants or the owner *is* lying about the incident.)

9. A. pro ref (I filled out the application with a pink pen and then put *the pen* in my backpack.)

10. A. ro (Many community college students plan to transfer; they want to get . . .)

11. A. s/v agr (Each of the teams' speeches *was* the same length.)

12. A. cliché (Once *it started to rain heavily* . . .)

13. B. dm (One of my knees was sore after *I jogged* all morning.)

14. A. ro (My supervisor evaluated my work, and she offered a few suggestions.)

15. A. shift (People enjoy e-mailing each other because *they* can communicate so much faster than before.)

Your revisions may differ, but here is one possibility:

Getting Involved

Getting involved in other people's business can be both right and wrong, depending on people's relationships and situations. For example, if one friend is in a bad relationship and the other is concerned, it may be time for the concerned friend to get involved. Stepping in not only shows real friendship but might also lead to solutions.

On the other hand, some people just like to be nosey, and they get involved in other people's business for fun. Such people need to know the details of others' lives to make their own lives more interesting. I have been in situations where peers have tried to learn about my life and problems. All of their discoveries turned into rumors.

Since I have learned from others' mistakes, I would never get involved in other people's business if it could not benefit them in some way. People should better their own lives rather than worry about anyone else's.

PUNCTUATION AND CAPITAL LETTERS

PERIOD, QUESTION MARK, EXCLAMATION POINT, SEMICOLON, COLON, DASH (PP. 164–169)

EXERCISE 1

1. On July 31, 2000, Sarah George and her friend Megan Freeman climbed to the top of Table Mountain in Wyoming.

2. After reaching the six-mile-high summit, George became ill; she was dehydrated and unable to climb down.

3. Freeman used a cell phone to call for help; then she and George waited for a helicopter to rescue them.

4. They had no idea that the pilot of that helicopter would be an incredibly famous movie star: Harrison Ford.

5. Ford volunteers as an emergency pilot when he stays at his vacation home in Jackson Hole, Wyoming.

6. Taking George and Freeman to the hospital was Harrison Ford's first mission as a rescue pilot.

7. George was relieved to see the helicopter bringing medical help to her and Freeman; she was also impressed when the paramedic told her who was flying the chopper.

8. Her enthusiasm was dampened, however, when she got airsick on the way to the hospital.

9. The only conversation George and Ford had was when he asked her how she was feeling; she said, "Fine."

10. Sarah George and Megan Freeman have something to tell their family and friends about for years to come.

EXERCISE 2

1. What have spiders done for you lately?

2. In the near future, a spider may save your life. (or !)

3. Researchers in New York have discovered the healing power of one species in particular: the Chilean Rose tarantula.

4. This spider's venom includes a substance that could stop a human's heart attack once it begins.

5. The substance has the ability to restore the rhythm of a heart that has stopped beating.

6. A scientist in Connecticut is experimenting with the killing power of another arachnid; the creature he is studying is the Australian funnel-web spider.

7. Currently, pesticides that destroy insects on crops also end up killing animals accidentally.

8. The funnel-web spider's venom is lethal to unwanted insects; however, it's harmless to animals.

9. Scientists would have to reproduce the funnel-web spider's venom artificially in order to have enough to use in fields.

10. As a result of these studies into the power of spider venom, you may live longer and enjoy pesticide-free foods.

EXERCISE 3

1. The change from one millennium to another has prompted us to look back over the twentieth century and wonder what its most important elements were.

2. Writers of history books—whose usual topics are influential people—are choosing these days to write about indispensable things.

3. The twentieth century saw the rise of two particularly important objects: the banana and the pointed screw.

4. Virginia Scott Jenkins has written *Bananas: An American History*.

5. And Witold Rybczynski is the author of *One Good Turn: A Natural History of the Screwdriver and the Screw*.

6. Jenkins' book includes facts and stories about the banana's rise in popularity during the twentieth century in America.

7. Before 1900, the banana was an unfamiliar fruit in the United States; now each American consumes about seventy-five bananas per year. (or !)

8. Rybczynski points out that the basic ideas for the screwdriver and the screw have been around since the ancient Greeks; however, screws did not have sharpened points until the twentieth century.

9. So for thousands of years, builders had to drill holes first; only then could they get the screws' threads to take hold.

10. Where would we be without bananas and self-starting screws?

EXERCISE 4

1. My friend Jason and I went to the beach yesterday; it was a really beautiful day. (or !)

2. We had finished our homework early so that we could enjoy ourselves.

3. Our English teacher had given us a special homework assignment: to draw a family tree.

4. I completed my drawing easily since I know my extended family very well; however, I kept thinking about it after I finished it.

5. I wondered how the other students' family trees would look compared to mine.

6. Would theirs be as big?

7. The two sides of my family tree—starting at my grandparents—have the same structure: both sets of grandparents had seven children.

8. From that level down, the two sides differ quite a bit; my mom's brothers and sisters didn't have many children, but my dad's siblings did—four each, to be precise.

9. I had mixed feelings—some good and some bad—about bringing my family tree to class.

10. I shouldn't have worried, however; several students' families were even bigger than mine. (or !)

EXERCISE 5

1. "Daddy, am I going to get old like Grandpa?"

2. This question is typical of the ones children ask their parents about aging; luckily, there are books that help parents answer them.

3. Lynne S. Dumas wrote the book *Talking with Your Children about a Troubled World;* in it, she discusses children's concerns and suggests ways of dealing with them.

4. In response to the question about getting old "like Grandpa," Dumas stresses one main point: be positive. (or—be positive.)

5. Too often, Dumas says, parents pass their own fears on to children; parents who focus on the negative aspects of aging will probably have children who worry about growing old.

6. Other subjects—homelessness, for instance—require special consideration for parents.

7. Dumas explains that children carefully observe how parents deal with a person asking for spare change or offering to wash windshields for money.

8. The unplanned nature of these encounters often catches parents off guard; therefore, they should try to prepare a uniform response to such situations.

9. Dumas also suggests that parents take positive action—involving children in charitable donations and activities, for example—in order to illustrate their compassion for the homeless.

10. The most important aspect in communicating with children is honesty; the second and third most important are patience and understanding.

PROOFREADING EXERCISE

The ingredients you will need for homemade brownies are flour, butter, eggs, sugar, baking chocolate, vanilla, baking powder, and salt—nuts are optional. First, you should combine the dry ingredients; then you can blend the wet ingredients in a separate bowl. Once the wet and dry ingredients are ready, you are ready to mix them. Your square baking pan needs to be greased on the bottom so that the brownies don't stick to it. Finally, you can spread the batter into the pan and bake them for half an hour. And when they come out of the oven, be prepared to eat them right away! (or .)

COMMA RULES 1, 2, AND 3 (PP. 171–175)

EXERCISE 1

1. Chickens are the subject of riddles, jokes, and sayings.

2. We think of funny ways to respond to the "Why did the chicken cross the road?" question, and we endlessly ponder the answer to "Which came first—the chicken or the egg?"

3. A person who runs around in a hurry is often compared to "a chicken with its head cut off."

4. Although we try not to visualize the image of the last comparison, most people understand the reference to a fowl's final moments of frantic activity.

5. Anyone who has heard the story of Mike "the headless chicken" will consider the popular saying differently from that moment on, for it will come to mean having a strong determination to live in spite of major setbacks.

6. On September 10, 1945, a farmer in Fruita, Colorado, chose one of his chickens to have for dinner that night.

7. But after having his head cut off, the rooster didn't die, didn't seem to be in pain, and continued to act "normally."

8. In fact, Mike went on to become a national celebrity, and his owner took him around the country so that people could see him for themselves.

9. When both *Time* and *Life* magazines ran feature stories complete with photos of Mike in October 1945, the public became fascinated by the details of Mike's ability to eat, drink, hear, and move without a head.

10. Mike lived for eighteen months after his date with a chopping block and would have lived longer, but he died by accidentally choking in 1947.

EXERCISE 2

1. Whenever I need advice about money, I ask my friend Janice.

2. Once she hears my problem, Janice knows exactly what to do.

3. The first time I needed help, I had more bills than my paycheck could cover.

4. Instead of lecturing me on unwise spending as I imagined my parents would do, Janice explained a strategy to avoid the same problem the next month.

5. Last month, I got into trouble with money again, but Janice was on a trip to Italy, so I couldn't ask her for help.

6. The only people available to guide me were my parents, but I didn't want to bother them at first.

7. I knew that they would worry and would ask, "You can't support yourself very well, can you?"

8. I didn't want to hear that lecture again, so I tried to work the problem out myself.

9. Finally, I asked my mom and dad for advice, and they had the answer to my problem.

10. The next time I need help with money, I will listen to them as much as I listen to Janice.

EXERCISE 3

1. As if people didn't have enough to worry about, Melinda Muse has written a book called *I'm Afraid, You're Afraid: 448 Things to Fear and Why*.

2. In her book, Muse points out the dangers of common places, objects, foods, months, days, and activities.

3. One place that the author warns about is Las Vegas casinos, and the reason is that paramedics can't get to ailing gamblers due to the crowds and huge size of the buildings.

4. Another dangerous spot is the beauty parlor, where people suffer strokes caused by leaning their heads back too far into the shampoo sink.

5. New clothes need to be washed before they are worn, or they may transfer dangerous chemicals to the wearers' eyes, skin, and lungs.

6. Grapefruit juice can interfere with certain medications' effectiveness, and nutmeg contains hallucinogenic substances, so these are among the foods to be avoided.

7. The sentence is correct.

8. Mondays have two dangerous distinctions, for more suicides and heart attacks occur on Mondays than on any other day of the week.

9. The sentence is correct.

10. After reading *I'm Afraid, You're Afraid,* it's possible to be afraid of almost everything.

EXERCISE 4

1. Speaking of worst-case scenarios, there is a book about how to survive them, and it's called *The Worst-Case Scenario Survival Handbook.*

2. The coauthors of this self-help book are aware that most of us will never have to overpower an alligator or make an emergency landing on an airplane, yet they want us to be prepared nonetheless.

3. In the "About the Authors" section of the book, readers learn that Joshua Piven is a first-time writer, but he has survived encounters with robbers, muggers, and stalled subway trains.

4. About Piven's coauthor, we discover that David Borgenicht has written two other books and has had his share of worst-case scenarios, especially while traveling.

5. Although the overall tone of the book is somewhat humorous because it covers such outlandish topics, the information it shares is deadly serious and could save a life.

6. The sentence is correct.

7. One of the best examples illustrates a way to avoid being attacked by a mountain lion, and that is to try to appear as large as possible, so the drawing shows a man holding the sides of his jacket out wide like bat wings to scare the lion away.

8. If readers wonder whether they can trust the advice on escaping from quicksand, they can just flip to the list of sources consulted for each section, in this case an expert on the physics of natural phenomena at the University of Sydney, Australia.

9. Wisely, Piven and Borgenicht begin the book by warning readers to seek professional help whenever possible instead of trying the survival techniques themselves.

10. The authors know that if people go looking for trouble, they'll probably find it.

EXERCISE 5

1. Fish may be considered "brain food," but I've never liked it.

2. While everyone is saying how delicious a big salmon steak is or how yummy the shrimp tastes, you'll find me grimacing and munching on a piece of bread and butter.

3. Part of the problem with fish is the smell, but my friends who love to eat fish also love the smell of fish cooking.

4. I always thought that was strange, but it makes sense, doesn't it?

5. If someone hates the taste of onions, that person probably also hates the smell of onions cooking.

6. Come to think of it, my husband hates to eat sweets and doesn't like the smell of them either.

7. When we walk into a bakery together, he practically has to hold his nose the way I would in a fish market.

8. To me, that's odd, but my aversion must be just as odd to someone who loves fish.

9. Our daughter loves the taste of bacon, but she hates the smell of bacon frying.

10. The sentence is correct.

PROOFREADING EXERCISE

I belong to a very large family, and we have trouble keeping up with each others' birthdays. In the past, we've tried to buy presents for every niece, nephew, uncle, and cousin, but we can't afford to continue, or we'll go broke. Recently, my extended family members and I have decided to hold a yearly birthday drawing so that each of us can plan to give and receive only one or two nice birthday gifts a year. For example, my Aunt Josephine and I were chosen to exchange gifts this year. We were both born in March, so our two birthdays fall close together. Of course, my immediate family—mother, father, sisters, and brothers—will buy presents for each other as usual.

SENTENCE WRITING

Here are some possible revisions. Yours may differ.

I'm a good bowler, but I've never joined a bowling league.

When the bell rings, I leave my math class and rush to my English class.

Although she currently teaches dance at a local college, she was a professional dancer in the 1970s and even performed in several movies.

Since Alex and Giselle are both intelligent and well-organized students, they will graduate with honors.

COMMA RULES 4, 5, AND 6 (PP. 178–181)

For Exercises 1 and 2, correct sentences remain in the answers without commas for the sake of comparison.

EXERCISE 1

1. This year's office party, I believe, was worse than last year's.

2. I believe this year's office party was worse than last year's.

3. Lee's lasagna, however, was better than ever.

4. However Lee's lasagna was better than ever. (or However, Lee's lasagna was better . . .)

5. The clerk who works in the claims division didn't bring a dessert even though he signed up for one.

6. Justin Banks, who works in the claims division, didn't bring a dessert even though he signed up for one.

7. And Mr. Hopkins, who planned the party, needed to think of a few more party games.

8. And the person who planned the party needed to think of a few more party games.

9. As usual, no one, it seems, had time to decorate beyond a few balloons.

10. As usual, it seems that no one had time to decorate beyond a few balloons.

EXERCISE 2

1. We hope, of course, that people will honor their summons for jury duty.

2. Of course we hope that people will honor their summons for jury duty.

3. People who serve as jurors every time they're called deserve our appreciation.

4. Thelma and Trevor Martin, who serve as jurors every time they're called, deserve our appreciation.

5. We should therefore be as understanding as we can be about the slow legal process.

6. Therefore, we should be as understanding as we can be about the slow legal process.

7. A legal system that believes people are innocent until proven guilty must offer a trial-by-jury option.

8. The U.S. legal system, which believes people are innocent until proven guilty, offers a trial-by-jury option.

9. With that option, we hope that no one will receive an unfair trial.

10. With that option, no one, we hope, will receive an unfair trial.

EXERCISE 3

1. In 1998, Kevin Warwick, an expert on cybernetics at the University of Reading, did something that no one had ever done before.

2. The sentence is correct.

3. Warwick was therefore the earth's first "cyborg," a being that is part human and part computer.

4. For two decades at Reading University, which is in England, Professor Warwick had helped design "smart" buildings, structures controlled by computer commands.

5. The sentence is correct.

6. Building doors, which needed to be entered with a card key by anyone else, opened by themselves as Professor Warwick approached. (This sentence could also be written without commas for emphasis on precisely which doors they were.)

7. The building's computer, which recognized Warwick's signal as he walked down the halls, greeted him by turning on lights and announcing the arrival of his e-mail.

8. For safety's sake, despite the small size of the device, about as large as a pea, Warwick had planned to and did have it removed after just nine days.

9. People in England and around the world, experts and laypeople alike, have reacted to Warwick's advances in a variety of ways.

10. Those who believe in taking all steps toward the future applaud his research, but others, who may be wary of the dangers involved in tracking people's movements by computer, remain skeptical. (This sentence could also be written without commas at the end to emphasize which people remain skeptical.)

EXERCISE 4

1. The Ironman competition, one of the most grueling athletic races in the world, takes place in Hawaii every year.

2. The sentence is correct.

3. The sentence is correct.

4. As if that race weren't enough for some fitness fanatics, it is followed soon after by the XTerra World Championship, another attraction for triathletes from around the world.

5. The Xterra, an obstacle course through the extreme Hawaiian landscape, takes participants over ocean waves, blistering sand, dried lava, fallen tree limbs, exposed roots, and huge chunks of coral.

6. The sentence is correct.

7. Some triathletes participate in both races, Ironman and Xterra, in what triathletes refer to as The Double.

8. The sentence is correct.

9. The sentence is correct.

10. However, the male and female athletes with the best times overall in both races are considered winners of the The Double; they earn a thousand dollars and an invaluable title, World's Toughest Athlete.

EXERCISE 5

1. The sentence is correct.

2. Cloning experts believe that Noah, like his namesake with the ark, has the potential to save the endangered species of the world.

3. The sentence is correct.

4. Noah's species is known as a gaur, a type of wild ox.

5. Since there are relatively few gaur left, scientists turned to the reproductive techniques that produced Dolly, the first mammal ever cloned by man.

6. However, Noah will be different from Dolly, who was a sheep cloned from sheep DNA and born by a sheep.

7. Noah will be a rare wild ox in every way genetically, but he has been developing within the egg of a normal cow, a completely different species, which has been acting as his surrogate mother.

8. The sentence is correct.

9. On the horizon is another first, the cloning of a bucardo, an extinct mountain goat.

10. Cloning scientists have received the go-ahead to produce a clone from DNA in the remaining tissue of Celia, the last living bucardo, who was crushed by a tree limb, leaving her species extinct.

PROOFREADING EXERCISE

There are two types of punctuation, internal punctuation and end punctuation. Internal punctuation is used within the sentence, and end punctuation is used at the end of the sentence. There are six main rules for the placement of commas, the most important pieces of internal punctuation. Semicolons, the next most important, have two main functions. Their primary function, separating two independent clauses, is also the most widely known. A lesser-known need for semicolons, to separate items in a list already containing commas, occurs rarely in college writing. Colons and dashes have special uses within sentences. And of the three pieces of end punctuation—periods, question marks, and exclamation points—one is obviously the most common. That piece is the period, which signals the end of the majority of English sentences.

SENTENCE WRITING

Here are some possible combinations. Yours may differ.

> Some people attend performances of *The Nutcracker*, a holiday tradition, every year with their families.

> I think I could learn to speak Italian fluently. (or) I could, I think, learn to speak Italian fluently.

> Joan, the student whos sits in the front row and has black hair, asks the best questions.

COMMA REVIEW EXERCISE

I'm writing this letter, Mr. Hampton, to ask you for a favor. [4] I know you are very busy, but would you mind writing a letter of recommendation for me? [1] When I visited the financial aid office yesterday, I noticed that there were many scholarships that I qualify for. [3] All of them, however, require the same form of references: two letters of recommendation from current professors. [5] Dr. Trent, my math teacher, is the other person that I plan to ask. [6] I have enclosed my application, my personal essay, and a copy of my transcript to help you write the letter. [2] Thank you in advance for your help.

QUOTATION MARKS AND UNDERLINING/*ITALICS* (PP. 185–189)

EXERCISE 1

  1. The Andy Griffith Show is still a popular television series.

  2. "You make me laugh," my friend Jennifer said.

  3. The movie version of To Kill a Mockingbird is just as good as the book.

  4. Last night we watched the movie JFK on video.

  5. Sam Shepard wrote the play True West, costarred with Diane Keaton in the movie Baby Boom, and played the part of Hamlet's father's ghost in the latest film version of Hamlet.

  6. "Do I have to pay for all of the groceries myself?" my roommate asked.

  7. I found her in the library reading the last issue of George magazine.

  8. My teacher assigned E. B. White's essay "Once More to the Lake" as homework.

  9. "The movie can't be over," said my brother; "I was only gone for a minute getting popcorn."

  10. Some children misunderstand the words to "The Pledge of Allegiance."

EXERCISE 2

1. "Have you been to the bookstore yet?" Monica asked.

2. "No, why?" I answered.

3. "They've rearranged the books," she said, "and now I can't find anything."

4. "Are all of the books for one subject still together?" I wondered.

5. "Yes, they are," Monica told me, "but there are no markers underneath the books to say which teacher's class they're used in, so it's really confusing."

6. "Why don't we just wait until the teachers show us the books and then buy them?" I replied.

7. "That will be too late!" Monica shouted.

8. "Calm down," I told her, "you are worrying for nothing."

9. "I guess so," she said once she took a deep breath.

10. "I sure hope I'm not wrong," I thought to myself, "or Monica will really be mad at me."

EXERCISE 3

1. "Stopping by Woods on a Snowy Evening" is a poem by Robert Frost.

2. "Once you finish your responses," the teacher said, "bring your test papers up to my desk."

3. I subscribe to several periodicals, including Time and U.S. News & World Report.

4. "Our country is the world," William Lloyd Garrison believed, "our countrymen are all mankind."

5. "Do you know," my teacher asked, "that there are only three ways to end a sentence?"

6. Edward Young warned young people to "Be wise with speed. A fool at forty is a fool indeed."

7. In Shakespeare's play Romeo and Juliet, Mercutio accidentally gets stabbed and shouts, "A plague on both your houses!"

8. "There is no such thing as a moral or an immoral book," Oscar Wilde writes in his novel The Picture of Dorian Gray; "Books are either well written, or badly written."

9. Molière felt that "One should eat to live, and not live to eat."

10. Did you say, "I'm sleepy" or "I'm beeping"?

EXERCISE 4

1. For my birthday, my mother gave me a copy of The Promise of a New Day, a book of quotations and inspirational discussions to get me through the year.

2. Thomas Merton believed that "We must be true inside, true to ourselves, before we can know a truth that is outside us."

3. "Injustice anywhere," said Martin Luther King, Jr., "is a threat to justice everywhere."

4. "When you hold resentment toward another," Catherine Ponder tells us, "you are bound to that person or condition by an emotional link that is stronger than steel."

5. Ellen Key feels that "At every step the child should be allowed to meet the real experiences of life; the thorns should never be plucked from the roses."

6. Randall Jarrell had this to say about the effects of oppression: "If you have been put in your place long enough, you begin to act like the place."

7. Amelia Earhart pointed out that "It is far easier to start something than it is to finish it."

8. "There are two ways of spreading light:" wrote Edith Wharton, "to be the candle or the mirror that receives it."

9. "Putting a question correctly is one thing," observed Anton Chekhov, "and finding the answer to it is something quite different."

10. Nikki Giovanni realizes that "Mistakes are a fact of life. It is the response to error that counts."

EXERCISE 5

1. In his book Who's Buried in Grant's Tomb? A Tour of Presidential Gravesites, Brian Lamb records the final words of American presidents who have passed away.

2. Some of their goodbyes were directed at their loved ones; for example, President Zachary Taylor told those around him, "I regret nothing, but I am sorry that I am about to leave my friends."

3. Other presidents, such as William Henry Harrison, who died after only one month in office, addressed more political concerns; Harrison said, "I wish you to understand the true principles of the government. I wish them carried out. I ask for nothing more."

4. John Tyler became president due to Harrison's sudden death; Tyler served his term, lived to be seventy-one, and said, "Perhaps it is best" when his time came.

5. At the age of eighty-three, Thomas Jefferson fought to live long enough to see the fiftieth anniversary of America's independence; on that day in 1826, Jefferson was one of only three (out of fifty-six) signers of the "Declaration of Independence" still living, and he asked repeatedly before he died, "Is it the fourth?"

6. John Adams, one of the other three remaining signers, died later the same day—July 4, 1826—and his last words ironically were "Thomas Jefferson still survives."

7. The third president to die on the Fourth of July (1831) was James Monroe; while he was president, people within the government got along so well that his time in office was known as "the era of good feelings."

8. Doctors attempted to help James Madison live until the Fourth of July, but he put off their assistance; on June 26, 1836, when a member of his family became alarmed at his condition, Madison comforted her by saying, "Nothing more than a change of mind, my dear," and he passed away.

9. Grover Cleveland, who had suffered from many physical problems, was uneasy at his death; before losing consciousness, he said, "I have tried so hard to do right."

10. Finally, George Washington, our first president, also suffered greatly but faced death bravely; "I die hard," he told the people by his bedside, "but I am not afraid to go. 'Tis well."

PROOFREADING EXERCISE

We read Langston Hughes' essay "Salvation" in class the other day. It is part of his autobiography The Big Sea. In the essay, Hughes tells the story of a church meeting that he went to when he was a child. "The preacher preached a wonderful rhythmical sermon," Hughes explains, "all moans and shouts and lonely cries and dire pictures of hell. And then he sang a song about the ninety and nine safe in the fold, but one little lamb was left out in the cold." Once Hughes realizes that he is the "little lamb left out in the cold," he feels that "Now it was really getting late. I began to be ashamed of myself, holding everything up so long." Hughes eventually pretends to see the light to save everyone the trouble of waiting for him to have his religious experience, but afterwards he feels even worse because he lied: "That night, for the last time in my life but one—for I was a big boy twelve years old—I cried. I cried, in bed alone, and couldn't stop."

CAPITAL LETTERS (PP. 191–194)

In this section, titles of larger works are italicized rather than underlined.

EXERCISE 1

1. Robert Redford's daughter is following in her father's footsteps.

2. Her name is Amy Hart Redford, and she has already been in a few movies and has played a small part on *The Sopranos.*

3. Robert Redford, though mostly a film actor, acted on Broadway in the early 1960s in the stage version of *Barefoot in the Park.*

4. Amy Hart Redford has been in Off-Broadway productions but hopes her big break will come soon.

5. In the play *The Messenger,* the younger Redford starred with Jane Fonda's son, Troy Garity.

6. Amy has studied at acting schools in New York, San Francisco, and London.

7. Amy's mother, Lola, a historian, has been divorced from Robert Redford since 1985.

8. Seeing his daughter on stage has prompted Robert Redford to think of trying it again himself.

9. When Amy Redford was growing up, she didn't always like the special treatment that a celebrity's child receives.

10. Now, however, she may become a celebrated actor herself.

EXERCISE 2

1. When people think of jazz, they think of *Down Beat* magazine.

2. *Down Beat's* motto may be "Jazz, Blues & Beyond," but some people think that the magazine has gone too far "beyond" by including two guitarists in the *Down Beat* Hall of Fame.

3. The two musicians in question are Jimi Hendrix and Frank Zappa.

4. Jimi Hendrix was inducted into the Hall of Fame in 1970.

5. *Down Beat* added Frank Zappa to the list in 1994.

6. Since then, readers and editors have been debating whether Hendrix and Zappa belong in the same group as Duke Ellington, John Coltrane, and Miles Davis.

7. Those who play jazz guitar have some of the strongest opinions on the subject.

8. Russell Malone, Mark Elf, and John Abercrombie all agree that Hendrix and Zappa were great guitarists but not jazz guitarists.

9. Others like Steve Tibbetts and Bill Frisell don't have any problem putting Hendrix on the list, but Tibbetts isn't so sure about including Zappa.

10. It will be interesting to see who *Down Beat*'s future inductees will be.

EXERCISE 3

1. I grew up watching *It's a Wonderful Life* once a year on TV in the winter.

2. That was before the colorized version and before every station started showing it fifteen times a week throughout the months of November and December.

3. I especially remember enjoying that holiday classic with my mother and brothers when we lived on Seventh Avenue.

4. "Hurry up!" Mom would yell, "You're going to miss the beginning!"

5. My favorite part has always been when Jimmy Stewart's character, George Bailey, uses his own money to help the people of Bedford Falls and to save his father's Building and Loan.

6. George's disappointment turns to happiness after he and Donna Reed's character, Mary, move into the abandoned house on their honeymoon.

7. Of course, mean old Mr. Potter takes advantage of Uncle Billy's carelessness at the bank, and that starts George's breakdown.

8. In his despair, George places the petals of his daughter Zuzu's flower in his pocket, leaves his house, and wants to commit suicide.

9. Luckily, all of George's good deeds have added up over the years, and he is given a chance to see that thanks to a character named Clarence.

10. When George feels Zuzu's petals in his pocket, he knows that he's really made it home again, and the people of Bedford Falls come to help him.

EXERCISE 4

1. Tracy Chapman grew up in Cleveland, Ohio, with her sister and her mother.

2. Even though they were poor enough to need food stamps at times, Tracy received a scholarship and attended the private Wooster School in Connecticut, where her interest in music grew.

3. When Tracy was a young girl, she would watch country music stars like Minnie Pearl and Buck Owens on TV.

4. Their ornate guitars inspired Tracy to play the instrument herself.

5. She first performed for other people during Thanksgiving break when she was studying at Tufts University in Massachusetts.

6. On a street in Boston with time to kill but no money to spend, Tracy's friend urged her to play and sing for the crowd.

7. By the end of the set, Chapman had made enough money to buy them both a good meal for the holiday.

8. Chapman's first recording, called simply *Tracy Chapman,* sold ten million copies, but she wasn't ready for the pressures of fame.

9. She found the cycle of making records and then touring with the songs very unsettling; now she calls San Francisco her home and tries to stay focused on what's real.

10. In 1996, Tracy Chapman joined Lilith Fair and in 2000 released her latest CD, *Telling Stories.*

EXERCISE 5

1. Helen Hunt has been acting on TV and in movies since she was nine years old.

2. She portrayed the cyclone-chasing scientist named Jo Harding in *Twister.*

3. She gave an Oscar-winning performance alongside Jack Nicholson in *As Good as It Gets.*

4. Her most recognizable and long-lasting TV character so far has been Jamie Buckman in *Mad about You,* which costarred Paul Reiser.

5. Having wanted to act with Kevin Spacey since she saw *American Beauty,* Hunt took the part of Haley Joel Osment's mom in *Pay It Forward.*

6. She also worked with famous director Robert Altman and actor Richard Gere on the film *Dr. T and the Women.*

7. Hunt played Tom Hanks' love interest in *Cast Away.*

8. She and Mel Gibson starred together in the romantic comedy *What Women Want.*

9. In addition to acting, Hunt loves the Olympics and even worked event tickets into her contract with NBC while she was making *Mad about You.*

10. Hunt has collected souvenir pins like any normal fan at the Olympic games in Atlanta and in Sydney, Australia.

REVIEW OF PUNCTUATION AND CAPITAL LETTERS (PP. 195–196)

1. The Eiffel Tower is one of the most famous structures in Paris.

2. Have you ever read Flannery O'Connor's short story "A Good Man Is Hard to Find"?

3. We camped out at the beach all weekend; we were ready to get warm and stay dry.

4. "How many doughnuts can I buy with five dollars?" she asked.

5. We received your letter, Mr. Jenkins, and have forwarded your concerns to our claims department.

6. The person who guesses the exact weight of the pumpkin will win first prize.

7. Dr. Flores teaches the film class, and Professor Duncan teaches Introduction to Critical Theory.

8. Because of the water shortage, we have to take shorter showers.

9. I need new pants, new socks, new shoes, and a new coat if you want me to go the the art opening with you.

10. Hamlet doesn't say the famous line "Something is rotten in the state of Denmark," but he knows it.

11. My math tutor gave me the following advice: "Don't think so much; just follow the directions."

12. Whenever I shop at the grocery store, I pick up the <u>TV Guide</u> and look at it, but I never buy it.

13. I bought two new textbooks this morning; however, I found out later that I didn't need either one of them.

14. "Is that what you're wearing to the play?" my father asked.

15. "You can lead a horse to water," the old saying goes, "but you can't make him drink."

COMPREHENSIVE TEST (PP. 196–198)

1. (ww) The scary scenes in the movie really *affected* me; I couldn't sleep that night.

2. (sp) The police asked us what time the theft had *occurred*.

3. (wordy and awk) *We can solve our money problems.*

4. (cap) Last semester, I took art history, *Spanish,* and geography.

5. (pro) The department store hired my friend and *me* as gift wrappers for the holidays.

6. (//) In just six weeks, we learned to find main ideas, to remember details, and *to integrate* new words into our vocabulary.

7. (ro) The chairs should be straightened, and the chalkboard should be erased before the next class.

8. (mm) The students noticed *a tiny frog hopping into the room* from the biology lab.

9. (shift in time) He tells the same joke in every speech, and people *laugh*.

10. (pro ref) I bring pies to potluck parties because *pies* are always appreciated.

11. (p) We don't know if the buses run that late at night.

12. (apos) The *women's* teams have their own trophy case across the hall.

13. (dm) *When I turned twenty-one,* my mom handed me a beer.

14. (ro) Their car wouldn't start; the battery was dead.

15. (cliché) I asked the car salesman about the actual price.

16. (wordy) That restaurant serves terrible food.

17. (pro agr) *All of the people* in the audience raised their *hands*.

18. (frag) *We left* because the lines were long and we couldn't find our friends.

19. (cs) I plan to stay in town for spring break; it's more restful that way.

20. (s/v agr) Each of the kittens *has* white paws. (or *All* of the kittens have white paws.)

WRITING

ORGANIZING IDEAS (P. 215)

EXERCISE 1 THESIS OR FACT?

1. FACT

2. THESIS

3. FACT

4. THESIS

5. THESIS

6. FACT

7. THESIS

8. FACT

9. THESIS

10. THESIS

ADDING TRANSITIONAL EXPRESSIONS (P. 218)

This year, my family and I decided to celebrate the Fourth of July in a whole new way. *Previously,* we always attended a fireworks show at the sports stadium near our house. The firework shows got better every year; *however,* we were getting tired of the crowds and the noise. *In addition,* we were starting to feel bad about our own lack of creativity. The goal this time was to have each family member think of a craft project, recipe, or game related to the Fourth. The result was a day full of fun activities and good things to eat—all created by us! *First,* my sister Helen taught us to make seltzer rockets from an idea she found on the Internet. We used the fireless "firecrackers" as table decorations until late afternoon when we set them off. *Then,* we ate dinner. Mom and Dad's contribution was "Fourth of July Franks," which were hot dogs topped with ketchup, onions, and a sprinkling of blue-corn chips. For dessert, my brother Leon assembled tall parfaits made with layers of red and blue Jell-O cubes divided by ridges of whipped cream. *Finally,* we played a game of charades in which all of the answers had something to do with the American flag, the Declaration of Independence, Paul Revere's ride, and other such topics. We all enjoyed the Fourth so much that the events will probably become our new tradition.

WRITING ABOUT WHAT YOU READ (PP. 235–239)

ASSIGNMENT 17

100-Word Summary of "Cat Lovers vs. Dog Lovers"

Certain characteristics make people prefer either cats or dogs as pets. The first is whether people seek solitude or companionship. Cat people like to be alone, and dog people like to be with others. Also, studies show that women prefer cats and men prefer dogs. This division goes back to the cave-dwelling days of our ancestors. Obviously, some people like both animals and have no preference. And most people exhibit catlike and doglike qualities in the ways they behave. So there is really no simple answer to whether a particular person would like a cat or a dog the best.

ASSIGNMENT 18

Sample 100-Word Summary of
"Test Case: Now the Principal's Cheating"

Kids are learning more than parents want them to in schools these days. They are learning to cheat. It's a complicated problem that's made worse because of the tests that students have to take to graduate from one level to another. The government uses the scores of these tests to reward or punish students, schools, and teachers. That's one reason why people think that teachers and schools are now cheating on behalf of their students and themselves. No one is happy about the increase in schools' cheating, but no one can figure out how to fix this complex problem either.

Index